the smoking gun

the

A DOSSIER OF
SECRET, SURPRISING, AND SALACIOUS
DOCUMENTS

smoking gun

William Bastone, Daniel Green & Barbara Glauber
creators of www.thesmokinggun.com

Little, Brown and Company
Boston • New York • London

First Edition

For information on Time Warner Trade Publishing's online
publishing program, visit www.ipublish.com.

ISBN 0-316-61110-7
LCCN 2001092813

10 9 8 7 6 5 4 3 2 1

Design: Barbara Glauber & Beverly Joel/Heavy Meta

COM-NJ

Printed in the United States of America

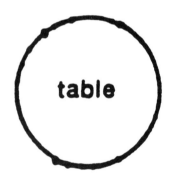

table

 hile journalism is generally regarded as "history's first draft," that distinction actually belongs to the primary-source documents on which many of those news accounts are based. Police reports, lawsuits, FBI memos, depositions, and other records often provide the firsthand accounts and narrative drive behind today's front pages. That's because every important, scandalous, or bizarre story—whether it's the assassination of a president or the arrest of a starlet—has its own paper trail, a fascinating mix of the mundane and the mesmerizing.

Since April 1997, The Smoking Gun (www.thesmokinggun.com) has been gathering, scanning, and posting these documents on the Internet, a place where fiction has often trumped fact. While most sites tout their bells and whistles, The Smoking Gun is just documents—a black-and-white "journalistic curio shop," as *The New York Times* called us (apparently it was a compliment). We spend time in dusty archives and dingy clerks' offices, places where you need a miner's helmet and one of those surgical masks preferred by Michael Jackson. The distinctive aroma of aged paper—a mixture of tube socks and vinegar—hangs on your clothes like cigarette smoke from a nightclub. Still, the promise of a paperless office remains a frightening prospect.

When not combing through files, we're writing letters requesting documents. And while The Smoking Gun is probably not what he had in mind, President Lyndon B. Johnson deserves credit for the single most important piece of legislation aimed at opening government records. On July 4, 1966, LBJ signed into law the Freedom of Information Act, noting that the legislation "springs from one of our most essential principles: a democracy works best when the people have all the information that the security of the Nation permits." Previously, a requester had to demonstrate a need for government documents and, if denied, had no judicial remedy available.

With FOIA, that "need to know" was flipped. Citizens suddenly had a right to this material, and the burden to prove why documents should not be released had shifted to Uncle Sam. In 1974, after Watergate drove Richard Nixon from the White House,

Congress fortified FOIA, overriding a veto from President Gerald Ford in the process. Following the federal lead, states soon adopted similar open records laws.

But that doesn't mean it's easy to get this stuff. File a FOIA request with the FBI and it could take forever to be fully processed (our personal best spanned seven years, two months). And then there are the redaction-happy censors who thrill to blacken the life out of documents. Our favorite is the court clerk we encountered when searching for a criminal case filed against some deviant who had gotten too friendly with a horse at a New York racetrack. After initially refusing to release the animal cruelty complaint, the clerk and her supervisor relented, but not before taking a Sharpie marker to the single page. She had obliterated the horse's name, explaining that "we don't release the names of victims" in sex crimes cases. Luckily, we didn't mention that the poor filly, one Saratoga Capers, was a four-year-old —or they might have tried to deny release on the grounds that she was a minor.

As with all other documents in this book, that criminal complaint is reproduced here in the form that it was obtained by The Smoking Gun. With the exception of a couple of instances where we've obscured certain identifying information such as Social Security numbers, all the redactions were made by the government agency releasing the particular record. While annoying, the redactions do offer the chance to play our favorite parlor game—Guess What's Under The Black Box.

Along with the book's uncredited collaborators—the cops, FBI agents, spies, bureaucrats, lawyers, and aggrieved citizens responsible for these documents— the authors would like to thank our editor, Terry Adams; Sloan Harris at ICM; Beverly Joel at Heavy Meta; Mike Essl and Matt Richmond at The Chopping Block; Andrew Goldberg; Joseph Jesselli; Kevin Dresser; Jonathan Hoefler; Richard Frenkel at Infoboard; Ken Cobb; Don Forst; Galen Jones and Jim Lyons at Court TV; Tom Apple; Wayne Barrett; Geoff Smith; John Hempill; Jon Bowles; Sam Bretzfield; and Ed Borges. Finally, special thanks to our families—Andrea and Siena, and Andrew.

CELEBRITY CIRCUS

Lou

Courtney

MAE

DEAN

SAMMY

Martha

Jack

MICK

BURT

George

Tom

Parker

Nicole

Kurt

Gracie

Kirstie

FRANK

"Puffy"

HOWARD

Roseanne

Fame may be fleeting, but foolish is forever.

Robert A. Adair, M.D., P.A.

☒ 41 West 96th Street
New York, NY 10028
Telephone (212) 866-2000
Fax (212) 749-6823

☐ 1066 Teaneck Road
Teaneck, NJ 07666
Telephone (201) 837-2111
Fax (201) 837-5875

January 10, 1998

Handprint Entertainment
Attention: Benny Medina
8436 West Third Street
Suite 650
Los Angeles, California 90048

Re: Sean "Puffy" Combs

Dear Mr. Medina:

This is to inform you that Sean "Puffy" Combs is under my medical care for acute and chronic symptoms and medical problems. Mr. Combs was most recently examined in my office on January 5, 1998. At that time, he was found to be suffering with hypertension, exhaustion, headaches, insomnia, anxiety reaction and dehydration.

As a result of my physical examination on that date and the patient's symptoms, Mr. Combs has been placed on bed and house rest and has been unable to travel and/or perform all of his normal work activities. The patient will be re-evaluated by us on January 15, 1998. At present, Mr. Combs' condition is fair and his prognosis is guarded.

Thank you.

Sincerely yours,

Robert A. Adair, M.D.
RAA:ch
via telecopier: 213-655-8555

When Sean "Puffy" Combs canceled a European tour at the last minute, he secured this doctor's letter for insurance purposes. Perhaps Midol would have helped Puff cope with those nagging PMS-like symptoms.

000062

1.   **"Confidential Information."** "Confidential Information,"
as the term is used in this agreement, includes any material or
information relating to Tom Cruise, Nicole Kidman or any other
member of the Cruise Family, his or her personal life, characteristics, views, conduct or background, or his or her business or
financial condition, affairs or operations, or the business or
financial condition, affairs or operations of any entity owned or
controlled by any member of the Cruise Family ("Cruise Entities").
By way of example but not limitation of the foregoing, Confidential
Information includes personal knowledge of Employee, as well as
physical items, such as negatives, masters, prints and copies of
photographs, films, videos, tapes and other records or recordings
of or relating to any member of the Cruise Family or his or her
voice or likeness, or any of his or her assets or activities. The
material and information described hereinabove are Confidential
Information no matter how obtained. By way of example but not
limitation of the foregoing, such information may be acquired by
observing documents, things, people or events, by direct communications with a member of the Cruise Family or others or by overhear-
ing conversations in the home, on the telephone or otherwise.

Employee acknowledges, and the parties agree, that priva-
cy and the non-disclosure of Confidential Information are vitally
important to the members of the Cruise Family and to Employer, that
Tom Cruise and Nicole Kidman are internationally well known figures
who will be seriously harmed both professionally and personally by
the unauthorized disclosure of Confidential Information, with the
amount of such harm likely to be very substantial and to vary with
the type and extent of disclosure and/or use of such information,
and that it would be extremely difficult and impractical, if not
impossible, to measure the full extent of the actual damages caused
by Employee's violation of this agreement. Accordingly, the parties agree upon the following schedule of liquidated damages, which
they acknowledge and agree is reasonable in light of the circumstances existing at the time this contract is made:

a.   Private disclosure or repetition of Confidential
Information, $50,000 for each person to whom each such disclosure
or repetition is made.

b.   Causing, participating or cooperating in, aiding or
abetting publication, broadcast or other public disclosure or
repetition of Confidential Information:

(1) In a newspaper or magazine, $20 for each copy
printed, with a minimum of $1,000,000 per publication.

(2) In a book, $250 for each copy printed, with
a minimum of $1,000,000 for publication in the United States,
$500,000 per territory for publication in Japan, U.K., Germany,
Italy, France, Canada, Australia, Scandinavia or Spain (the "major
territories"), and $250,000 per country for publication in other
countries.

(3) By theatrical exhibition, $20,000 per showing.

(4) In a U.S. network television broadcast,
$5,000,000 per broadcast.

(5) In a U.S. non-network television broadcast,
$2,000,000 per broadcast.

(6) In a foreign television broadcast (a) in major
territories, $1,000,000 per broadcast; (b) other foreign television
broadcasts, $500,000 per broadcast.

(7) In video cassettes, discs or other video
devices, $30 for each unit manufactured, with a minimum of
$1,000,000.

(8) On audio records (tape, disc or otherwise),
$10 for each unit manufactured, with a minimum of $1,000,000.

(9) By other public disclosure or repetition,
$1,000,000 for each such disclosure or repetition.

c.   With respect to the first time, unintentional
disclosure of Confidential Information, only one-half of the sums
specified above shall be payable.

d.   In addition to the foregoing liquidated damages, any
payment or other consideration payable to or received by Employee
for causing, participating or cooperating in, aiding or abetting
publication, broadcast or other disclosure or repetition of
Confidential Information shall be the property of Employer and, if
received by Employee, shall be held in trust for Employer.

Just in case any of Tom Cruise and Nicole Kidman's household workers wanted to spill the beans on the couple's fractured marriage, the Draconian penalty provisions in this employee confidentiality agreement would likely keep them quiet. For example, a leak to the *National Enquirer* would set a maid back $55.2 million.

DECLARATION OF RICHARD S. PARKER, JR.

1   I, RICHARD S. PARKER, JR., declare as follows:

2   1.   I am the Petitioner herein and the father of William T. Parker, born

3 September 28, 1992 (hereinafter "True") and Lillie P. Parker, born June 15, 1994 ("hereinafter

4 "Lillie"), the only children of my marriage to Respondent, Kirstie L. Alley, (hereinafter

5 "Kirstie").

6   2.   This Declaration is prepared and submitted in support of my Order to Show

7 Cause for Spousal Support, Child Support, Attorneys' Fees, Accounting Fees, and other

8 miscellaneous relief.

Lifestyle:

16.   Our lifestyle became lavish at or about the time Kirstie obtained her *Cheers* series in 1987. I was familiar with Kirstie's contracts and remuneration. At that time, Kirstie was earning $65,000 a week (which ultimately peaked at $150,000 per week) for 26 weeks of episodes. In or about 1993, at the end of the *Cheers* series, Kirstie's "loan out" corporation earned nearly $6 million for that year. Respondent and I maintain over 13 vehicles. We enjoyed private tennis lessons, personal trainers and almost-nightly masseuses. Money was, and remained, no object throughout our marriage. We spared no expense when it came to our lifestyle. Kirstie and I always had the financial wherewithal to pamper ourselves with gifts

When his marriage to Kirstie Alley cratered, Parker Stevenson sought support payments so that he'd be able to maintain the lavish lifestyle—detailed in this Los Angeles court declaration—he previously shared with the *Cheers* star. The image of a Hardy Boy as a kept man is unavoidable.

1 and "toys." Kirstie's extravagances included clothing, a golf cart, personal beauty services,

2 jewelry and entertainment, while mine included fancy cars and boats, including a 40-foot

3 power boat, a sailboat, a 25-foot Boston Whaler, and 10-foot and 12-foot runabouts. Our

4 children, True and Lillie, were provided with bountiful material possessions. Kirstie and I

5 made a conscious decision to expose our children to a myriad of opportunities. I anticipate

6 that the children will continue to be provided every educational, extracurricular and travel

7 opportunity. Kirstie and I generally spoiled each other with expensive gifts. Among the gifts

8 I received from Kirstie in the past were a 1984 Ferrari 512BBi, an antique wooden sailboat,

9 and a rowing shell. I gave Kirstie multiple art pieces, bronzes, antiques, exotic animals and

10 jewelry.

11   17.   Kirstie and I generally traveled in private jets and/or luxury private buses, with

12 every possible amenity. The times we used the private buses, we preferred chartering the bus

13 used by the Prime Minister of Canada on his campaign tours; it had every amenity. When we

14 would travel to New York, we would always stay in a $2,000-a-night suite at the Hotel Pierre.

15 We would always have security accompanying us on our excursions and traveled in "stretch"

16 limousines. When we would arrive in New York, we would generally go directly from the

17 airport to the FAO Schwartz store, which opened after hours exclusively for us. FAO

18 Schwartz would keep a staff and the store open for two hours exclusively for Kirstie and me.

19 We spared no expense, as we enjoyed our "private" shopping spree. Our FAO Schwartz

20 private jaunts would cost us approximately $15,000. Kirstie and I also enjoyed lavish,

21 frequent shopping sprees for ourselves, in Europe, New York and other cities to which we

22 traveled.

23   18.   Throughout the course of our marriage, we traveled around the world on both

24 business and pleasure, attended countless openings of theatrical events, movies, fund raisers

25 and award shows, as well as various major film and entertainment events. Whenever we

26 traveled, we would fly either first class and/or in private jets, and our accommodations were

27 extremely luxurious. By way of example, when in Italy in the summer of 1996, we rented a

28 villa in Florence for a month, and also a villa adjacent to Lake Gardo, for a month (costing

approximately $20,000 a month), with a complete staff, including a caretaker, cook, chauffeur/ body guard, and nannies.

19.   When we traveled to Florida, we did not rely simply on luxurious hotels, but rather "personalized" our accommodations. Kirstie was never satisfied with any accommodation or rental property "as is." Rather, she historically recarpeted, refurnished, and relandscaped the houses we leased, even on a short-term basis, and in Florida, we leased two adjacent properties. During our travels, we maintained our own personal chefs and full-time housekeepers.

20.   This summer when I traveled to see the children in Baltimore, where Kirstie was shooting the film, *Richer or Poorer*, I went to the luxurious property she rented during such filming. Kirstie had rented a huge equestrian estate, on an expansive piece of property with thoroughbred horses.

21.   When it came to our children, no expense was spared. In addition to giving Lillie a life-size baby giraffe rocking horse, at a cost of $10,000, we built True "The Little Homer," a down-scaled exact replica of "The Down Homer," a working lobster boat. In fact, at Lillie's recent birthday at my residence, on June 15, 1997, Kirstie sent over an extravagant display of balloons and birthday cake, a driveable electric Barbie car as a gift for Lillie, and a pool/air hockey/ping pong table for True. Like birthdays in the past, Lillie's birthday party included extravagant food, clowns, "moonbouncers," etc.

22.   Kirstie and I were famous for our children's parties, and most famous for our annual Halloween and Easter parties. At our annual Halloween parties at the Encino property, hosting up to 200 guests, we hired a 150-piece marching band and six cavalrymen on horseback shooting blanks from guns to commence the festivities. The parties would last approximately six hours and in the past have included petting zoos, camels, ponies, chimps and performers. Formal dining tables would be set up on the property for the children, including formal crystal place settings. After the marching band and six horsemen entered the one-acre circular driveway of the Encino residence, we had a traditional "rope-cutting" ceremony to commence the festivities and all the guests would scurry for the food and other

gifts which were hidden on the property for them to find. The Halloween parties cost approximately $20,000-$25,000 each. We spared no expense with entertainment for such parties, often times flying the entertainment in from across the country. Kirstie and I flew in a special puppeteer that we had admired in New York's Central Park when we had traveled there.

23.   For the past four or five years, we have flown in the "Santa Claus to the Stars," generally on Christmas Eve or Christmas Day to the location of our holiday party. This is the same "Santa Claus to the Stars" that has been utilized at White House functions. We also paid for flights of our families and friends for holidays. We would generally spend approximately $30,000 to $40,000 on Christmas gifts alone. One year, while Kirstie was filming *Look Who's Talking III*, we recreated "Santa's Village," as pictured in that film, utilizing the studio's blueprints. We created this on the grounds of the Ballfield in Maine, replete with lights, reindeer, Santa, and giant candy canes which surrounded the pond, which would be open for nightly ice-skating for the entire island of Isleboro.

24.   Easter celebrations, like Halloween, were extravagant and consisting of food, entertainment, bountiful gifts and an Easter egg hunt.

25.   For Thanksgiving, we traditionally flew our entire families to either Encino or Oregon for an elaborate Thanksgiving celebration and feast. Our Thanksgiving celebration would generally cost us approximately $10,000.

26.   I desire to maintain a lifestyle commensurate to that which Kirstie and I had enjoyed during our marriage, and am requesting sufficient support to accomplish same. To lease and/or purchase a property equivalent to the Encino property alone (without consideration of other properties owned and enjoyed by Kirstie and me), will cost approximately $18,000 a month. I am currently in a rental home in Bel Air, comparable to the Encino residence. The children have grown familiar with the Bel Air rental residence during their summer custodial periods with me, and the Bel Air residence is where I desire to continue to reside. The landlord is requesting $18,000 a month from me to stay in the residence after September 1, 1997 and I would prefer to remain there so that the children will

STATE OF NEW YORK)
) ss:
COUNTY OF SUFFOLK)

I, MATTHEW JOHN MUNNICH

_____, being duly sworn, deposes and says:

I am 23 years old. I was born on March 4, 1974. I live at 8 Sage Road, Port Jefferson Station, New York 11776. I live there with my parents and I have lived there my whole life. The phone number is 516-928-████. I graduated from SUNY Cobbleskill in December 1996. _I have a Bachlor's degree in Plant Science and an Associate's degree in Ornamental Horticulture. I started work for Whitmore's Landscaping on March 3, 1997, which is located on Montauk Highway in Amagansett, New York. I was hired as a Foreman Trainee, so when the foreman is not on the job, I'm in charge of the crew.

On Wednesday, May 21, 1997, at about 9:30 PM, I was working at 87 Georgica Close Road, the Harry Macklowe residence. My foreman was not on the job so I was in charge of the crew. I had at least eight (8) men working on this job. As we were loading up the truck, we were walking back and forth from the property to the road. As I was walking on the driveway, I saw headlights pulling into the driveway. I walked up to the driver's side of the car, to the driver's window, and I said, "May I help you?" The car was a dark colored big suburban, I think it was 4-door. There was a lady driving. She asked me if we, meaning Whitmore's, had put up a fence and I told her no. At that point she started to get extremely angry and she called me a "Fucking liar". She asked, "Who put up the fence?" and I said that I didn't know. She then started yelling, "All you Whitmore guys are fucking liars, you're all no good, the bunch of you". She was just screaming at me and yelling that "you and all your fucking illegal aliens are no good". She said she was going to call the police. I said go ahead. The whole time she was yelling at me, I said, "This is not really necessary to be talking like this and don't talk about my guys like that." I kept telling her, "I'm sorry there is nothing I can do about it". She said, "Don't you leave, I'm calling the police and you're going to take that fence down." At this point, she picked up her car phone. Right around that point, I realized that this person was Martha Stewart, who has a house next door. I recognized her from TV.

I was getting ready to walk away and she was still yelling at me and then she started to back out of the driveway. As she started

Witnessed/Sworn to before me this
23 day of MAY, 1997.

Gerald Larsen
GERARD LARSEN
Notary Public, State of New York
No. 499-1361

False statements made herein are punishable as a Class "A" Misdemeanor pursuant to Section 210.45 of the New York State Penal Law.

_____   5-23-97
Signature   Date

I, MATTHEW JOHN MUNNICH
_____, *being duly sworn, deposes and says:*

to back out, I was standing next to the driver's door. I was between the driver's door and the security entrance keypad which sticks up out of the ground. It controls the electronic gate on Mr. Macklowe's property. As she started to back out, she was trying to dial the phone, close her window and turned the steering wheel to the right and the front of the car moved to the left and pinned me against the electronic security box. I was trapped against the electronic box, the sideview mirror on the driver's door and the driver's door. I started to yell, "You're fucking crushing me, stop the car, let me out." She looked right at me and kept backing. As the car was crushing me more into the security device, the mirror collapsed forward and I was able to go into the bushes and avoid getting hit by the front of her car. She backed out into the road and at that point, I saw two men standing in the road with smirks on their faces as if they thought the whole thing was funny. I saw her motion to them to get in the car and they did. As they were getting in, I ran out to get the license plate number. I saw it was Connecticut 420-JB. I ran to my truck and got a piece of paper and wrote the license plate number down. I went back to the street and the car was parked right in front of her driveway and I then realized I had the wrong plate number written down and I then wrote the correct one down, Connecticut 420-JLB. I am now giving that piece of paper to Sergeant Larsen and I am placing today's date, 05/22/97, at this time, 1:35 PM, and I have initialed it. I am also giving Sergeant Larsen the sweatshirt I was wearing last night. It's a gray sweatshirt with a Whitmore's emblem, size large and my initials are on the label. I finished loading up the truck and then I left.

At that point I didn't know what to do. If I should call the police on my own or I should talk to my boss. This morning, I talked to Keith Tikkanen, my foreman, and Jack Whitmore, the owner. They said they would contact Mr. Macklowe's attorney or Mr. Macklowe himself to see what I should do.

I received an injury from this incident to my right side from the electronic security box. It is black and blue. It was giving me some pain last night and it was giving me some discomfort today. I have also noticed that it is still black and blue and that there

July 26, 1971

Jack Lord,

I hate You! I'm gonna fight and Kill You! You think You are the So-Called "terrific", But You just wait! I'm going to steal Your girlfriend away from You! SO, You Better Watch Out! To me You have B.O. (Body odor)! You have Various types of dieasse (Contagious kinds). I'm coming to Your studio Center and Kill You!!

As if the threats to murder him and steal his squeeze weren't enough, Jack Lord had to endure a B.O. rank-out in this letter the *Hawaii 5-0* star turned over to the FBI (but which he wanted to keep on the QT).

Mr. LORD requested that this matter be kept confidential in view of his type of employment, being that should something like this become known to the press, it might prejudice his career.

CITY MAGISTRATES' COURT,
BOROUGH OF MANHATTAN,

```
* * * * * * * * * * * * * * * * * * * * * *
THE PEOPLE OF THE STATE OF NEW YORK        *
on complaint of JAMES S. BOLAN,            *
              against-                     *
C. WILLIAM MORGANSTERN,EDWARD ELSNER,      *
MAE WEST,BARRY O'NEILL, EDNA VON           *
BEULOW,LYONS WICKLAND,PACIE RIPPLE,        *
GORDON BURBY,DAVID HUGHES, D.J. HAMILTON,  *
CONSTANCE MORGANSTERN,ANN READER,WARREN STERLING THOMAS
V. MORRISON,ALFRED L. RIGALI,FRANK R. WOOD *
MARYE MORRISEY, IDA MANTWELL,CONDE BREWER, *
FRED LE QUORNE,FLORENCE DOHERTY, AND PETE  *
SEGRETO.                                   *
                        DEFENDANTS.        *
* * * * * * * * * * * * * * * * * * * * * *
```

Act II "episode" 1 takesplace in the cafe in Hotel
Port au Prince,Trinidad, to which place the prostitute,
Margie LaMont, following out the request of Lieutenant Gregg,
in "episode"2, has come with Lieutenant Gregg. In this
"episode" the prostitute dances before the sailors of the
fleet and the officers in a way that causes Ensign Jones,
the same cahracter in which "episode"1 had solicited Margie
LaMont to commit an act of prostitution with him, to say

"You'd make a bulldog braek its chain", the said danceshaving
been performed by the defendant Mae West by moving her
buttocks and other partsof her body in such a way as to
sugget an act of sexual intercourse . In this scene defendant

New York cops once busted Mae West for the kind of rump-shaking that today would land her the lead in Snoop's next video.

HOWARD A. STERN - CONFIDENTIAL B

1   asshole in the newspaper, take out an ad. While I

2   was on the air there, they interrupted the

3   broadcast and had another guy talk about tune over

4   to the FM. They wouldn't pay me the money. These

5   are actual acts that affect people.

6   Q.   Let me just, at the risk of losing

7   memory of the tape and if you do, we can come back

8   to it. Let me just ask you a couple of questions

9   about that.

10   You say that Mr. Mancow sent you a

11   package containing excrement. How do you know it

12   was from Mr. Mancow?

13   A.   I received three or four letters. My

14   producer Gary opens the mail. I received three or

15   four letters from him on Loop -- not Loop, I forget

16   the name of the station he was on, with his various

17   paraphernalia. They have bumper stickers, they

18   have Mancow hats, this and that. He sent me a

19   plastic cow saying hey, asshole, you've lost in

20   Chicago, fuck you. This kind of stuff. Sent me

21   repeated things.

22   And I think Gary, I'm not sure who it

23   was that called over, they in fact even said yes,

24   it was us. We sent it to you. Go screw yourself,

HOWARD A. STERN - CONFIDENTIAL B

1   you lost in Chicago, you're a loser.

2   And in the same handwriting, same

3   boxes, he writes Mancow on the return address,

4   sends a box of what I believe to be either cow

5   excrement or human excrement. I'll continue.

6   He also then sent up a guy to defecate

7   in the lobby of my building where two female

8   interns were.

9   Q.   What's your basis for saying

10   Mr. Mancow did that?

11   A.   He was on the radio with it. And he

12   sent a guy named Turd -- not a guy named Turd,

13   there was another guy, a listener, with a hand-held

14   telephone -- you can see I get a little upset about

15   this, because this is beyond. This is enough

16   already. This they got to stop. Evergreen has got

17   to stop there this. You don't pay --

18   Q.   This is personally --

19   A.   With Evergreen's knowledge. He's an

20   employee of Evergreen, I assume.

21   Q.   I was going to say this is personally

22   upsetting to you.

23   A.   Oh, absolutely. Listen, I can take

24   jokes, I can talk on the air about anything. When

This excerpt from a court deposition of Howard Stern reveals what the King of All Media actually finds "shocking and appalling." Hint: It's not Baba Booey's breath.

```
1          HOWARD A. STERN - CONFIDENTIAL B
2     you expose young people, 18 years old, to guys
3     defecating in a lobby in front of them, women who
4     are sensitive to that, they don't want to see some
5     guy pull down his pants and make excrement on a
6     floor of a studio, that's different.
7          Q.      That's a vile thing to do.
8          A.      I think it's vile.  I think it's
9     wrong.  Somehow through my comedy -- listen, I'm
10    the type of guy that doesn't just sort of lay back
11    and take it.  I try to mix it up a little bit on
12    the air and try to do it in such a way to be
13    entertaining as well as provocative.
14              But would I move my bowels in front of
15    a teenage intern who doesn't even want to see this
16    kind of thing, hasn't asked to see this kind of
17    thing, without knowing who's going to open the
18    mail -- I think that might be a violation of
19    federal law, sending excrement through the mail.  I
20    don't know.  You tell me.
21         Q.      I'm happy to say I don't know the
22    answer to that question.
23         A.      It was shocking and appalling.
24         Q.      Did you know that people calling
25    themselves fans of your show sent excrement through
```

INTERIM/NOON & PRATT COURT REPORTING

AS THE WORM TURNS

Trouble just seems to follow Dennis Rodman, as these excerpts from lawsuits filed against the former NBA star reveal. Most of the suits charge the Vegas-loving Worm with illegal use of the hands (and other appendages).

14.   Plaintiff went to the bathroom to call her fiancé again and emerged from the bathroom to find RODMAN stripped down to his boxer shorts and exposed his penis.

15.   Plaintiff yelled, "What are you doing? You're disgusting!"

16.   RODMAN grabbed Plaintiff and began fondling her breasts and entire body. RODMAN quickly jammed his hand under her dress and sexually assaulted Plaintiff.

Chaker v. Rodman, Los Angeles Superior Court, 1999
1 in a series of 10

(62-81518-477)

13. CALL GIRLS, OBSCENE FILM, RAIDEN MATTER

(62-75147-26 section 17, serial 243) b7C b7D

During the White Slave Traffic Act Investigation in March, 1949, of ▮▮▮▮▮▮▮▮▮▮▮▮▮▮▮▮▮▮▮▮▮▮ it was ascertained that the victim, a prostitute named ▮▮▮▮▮▮▮▮▮ was in contact with George Raft while the latter was staying at the Sherry Netherlands Hotel in New York. (31-74879)

(66-16453-1) b7C b7D

In 1952 and 1953, the Los Angeles Office reported that George Raft was interviewed by Bureau Agents in connection with another investigation. In an attempt to locate Raft at his residence in Beverly Hills, it was determined that his house was occupied by a young woman who Raft later advised was his girl friend. He stated he allowed the girl to live in his house with her parents while he was absent from California, and upon returning found that her parents were ill and he could not move them from the house so he took an apartment in Beverly Hills where he was interviewed. At the time of the interview, Raft was accompanied by two male associates one of whom was recognized as ▮▮▮▮▮▮▮▮ Agents observed that Raft is small in stature, has a very limp hand shake and gives the personal impression quite contrary to that which he portrays in motion pictures and television shows. (62-75147-26-37-445) b7C

(72-472-1556) b2 b7D

- 17 -

Price to Rosen memorandum dated 11-28-44, captioned ▮▮▮▮▮▮▮▮▮▮▮ et al., Interstate Transportation of Obscene Matter" stated it has been reliably reported that sizeable libraries of obscene motion picture films are possessed by ▮▮▮▮▮▮▮▮ Lou Costello, George Raft and others. (71-1788-95) b7C

Q   Tell me again how were your pants tailor made; what did you say?

A   Why don't you go back and reread the testimony?

THE COURT: Answer the question.

A   To the best of my recollection I testified that they were custom made leather pants that tightly contoured the lower part of my body.

Q   You also testified that you don't usually wear undergarments, isn't that a fact?

A   Right.

Q   These pants were tailor made for your performance, isn't that a fact?

A   No, just for wearing. I don't wear anything difference in a performance than I would on the street.

Q   In other words, your pants were tailor made to give maximum exposure of your genital area, isn't that a fact?

A   Huh-uh.

Q   Yes or no.

A   No.

Q   Why did you have them tailor made

to tightly fit, tightly cover the lower part of your body?

A   Well, it looks better and it feels better that way.

Q   Now, when you put your thumbs in your pants, is that as far as they went, just your thumbs over the edge of your pants?

A   No, what I meant was the four fingers inside with the thumb hooked on the waist of the pants.

Q   But you never got down as far as your wrist, all the way down into your pants, did you?

A   No.

Q   You remember the events that evening, isn't that a fact?

A   Well, I do, but I could explain that a little further if you would like.

(Discussion.)

A   If you ask me if I remember that concert, there have been years when I have done 200 concerts in 365 days. I have memories of all of them but the memory of this concert a year and a half ago does not stick out in my mind any more than a score of other concerts I have performed at.

Q   You haven't thought about this one

Hauled before a Florida court on an obscenity charge, Jim Morrison endured a prosecutor's searing cross-examination on the contour-hugging nature of his pants.

Int. Cl.: 16

Prior U.S. Cl.: 38

United States Patent and Trademark Office

Reg. No. 1,871,900
Registered Jan. 3, 1995

TRADEMARK
PRINCIPAL REGISTER

Worried that someone else might be thinking of replacing his or her name with this tangled mess, Prince hightailed it to Washington and trademarked his symbol.

PAISLEY PARK ENTERPRISES (MINNESOTA CORPORATION)
7801 AUDUBON ROAD
CHANHASSEN, MN 55317

FOR: POSTERS AND PUBLICATIONS; NAMELY, FAN CLUB MAGAZINES, COMIC BOOKS, ACTIVITY BOOKS AND BOOKS PERTAINING TO A VARIETY OF SUBJECTS;

BUMPER STICKERS AND STICKERS, IN CLASS 16 (U.S. CL. 38).
FIRST USE 3-1-1992; IN COMMERCE 3-1-1992.

SN 74-343,333, FILED 12-28-1992.

GERALD C. SEEGARS, EXAMINING ATTORNEY

OPTIONAL FORM NO. 10
MAY 1962 EDITION
GSA FPMR (41 CFR) 101-11.6

UNITED STATES GOVERNMENT

Memorandum

TO :   SAC, LAS VEGAS (92-   DATE: 1/8/73

FROM :   SAC, CHICAGO (92-3773)(RUC)

SUBJECT: SAMMY DAVIS, JR.   92-4265
             AR
             (OO: LAS VEGAS)

Re Las Vegas letter to Chicago dated 11/6/72.

Enclosed for the investigative information of the Las Vegas Division is one copy each of a memo to SAC, Chicago, dated June 11, 1968; one copy of memo to SAC, Chicago, dated September 2, 1969, and one copy of a memo to SAC, Chicago, dated November 20, 1972.

Chicago indices negative ▇▇▇▇▇▇▇▇▇▇▇▇▇▇ b7c

For information of Las Vegas, a review of Chicago indices and records reflect the only contact DAVIS had with Chicago organized figures was in 1962, when DAVIS personally appeared at the reopening of the Villa Venice, Chicago, Illinois, which establishment was then owned by SAMUEL M. GIANCANA. In this regard, DAVIS was interviewed by the Chicago Division on November 30, 1962, and DAVIS was cooperative stating that he was hired there to entertain by an entertaining agency. DAVIS added that his close friends FRANK SINATRA and DEAN MARTIN were also entertaining at the same club. For additional information, see enclosed memo dated June 11, 1968. During the same interview, DAVIS comically pointed out that he realized that things were tough in Chicago and that the appearance of some of the club guests confirmed this and that he, DAVIS, having only one eye, was not about to run the risk of loosing it by getting involved with organized crime figures. DAVIS added that had he known that the club was any way connected with an organized crime figure, that he would not have accepted the invitation to entertain there.

② - Las Vegas (Encl 3)
1 - Chicago
JPD/bkb
(3)

92-4265-9

SEARCHED ____ INDEXED ____
SERIALIZED ____ FILED ____
JAN 18 1973
FBI—LAS VEGAS

Buy U.S. Savings Bonds Regularly on the Payroll Savings Plan

3010-108-02

While Sammy Davis, Jr., probably could have spared a tooth or two, he wasn't eager to screw around with the Mafia, members of which actually believe that "eye for an eye" crap.

BURT REYNOLDS PRODUCTIONS, INC.
PAYMENTS TO CREDITORS WITHIN LAST 90 DAYS
AGGREGATING MORE THAN $600

AMERICAN FEDERAL OF TV	792.50
APOLLO HAIR SYSTEMS, INC.	1,950.00
AT&T WIRELESS	1,499.76
COHEN PRIMIANI & FOSTER	1,000.00
ED KATZ HAIR DESIGN	5,647.20
FEDERAL EXPRESS	1,030.42
FORD MOTOR CREDIT	697.47
FOUR SEASONS	5,349.87
LA MUNICIPAL SERVICES	642.16
MID–WEST NATIONAL LIFE	1,217.00
PACIFIC BELL	487.17
PRIME MATRIX	3,806.71
SCREEN ACTORS GUILD	1,130.00
WILLIAM MORRIS AGENCY, INC.	15,000.00

D uring the depths of his bankruptcy, Burt Reynolds even had to repay debts to two hair merchants, in effect confirming what was the worst-kept secret in Hollywood history.

October 20, 1998

Larry Ish
7800 Beverly Boulevard
Los Angeles, CA 90036
Phone: (213)852-2536

Theodore Kaczynski
P.O. Box 8500
Florence, CO 81226

Dear Mr. Kaczynski:

Since your arrest, the world has been waiting to hear your side of the story. I understand how the press and media can warp or outright lie about a person's history because it makes for a better story. "The Roseanne Show" would like to offer you a platform from which you can speak out about the injustices that you feel have been dealt to you and your family.

If you know anything about Roseanne, you must know that she is a non-conformist and rarely does what society expects of her. I believe that you and her would definitely "hit it off" and the conversation would definitely be interesting and fulfilling for the both of you.

I also understand that you are attempting to have a book about your life published and a show like "The Roseanne Show" with its international audience could only help your prospects. A woman who was recently jailed for having the babies of a young boy recently had her book published in France after having it rejected by American publishers. Personally, I think it will soon be on American shelves because of the interest in the story and because of all the media play the release received here. Since, as I've said, our show is broadcast internationally, there is a very good chance that publishers outside the U.S. will want to produce your story as well.

Thank you for taking the time to review my request and please feel free to write back to me at the address above or, if you are able to, you can call me at the phone number I've listed above between 6am and 6pm, Monday through Friday, collect. I promise you, anything that we discuss or any letters you may send will remain off the record and will be held in complete confidentiality.

Sincerely,

Larry Ish
Producer

CBS Television City • 7800 Beverly Blvd. • Los Angeles, CA 90036
Phone (323) 575-2626 Fax (323) 575-2674

FORM 9 27
CS 21 67 REV 9/78

SEATTLE POLICE DEPARTMENT

INCIDENT NUMBER
94-156500

DATE 04/08/94   TIME 1340   PLACE HOMICIDE OFFICE

STATEMENT OF V.Levandowski #5326

On 04/08/94 I was working a one man marked patrol car in uniform, 1C4. At about
0856 Hrs. I was dispatched to 171 Lake Washington Blvd. E. to investigate a dead
body. On arrival, I was contacted by ▮▮▮▮▮▮▮▮▮▮▮▮▮▮▮▮▮▮▮▮ of ▮▮▮▮▮▮▮▮▮▮▮
I saw ▮▮▮▮ work truck parked in the driveway of the house. ▮▮▮▮ stated he had
arrived at the house to do some electrical work on contract for ▮▮▮▮▮▮▮ the
security company for the residence. Smith stated he had stepped onto a west facing
deck at the second floor level of the garage, and had observed a dead male on the
floor. ▮▮▮▮ said he was see the body through the french doors, but that the doors
were locked. ▮▮▮▮ took me to the doors, and I observed through the door a W/M, with
long blonde hair, laying on the floor, on his back. A shotgun was laying across
the victim's body; the butt of the gun was between the victim's feet, and the muzzle
was at about the mid-chest level of the victim. The victim appeared to be Kurt Cobain,
who I knew to be the resident of the house, and who I had contacted in the recent past.
Seattle Fire units arrived, and forced entry by breaking a pane in the french door.
On entry, SFD announced the W/M as dead on arrival, and cleared the scene, leaving
Engine Company 34 behind. SFD asked for I.D. from the nearby wallet, and I opened
the wallet which was within a couple feet of the victim's body. Inside I found a
Washington state driver's license in the name of Cobain, Kurt Donald DOB/022067.
I had called for 1G, Sgt. Getchman enroute to the call, and Sgt. Getchman and A/Sgt.
Fewel arrived. I used Getchman's polaroid to photograph the scene, while Fewel and
Getchman used 35mm cameras to document the scene. Lt. Zimnisky arrived, and notified
Homicide. Lt. Marberg stated his Detectives would respond. I maintained the scene
until Homicide's arrival.

    As I waited, ▮▮▮▮▮▮▮▮▮▮▮▮▮▮▮▮▮▮ arrived and contacted me. ▮▮▮▮ is
the president of ▮▮▮▮▮▮▮▮▮▮▮▮▮▮▮, the company which had arranged for the

STATEMENT TAKEN BY: self   SIGNED: *V. Levandowski #5326*

WITNESS: WITNESS:

PAGE   1   OF   3

This is the incident
report written
by the Seattle cop
who first responded
to the scene of
Kurt Cobain's 1994
suicide.

SEATTLE POLICE DEPARTMENT

DATE   04/08/94   TIME 1340   PLACE HOMICIDE OFFICE

STATEMENT OF: V. Levandowski #5326 -continued-

electrical work to be done by ███ ███ stated he had been informed of the event
by ███ and had responded to see if he could be of assistance. ███ stated he had
                                who was in Los Angeles.
recently spoken with Courtney Love, Cobain's wife∧ Love had stated that they were
concerned that there might be unauthorized people staying in the house, and that Love
had arranged for Tim Grant, a private investigator in Los Angeles to go to Seattle to
check the house. Love stated that Grant had been given ███ name as a contact.
Pelly said this conversation occurred on 04/06/94. ███ stated he received a call
on 04/07/94 at about 0245 from Grant, who stated that Grant was in the driveway of
Cobain's house, and was going to check the interior of the house. At about 1400 hrs.
that same day, ███ and ███ surveyed the property to assess the wiring job that
███ was to perform. ███ stated that neither he, nor ███ looked into the room
over the garage. Later that day, at about 2140 hrs., ███ received another call
from Grant. Grant asked if ███ had locked the window that Grant had used to get
inside the house. ███ told Grant he had not, as ███ had not entered the house.
███ stated he had no information on Grant other than his name, and a cellular
phone number of ███████ ███ stated he had never met Grant. I told ███
that if he should hear from Grant, to have Grant call the Homicide office.

Once the detectives arrived, A/Sgt. Fewel and I checked the interior of the main
house. Nothing appeared to be amiss, and there was nothing of note discovered.

Inside the scene, I had observed a cigar box lying next to the victim. Inside the
box were syringes, a spoon, and other items of narcotics paraphernalia. On a nearby
table was a paper placemat, with a hand-written note in red ink. The pen was stabbed
into the note, holding it in place. The note was apparently written by Cobain to his
wife and daughter, explaining why he had killed himself. I stayed on scene, until
relieved by second watch patrol units, after Cobain's body had been removed by the M.E.

STATEMENT TAKEN BY: self   SIGNED: *V. Levandowski #5326*

WITNESS: _____   WITNESS: _____

PAGE   2   OF   3

SEATTLE POLICE DEPARTMENT

DATE 04/08/94   TIME 1340   PLACE HOMICIDE OFFICE

STATEMENT OF: V. Levandowski #5326 -continued-

I secured Cobain's main house, and responded to the Homicide office to prepare the major report and this statement.

As an addendum, I had been dispatched to the Cobain residence within the last month, to respond to a 911 hang-up call. On arrival, I had contacted Courtney Love, Cobain's wife, who had stated she had called 911 ███████████████ I saw no signs of injury to Love. I heard a small child's voice, and asked who was caring for the child. Love replied, "my husband-he's in the next room." I knocked on an adjoining room's door, and Kurt Cobain answered the door. Cobain had just recently recovered from a substance abuse induced coma in Rome. I asked Kurt what was going on, and he stated that there was a lot of stress in their relationship currently. Cobain stated that they should ██████████████████ and I advised him to do that. There was no apparent need for police intervention, and with Love and Cobain's assurances that they'd work thing out, I left the residence. End of statement.

STATEMENT TAKEN BY: self   SIGNED: W. Levandowski #5326

WITNESS: WITNESS:

PAGE 3 OF 3

JOHN EDGAR HOOVER
DIRECTOR

Mr. Colson
Mr. Nathan
Mr. E. A. Tamm
Mr. Clegg
Mr. Coffey
Mr. Crowl
Mr. Egan
Mr. Foxworth
Mr. Glavin
Mr. Harbo
Mr. Lester
Mr. McIntire
Mr. Nichols
Mr. Quinn Tamm
Mr. Tracy
Miss Gandy

Federal Bureau of Investigation
United States Department of Justice
Washington, D. C.

EAT:COH

Time: 2:05 p.m.

April 1, 1939

S id and Nancy.
Kurt and Courtney.
Burns and Allen?

MEMORANDUM FOR THE DIRECTOR

Inspector Foxworth called and furnished the following developments in connection with ▮▮▮▮▮▮▮▮▮▮▮▮ in the Jack Benny case: b7C,b7D

▮▮▮▮▮▮ has told Mr. Foxworth that he has been shaken down for ten or twelve thousand dollars by Morris Rosen, Oscar Moore, ▮▮▮▮▮▮▮ and ▮▮▮▮▮▮▮▮▮ these individuals having knowledge of ▮▮▮▮▮▮ past criminal record. ▮▮▮▮▮ went to ▮▮▮▮ who runs a night club in New York City, and told ▮▮▮▮ he was not going to stand any more shake-downs and was going to report to the authorities. ▮▮▮▮ told ▮▮▮▮ that he, ▮▮▮▮▮, and "John Edgar Hoover were just like that"; that you had sat at his table and ▮▮▮▮▮ exhibited to ▮▮▮▮▮▮ photograph from you signed "To my friend". ▮▮▮▮▮▮ states he did nothing further and that he is afraid of every one.

▮▮▮▮▮▮ says that Gracie Allen was just as guilty in the smuggling case as George Burns; that in fact Gracie Allen jointly signed the checks with Burns; and that Mary Livingston is the real one involved in the Jack Benny case and that she had personally given him the jewelry he was to bring over. George Burns, according to ▮▮▮▮▮▮ deducted from his income tax the amount he paid for the jewelry. Also that when the Customs officials raided Burns and Allen's apartment, certain narcotics were found. ▮▮▮▮▮ has been informed by an individual, presently in the Federal House of Detention from Alcatraz, that both Burns and Allen use narcotics and that this is the reason Gracie wears long sleeves all the time. The individual claims he has sold narcotics to George and Gracie.

▮▮▮▮▮▮ also mentioned ▮▮▮▮▮▮, a well-known bondsman in the Southern District, and stated ▮▮▮▮ is supposed to be a contact man of Assistant U. S. Attorney Delaney. He also stated he had been told that if he made certain payments to ▮▮▮▮▮▮ (mentioned in the Manton case) that ▮▮▮▮ would take care of his case for him. The payments were not made as he had a falling-out with ▮▮▮▮▮▮ ▮▮▮▮▮▮ also furnished Mr. Foxworth information concerning three other pay-off matters that ▮▮▮▮ is supposed to have originated but which did not go through. Mr. Foxworth is to send the details of these to the Bureau.   RECORDED & INDEXED

The records in the Director's office show that a photograph was furnished ▮▮▮▮ on ▮▮ b7C
4/1/37 autographed, "With most cordial regards from your friend."

Respectfully,

FEDERAL BUREAU OF INVESTIGATION
APR 7 1939
E. A. TAMM

that it was later when JIMMY JOHNSON did not show up at a NYC HAMC
run to the grave site of VINNY GIROLAMO and the subsequent
barbecue at the back of BIG JOE's tattoo parlor that he began to
worry about the whereabouts of JIMMY JOHNSON. He advised that
after that run on September 13, 1981, that when he returned to
NYC, MILLER went to the apartment of JIMMY JOHNSON and could not
locate him there. MILLER advised that several days later he
learned that JOHNSON had been murdered and observed SANDY
ALEXANDER to be explaining to small groups of HAMC members about
some serious matter. MILLER noted that after several of these
discussions certain members seemed to be highly agitated regarding
the conversation with ALEXANDER. MILLER stated that he never was
told by ALEXANDER what happened to JOHNSON, however advised that
he was close to JOHNSON and for that reason felt that members
might be reluctant to discuss JOHNSON's murder with him.

MILLER was questioned regarding any knowledge he might
have of a murder attempt on the life of MICK JAGGER of the ROLLING
STONES. MILLER advised that he was not a member of the NYC
Chapter when this attempt was made however has been told on a
number of occasions that SANDY ALEXANDER, HERBERT KITTEL, MICHAEL
MANFREDONIA, MICHAEL CICCETTI and other NYC members of the HAMC
made an attempt to kill MICK JAGGER at a residence which JAGGER
maintained in Long Island, NY. MILLER related that these HAMC
members utilized a boat to travel out to the Long Island estate of
JAGGER and were interrupted as a storm blew up capsizing the boat
and sinking it. MILLER stated that as a result of the storm
members of the HAMC barely escaped their lives. He advised that
no further attempts were made on the life of MICK JAGGER to his
knowledge.

MILLER was questioned regarding the hierarchy of the
HAMC in the United States (US) and responded that the main figure
was SONNY BARGER. He advised that possibly IRISH O'FARREL maybe
gaining power now to the status of that held by SONNY BARGER.
MILLER advised that on the East Coast of the US SANDY ALEXANDER is
the main HAMC member and that he is shown much respect by all

472

Before setting out on the high
seas to whack Mick Jagger,
as this FBI report notes, these
guys should have checked their
dinghy's owner's manual.
Because occupancy by more than
eight bloodthirsty Hell's Angels
is definitely not recommended.
No charges were filed against
these bike enthusiasts.

BUREAU OF INVESTIGATION
DEPARTMENT OF JUSTICE
COMMUNICATIONS SECTION

JUN 26 1969

TELETYPE

FBI WASH DC

4:38 URGENT 6/26/69 MAT

TO DIRECTOR AND LOS ANGELES

FROM BUFFALO (165-1519) (P)

also known as Interstate Transmission of Wagering Information
AKA ET AL BUFFALO
Office of Origin

SUBJECT UNDER INTENSIVE INVESTIGATION BY BUFFALO, AND

SPECIAL U.S. GRAND JURY ACTION CONTEMPLATED IN JULY, SIXTY-

NINE.

DURING REVIEW OF TELEPHONE CONVERSATIONS OBTAINED

THROUGH LEGAL COURT ORDER IN STATE COURT, SUBJECT ASCERTAINED

THAT LIBERACE, NOTED PIANIST AND ENTERTAINER, HAS BEEN MAKING

LONG DISTANCE BETS WITH ANOTHER BUFFALO BOOKIE FOR SEVERAL

YEARS. LIBERACE IS ALLEGED TO BET FROM FORTY TO SIXTY DOLLARS

TO WIN ON EACH HORSE HE BETS.

JOHN TARRANT, DEPARTMENT ATTORNEY, ADVISED THAT HE

WOULD CONSIDER SUBPOENAING LIBERACE BEFORE U.S. GRAND JURY

IN BUFFALO. TARRANT REQUESTED THAT

BE IMMEDIATELY OBTAINED.

LOS ANGELES IS REQUESTED TO OBTAIN

EXPEDITE.

END.

EBT

FBI WASH DC

CC: MR. GALE

JUL 10 1969

MR. DELOACH FOR THE DIRECTOR

Mr. Tolson
Mr. DeLoach
Mr.
Mr.
Mr. Casper
Mr. Callahan
Mr. Conrad
Mr. Felt
Mr. Gale
Mr. Rosen
Mr. Sullivan
Mr. Tavel
Mr. Trotter
Tele. Room
Miss Holmes
Miss Gandy

 WITH DOCUMENTS

If you loved *Quincy* as a child, you no doubt dreamed of the day when you could open up a corpse with one of those Y-shaped incisions and then root around for the cause of death. Here's the next best thing: Examine these autopsy excerpts and try to identify the stiff in question.

 A Marilyn Monroe

 B Dana Plato

 C John F. Kennedy

 D Robert F. Kennedy

 E John Belushi

 F Karen Carpenter

1

ABDOMINAL CAVITY: The abdominal organs are in their normal
                                     positions and relationships and there is
no increase in free peritoneal fluid. The vermiform appendix is surgically absent
and there are a few adhesions joining the region of the cecum to the ventral abdominal wall at the above described old abdominal incisional scar.

2

A partially erased tattoo is present on the left upper arm.
Multiple fresh needle puncture marks are seen in the left antecubital fossa. On incision of the skin these marks are surrounded by fresh hemorrhage. Two (2) small fresh superficial
contusions are seen on the inner surface of the right upper
arm. The right antecubital fossa contains multiple needle
puncture marks. On incision of the skin the marks appear
surrounded by dark red blood. No evidence of scarring or
thrombosis of veins is seen either on the left or in the
right side.

3

GASTROINTESTINAL TRACT:

The esophagus is dilated and contains gastric content to the
level of the midesophagus. The upper portions of the esophagus
are grossly normal. The stomach contains an estimated 50 to 60
cc. of a dark green, dry and hydrous material which has the consistency of dried tea leaves. No solid material or identifiable
food is seen. No pills, capsules or other forms of medications
are identifiable. The mucosa is rugose and intact and reveals
no ulcerations or other abnormalities. The duodenum is dilated

4

"Recently, one of the main objectives of her psychiatric treatment
had been the reduction of her intake of drugs. This has been
partially successful during the last two months. She was reported to be following doctor's orders in her use of the drugs;
and the amount of drugs found in her home at the time of her
death was not unusual.

5

BLOOD: (Heart)

Ethyl Alcohol - Negative
Methamphetamine - Positive (Less than 0.07 mcg/mL)
Benzoylecognine - Positive
Hydrocodone - Positive
Carisoprodol - Positive
Meprobamate - Positive
Diazepam - Positive
Nordiazepam - Positive

6

7)   There is a trapezoidally folded cotton handkerchief showing,
on what appears to be the presenting (anterior) surface, several
scattered dark red and somewhat brown spots ranging from a fraction
of a millimeter to about 4 mm (less than 3/16 inch) in greatest
dimension.

Put bluntly, Mr. Smith was drunk for most of this time

BIZARRE

what appeared to be a costume that was made to resemble a penis

one hundred pounds of pork buried in Horne's backyard

he had made a trip to Venus

defecating on a service cart

On May 26, 1996 at 10:00 a.m. Plaintiff began his daily routine of intoxication

Type of Weapon used: A Large Fish

HE HAD CUT OFF HIS PENIS

roommate bitten on the penis by a spider

Sure, in a polite society some things are better left unsaid.
That's why it's preferable to hide in your room and simply read about the
strange and sickening stuff that is clogging up America's glorious court system.

SENT TO
COUNTY ATTORNEY

State of New Hampshire

Supporting Affidavit for Arrest W/O Warrant

Hillsborough County   Manchester District Court

I Tyrone Guyse being duly sworn, depose and say:

1. I have arrested:

Joshua Dostis   09-19-41   235 Neilson Road; New Salem Mass

2. I have information that a crime (or offense) has been committed by the defendant as follows:

Lewdness RSA 645:1

3. That on January 26, 2000 while on routine bike patrol at about 3:20 P.M. myself and officer Brain O'Keefe were traveling North on Elm street in the area of Hanover street when we observed a subject walking South on Elm street with what appeared to be a costume that was made to resemble a penis.

4. That while observing the subject we saw that foot traffic and vehicle traffic was heavy on Elm street.

5. That our attention was drawn to the subject because he was yelling to the crowd that was around him, and the subjects who were standing at the bus station were looking at the subject.

6. That due to the manner the subject was dressed and the crowd he was causing to gather we rode our bikes up to the subject.

7. That upon our making contact with the subject he identified himself as: Joshua Dostis DOB 09-19-41.

8. That once contact was made with the subject we asked him what he was doing and he replied "I am a dick head".

9. That while speaking with the subject a female subject walked by Mr. Dostis and made a face that implied she was offended by what Mr. Dostis was wearing and or saying.

10. That when the female (Merrin Arnold DOB 02-07-83) made this face officer O'Keefe approached her.

11. That Ms. Merrin was asked if she made the face because she found Mr. Dostis manner of dress funny or offensive and she stated "because its offensive"

12. That after Ms. Merrin made this statement Mr. Dostis was advised that a citizen found his manner of dress offensive and he should take it off.

13. That Mr. Dostis was asked to remove the "penis and scrotum" costume but he again refused stating "its art".

14. That at this point Charles Holmes walked up to officer O'Keefe and stated that he found Mr. Dostis manner of dress offensive.

15. That I spoke with two persons (Georgie Hill DOB 04-10-81) & (Michael Curtis DOB 01-27-78) whom were standing at the City of Manchester bus stop, and they advised me that they found Mr. Dostis manner of dress offensive.

16. That Georgia Hill stated that she was "glad her kids were not here to see this".

17. That again I advised Mr. Dostis that he would have to remove the "penis & scrotum" costume, but he again refused.

18. That he was advised that if he did not remove the costume he was going to be arrested.

19. That because he refused to take off the "penis & scrotum" costume and it was deemed as lewd and offensive he was advised that his failure to remove the "penis & scrotum" costume was going to cause him to get arrested.

20. That after again refusing to remove the "penis & scrotum" he was arrested for lewdness under RSA 645:1

_____
(Signature)

Then personally appeared the above named Tyrone Guyse and made oath that the foregoing affidavit by him is true.

Before me on this 19 day of 01, 00

_____
(Justice of the Peace)

Geez, what's wrong with these New Hampshire cops? Surely this wasn't the first time they'd run into a dickhead.

Hubbard has corresponded with this Bureau and the Department of Justice on several occasions for various reasons, including complaints about his wife and about alleged communists. In one lengthy letter in May, 1951, it is perhaps noteworthy that Hubbard stated that while he was in his apartment on February 23, 1951, about two or three o'clock in the morning his apartment was entered. He was knocked out. A needle was thrust into his heart to produce a coronary thrombosis and he was given an electric shock. He said his recollection of this incident was now very blurred, that he had no witnesses and that the only other person who had a key to the apartment was his wife.

This excerpt from the late L. Ron Hubbard's FBI file provides a whole new insight into the man. While he is often described as the controversial and enigmatic founder of the Church of Scientology, a more accurate description of Hubbard would be COMPLETE LUNATIC.

AS THE WORM TURNS

8   18.   At approximately 5:00 a.m., plaintiff was awakened
9 suddenly and discovered that defendant RODMAN had entered the room
10 and was situated at the end of the bed.   Defendant RODMAN was
11 completely naked and attempted to kiss plaintiff.   Plaintiff pulled
12 away from defendant RODMAN in an obvious and apparent rejection of
13 his sexual advances.   As she became somewhat more awake plaintiff

New v. Rodman, Orange County Superior Court, 2000
2 in a series of 10

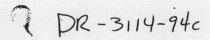

DR-3114-94c

MARITAL AGREEMENT

This document drawn on this ___23rd___ day of __September__ 1991 with the below affixed signatures of Yvonne Angenette Spires, Myles Spires, Jr. and a notary public, shall henceforth serve as the governing document for the continuance and, if applicable, the dissolution (including distribution of assets and placement of children) of the abovementioned parties' marriage, which began October 27, 1984, as per the husband's, Myles Spires, Jr., discretion.

The husband, Myles Spires, Jr., hereby agrees to continue in this marriage provided that the wife, Yvonne Angenette Spires, complies with the following articles of continuance and any addendums added bearing the notarized signature of the husband.

ARTICLES OF CONTINUANCE

1. Wife shall in no case obtain money from the joint bank accounts, individual accounts, or house emergency funds without express permission of the husband.

2. Wife shall in no case divulge information of any kind which concerns domestic relationships, i.e., marital difficulties, particulars concerning children, job status(es), and financial information to anyone outside of the marriage without the express permission of the husband. Anyone includes the wife's family, acquaintances, and friends and the husband's family, acquaintances and friends.

3. Wife shall in no wise attempt to influence the status/intensity of the relationships that husband has with other individuals outside of the marriage unless the husband verbally requests input from the wife. Moreover, the wife shall, at all times, treat the husband's family, friends, and acquaintances with the utmost respect.

4. Wife shall immediately divulge to the husband any input concerning the marriage or matters concerning the marriage given by outside parties.

5. In public, wife shall in no wise dispute husband on any matters; rather, shall present herself in full accordance with him at all times. Matters of dispute should be handled in private and with due respect, i.e., no yelling, profanity, or badgering.

6. Wife shall conduct herself in accordance with all scriptures in the Holy Bible applicable to marital relationships germane to wives and in accordance with husband's specific requests. Wife shall consult husband as to the applicability of scriptures.

7. Wife's sexual relationships shall remain spontaneous and solely with the husband.

8. Wife shall carry out requests of the husband in strict accordance, i.e., timeliness, sequence, scheduling, etc.

Wow, if Larry King had thought to draft an iron-clad post-nuptial agreement like this one, he might only be on Wife #12. The document was filed during the Washington, D.C., couple's divorce case.

Page 1 of 3

2. On or about September 19, 1997 Plaintiff went through what he believed to be a marriage ceremony in Daytona Beach, Florida, wherein Ducile M. Palermo was the bride at the ceremony.

3. Subsequently Mr. Pileggi learned that in fact the name on the marriage certificate from the September 19, 1997 ceremony was that of Carli Dene Buchanan, the daughter of Ducile M. Palermo.

8. In May, 1999, Mr. Pileggi learned he was not in fact married to Ducile M. Palermo but was married to her daughter, Carli Dene Buchanan.

9. Upon learning this fact Mr. Pileggi filed to have his marriage to Carli Dene Buchanan annulled in the Court of Common Pleas, Domestic Relations Division, of Summit County, Ohio, Case No. 99 06 1344.

Guy thinks he married this woman, but it turns out her daughter's name is on the marriage certificate. Bad news: Deceived by supposed loved ones. Good news: Second chance to consummate marriage.

On July 16, 1995 the Plaintiff was a patron at the Silver Star Casino in Philadelphia, Mississippi. The Plaintiff was suffering from a severe case of diarrhea which called him urgently to the restroom. In a moment of great haste, Plaintiff was using the men's restroom facility when his buttocks stuck to the commode seat due to the fact that someone had covered the seat with super glue, or a similar type clear, odorless substance. The Plaintiff was forced to stay on the seat until help could arrive.

After being physically pried from the seat, the Plaintiff was forced to drape a towel around his lower body and walk through the Casino accompanied by two Casino security personnel.

Most gamblers leave the Silver Star without their shirt, not their pants.

6. A male flight attendant then entered the first class section and saw FINNERAN with his pants and underwear down defecating on a service cart used by the flight crew. FINNERAN then used linen napkins as toilet paper and wiped his hands on various service counters and service implements used by the crew. FINNERAN also tracked feces throughout the aircraft.

7. The Captain of the aircraft was notified of FINNERAN's behavior. In response, the Captain suspended all food and beverage service on the flight due to the possibility of an infectious condition. At this time, the flight was approximately four hours from New York. In addition, the Captain suspended the

Finally, proof of what goes on behind the curtain separating First Class from the rabble in Coach.

THE MAGAZINE. ON THE DECEMBER 2000 PENTHOUSE ISSUE IT READS IN PERTINENT PART: "PAULA JONES UNCOVERED! SHOWS ALL AND TELLS ALL..."

THE MAGAZINE DISPLAYED NUDE PHOTOS OF PAULA JONES WHICH EXPOSES EVERYTHING BUT NOT HER <u>VAGINA</u>. WHILE AT THE SAME TIME THE FRONT COVER OF THE MAGAZINE BOLDLY READS "SHOWS ALL."
THE DEFENDANTS ALL KNEW THAT THIS FALSE, EXPLOITIVE, DECEPTIVE INFORMATION WOULD CAUSE ITS READERS OR CUSTOMERS TO PURCHASE THE MAGAZINE BELIEVING THAT PAULA JONES WAS 'SHOWING ALL' IN THE PUBLICATION.

Said reports further indicates that numerous officers approached the vehicle with their weapons drawn, ordering the driver out of the vehicle. She yelled through the closed driver's side window, "No, I'm not ready to come out." Again, officers ordered her to exit the vehicle, but she repeated that she was not coming out. As Officer Borenz approached, he could see that the driver was a white female, who appeared to not be wearing any pants or undergarments. Officers found the doors on the vehicle to be locked. When the driver began to bend over in the driver's seat and started grabbing at the floor, officers then used their batons to break the driver and passenger side windows. Once the windows were broken, an officer reached in and turned off the vehicle. Officers then had to forcibly pull the driver out of the vehicle and direct her to the ground, since she would not come out voluntarily. There was a brief struggle on the ground, but officers were finally able to secure her in handcuffs. Since she did not have any clothing on from her waist down, officers retrieved a blanket and used that to cover her.

Said reports further indicate that the driver was identified as Selma A. Troyanoski, the above-named defendant. Selma went on to give a statement, which is believed to be reliable inasmuch as it was made contrary to her penal interest. Selma said she had pulled into Lorleberg's parking lot to rest on her way from her residence in Steven's Point in Lake Geneva where she was going to attend a convention. Selma said she normally takes off her undergarments during long trips, because she sweats a lot. Selma said that because she wasn't wearing clothing from the waist down, and she was late for her check-in time in Lake Geneva, she decided to try her chances on fleeing the police.

COMMONWEALTH OF KENTUCKY
KENTON CIRCUIT COURT
DIVISION NO. *II*
CASE NO. 00-CI-01664

03.00

MACK WAYNE METCALF   PLAINTIFF

Vs.

DEBORAH HODGE   DEFEDANT

COMPLAINT

Come now the Plaintiff herein, Mack Metcalf, and for his cause of action, state as follows:

1) The Plaintiff is an individual residing in Kenton County, Kentucky.

2) That the Defendant, Deborah Hodge, is an individual residing in Kenton County, Kentucky.

3) That on or about August 7, 2000 the Plaintiff received the proceeds from the winning of the Kentucky Powerball Jackpot. At that time the Plaintiff was acquainted with the Defendant Deborah Hodge.

4] That the Defendant harassed and threatened the Plaintiff in order to obtain cash from the Plaintiff.

5] That as a result of that harassment and abuse the Plaintiff, while in an intoxicated state agreed to surrender the sum of $500,000.00 to the Defendant. The Defendant stated that she would cease her harassment of the Plaintiff upon the payment of that sum.

$500,000 to get rid of an obnoxious pest of an ex-girlfriend? Sure, he was liquored up, but most guys could be high on crack and grain alcohol and still wouldn't part with a penny more than $250K. Deborah denied the charges in Mack Wayne's lawsuit, which was later dismissed.

#
#
#
#
#
#
#   #
#   #
# # # # # # # # #

5. Mr. Smith informed me that following a period of domestic dispute he began drinking alcoholic beverages and that he patronized TD's on four (4) occasions: July 12-13; July 17-18; July 19-20; and July 21. Mr. Smith stated that he does recall some of his experiences at TD's but not all because of the excessive amount of alcohol he consumed during this period. Put bluntly, Mr. Smith was drunk for most of this time.

6. Subsequently, when Mr. Smith received his Diners Club credit card statement he found that TD's had charged his credit card account for a total of **$26,974.50.** Mr. Smith had no documentation of what these charges were for and no understanding or memory of how he alone could have incurred almost $27,000 in costs for four visits to a topless bar. Mr. Smith also informed me that TD's had reserved an additional $30,000 against his credit card which had not been charged against. I was, obviously, astounded by these allegations and considered whether they stated a probable violation of the UPA.

After "Mr. Smith" went on a drunken bender at a New Mexico strip club, he ran to the authorities when he got a whopping credit card bill, as this state investigative report shows. Yo, Smitty: Next time you have a falling out with wifey, don't console yourself with 1,327 lap dances in the nearest Champagne Room.

CONTINUED FROM:

[ ] OFFICER'S REPORT ONLY

[x] ARR./JUV. CON.

[ ] CRIME

[ ] OTHER _____

	INCIDENT NUMBER 99060031662	
PAGE 1 OF 2	CASE NUMBER 99039156	

CODE SECTION AND DESCRIPTION (ONE INCIDENT ONLY) PC / 245A1 / ASSAULT W/DEADLY WEAPON OTHER THAN FIREARM OR GBI	DATE 06/15/1999 - 06/15/1999	DAY OF WEEK TUE - TUE	TIME 01:30 - 01:31
LOCATION OF INCIDENT (OR ADDRESS) 8800 Villa La Jolla Dr	CITY SAN DIEGO	DISTRICT	BEAT 132

PERSON(S) INVOLVED: VICTIM

SUSPECT (IF NAMED)
Vitalich, Nicholas Anthony

PROPERY TAG NO.(S)

Officer's Statement:

Officers Scruggs #4407, Cook #5155, and I received a radio call of a violent disturbance at 8657 Villa La Jolla Dr. Officer Scruggs arrived at the scene before Officer Cook and myself. When we arrived Officer Scruggs was talking to a few of the employees outside the Ralph's Grocery Store. Officer Scruggs showed me a whole dead fish, laying on the side walk outside the Ralph's. ▓▓▓▓ ▓▓▓▓ walked out of the Ralph's. ▓▓▓▓ was crying and had several bruises and scratches on her arms and face. ▓▓▓▓ said her boyfriend had beaten her with the fish.

D rop the mackerel, sir, and nobody will get hurt.

Type of Weapon used: A Large Fish
Weapon(s) impounded?   [ ]YES [x]NO
Firearm impounded for safety?   [ ]YES [x]NO

PROPERTY TAG NUMBER :   N/A

REPORTING OFFICER J.Scruggs	I.D. # 4407	DIVISION N3		DATE OF REPORT 06/15/1999	TIME 07:30

ORIGINAL   CONTINUED [Y]

OFFENSE REPORT
JONESBORO POLICE DEPARTMENT

OF 1999 00519

| Complainant/Victim/Firm Name | AGE | Dob | RACE | SEX | Phone (Business) |
| LOOPER, AMY | 22 | 1976/01/31 | WHT | F | |

| Complainant/Victim/Firms Address | City/State/Zip | Phone (Residence) |
| 2209 PARKSIDE DR | JONESBORO, AR 72401 | |

| Complainant's Business, Employment/School | Object Of Attack |
| | TERRORISTIC THREAT |

| Place Where OFFENSE Occurred | Type of Building |
| 2209 PARKSIDE DR - | RESIDENTIAL |

| Reported By | Reported To | Arrival Time |
| LOOPER, AMY | LT B.J. SMITH - CID | |

| Date and Time of Offense | Date and Time of Report | How Reported |
| 1999/01/25 AT 16:00 TO 20:00 | 1999/01/26 AT 15:15 | PERSON |

| M.O. (How done, force used, at what point, tool or weapon, other acts or trademarks) | Will Complainant Prosecute |
| | YES |

SUSPECT INFORMATION

| Suspect's Name | Address | City/State/Zip |
| LOOPER, TODD ANTHONY | 2209 PARKSIDE | JONESBORO, AR 72401 |

Alias/AKA								
	RACE	SEX	Height	Weight	Hair	Eyes	Date Of Birth	AGE
	WHT	M	510	175	BLN	BLU	12/15/67	31

NARRATIVE

AMY LOOPER REPORTED TO LT SMITH THAT HER RESIDENCE AT 2209 PARKSIDE DRIVE WAS ENTERED SOMETIME BETWEEN 1600 AND 2000, 01 25 99. SHE SAID THE HOUSE WAS RANSACKED AND MUCH OF HER PROPERTY WAS DAMAGED. SHE SAID HER CAT WAS KILLED AND BEHEADED. SHE SAID A NOTE WAS ATTACHED TO THE CAT'S HEAD. THE NOTE SAID, " I'M GOING TO GIVE YOU A BIRTHDAY LIKE YOU NEVER WILL FORGET, YOU LITTLE WHORE." SHE SAID THE MESSAGE WAS WRITTEN ON THE BACK OF HER 4 YEAR OLD DAUGHTER'S COLORING BOOK.

MS. LOOPER SAID SHE KNEW THE WRITING TO BE THAT OF HER HUSBAND, TODD LOOPER. SHE SAID SHE AND TODD ARE SEPERATED. SHE SAID SHE HAS HAD AN ORDER OF PROTECTION ISSUED ON HIM, BUT THE ORDER HAS YET TO BE SERVED.

MS. LOOPER WAS ESCORTED BY LT SMITH TO THE CITY ATTORNEY'S OFFICE WHERE SHE FILLED OUT AN AFFIDAVIT FOR ARREST WARRANTS ON MR. LOOPER FOR TERRORISTIC THREATENING AND CRUELTY TO ANIMALS.

ON 01 28 99, LT SMITH ARRESTED TODD LOOPER ON THE WARRANTS. LT SMITH INTERVIEWED MR. LOOPER CONCERNING THE ALLEGATION. AFTER BEING ADVISED OF HIS RIGHTS UNDER MIRANDA, HE CONSENTED TO THE INTERVIEW. MR. LOOPER ADVISED SMITH HE DID NOT REMEMBER HURTING THE CAT, OR TRASHING THE RESIDENCE AT 2209 PARKSIDE. HE TOLD SMITH HE HAD BEEN DRINKING THE DAY OF THE INCIDENT. HE SAID HE DRANK ABOUT 14 BEERS WITHIN ABOUT 3 HOURS. HE SAID THE NOTE THAT HAD BEEN LEFT WITH THE CAT'S HEAD APPEARED TO BE WRITTEN BY HIM. HE SAID HE HAD "BLACKED OUT" AND DID NOT REMEMBER ANYTHING. HE SAID HE HAS HAD PERIODS IN THE PAST WHERE HE HAD DRANK TOO MUCH AND BLACKED OUT.

While fourteen beers in three hours might leave a guy impaired, that certainly doesn't excuse Mr. Looper's heinous act. It remains unclear how Todd chose to celebrate the couple's wedding anniversary.

| Reporting Officer | Investigating Officer | Current Disposition |
| LT B.J. SMITH - CID | LT B.J. SMITH - CID | CLOSED |

9. On May 26, 1996 at 10:00 a.m. Plaintiff began his daily routine of intoxication. He visited 7-11, Hooters, Chevron, Waterhole, Beef-O-Brady's, and Radiant.

10. Plaintiff's intoxication resulted in him entering a TECO substation at 10:00 pm on May 26, 1996. In a drunken stupor, he climbed up onto a transformer where he was electrocuted. Over 13,000 volts went through his body and threw him over 40 feet from the transformer.

26. Defendants knew or should have known that Plaintiff was a habitually addicted to alcohol due to: frequency of his visits, his continual consumption of alcoholic beverages, and his repeated behavior and appearance.

What's more embarrassing? That plaintiff got drunk, climbed a transformer, and was sizzled by 13,000 volts? Or that he hung out at a joint called Beef-O-Brady's?

```
RUN DATE: 7-JUL-00  BY: robb          Itasca County Sheriff's Dept                    PAGE    1
RUN TIME: 11:31                         * * * E N F O R S * * *  .
REPORT #: 14                            CALLS FOR SERVICE PRINT              cfs-print20r14t113132
DT-TM RPTD: ALL

                                  SORT SEQUENCE: (2) AGENCY, INCIDENT#, & INC SEQ NO
```

```
              Agency:  001
            Incident:  00005612  ISN: 02

   Date-Time Reported:  06/27/00  1520
         How Received:  911       -911

         Reported by:  steinhart, scott
             Address:  2502 midway ln  grand rapids
        Caller Phone:
   Incident Location:  2502 midway ln, APT 7  grand rapids  mn  55744-
        Common Place:

         ILI Activity:  9000      -ambulance call
         CFS Activity:  09000     -ambulanc call
         Patrol Area:  01        -grand rapids
               Grid:  005525     -grand rapids township
        Unit Assigned:  162       -meds 1 ambulance
   Officer Assigned #1:            -no entry
   Officer Assigned #2:            -no entry
                Misc:
       Time Received:  1520
     Time Dispatched:  1521
        Time Arrived:  1558
      Time Completed:  1635
         Disposition:  c         -exceptionally cleared
             Juris:  01
Environ/Weather Conditions:        -no entry
       Evidence Tech:  n
             Remarks:  roommate bitten on the penis by a spider
                       spider is a tarantula and did draw blood.
                       victim's breathing is fine, however he is very afraid.
                       victim: aaron jarva
                       upon arrival of ambulance 162, victim stated he had taken 2 grams
                       of crystal methamphetamine


   Created by Operator:  olso
ILI Last Update Operator:  robb
CFS Last Update Operator:  robb
```

Poor Aaron somehow forgot that crank + tarantula + penis = big fucking trouble. Hey, but now he'll have a fabulous story to tell the grandkids.

UNITED STATES DEPARTMENT OF JUSTICE

FEDERAL BUREAU OF INVESTIGATION
Baltimore, Maryland 21202

In Reply, Please Refer to
File No. BA 89-30

January 23, 1968

RE: DAVID F. JENKINS
      AIR FORCE SERIAL NUMBER 11986876
      AIRMAN FIRST CLASS, UNITED STATES
      AIR FORCE
      1002nd SECURITY POLICE SQUADRON

        DAVID F. JENKINS furnished the following infor-
mation to a Special Agent of the Federal Bureau of Investigation on January 19, 1968:

        JENKINS was interviewed in the psychiatric ward
of the Andrews Air Force Base Hospital and advised that he
knew who assasinated President KENNEDY. He clarified this
by saying that President KENNEDY was not assasinated in
Dallas, Texas, however, was seriously wounded by shots
fired by LEE HARVEY OSWALD and JACK RUBY. When the body
of the President was taken to the Parkland Memorial Hospital in Dallas, the heart of a dummy was transposed into
the President and the President's heart was taken out and
put into the dummy. It was the dummy that was buried in
Arlington National Cemetery. President KENNEDY is reincar-
nated in the person of his wife, JACQUELINE, and on occasions,
he assumes the identity of General WESTMORELAND, as well as
other figures of prominence.

        JENKINS stated that he has been working exhaustively
on the assasination for the past two weeks, in addition to
developing an M16 rifle which shoots filter-tip cigarettes.
The rifle is equipped with a flame thrower to light the
cigarettes as they come out of the barrel.

        JENKINS stated that there is a conspiracy against
him to prevent him from furnishing the appropriate authorities
the true facts of the assasination which was instigated and

ENCLOSURE

RE: DAVID F. JENKINS
     AIR FORCE SERIAL NUMBER 11986876
     AIRMAN FIRST CLASS, UNITED STATES
     AIR FORCE
     1002nd SECURITY POLICE SQUADRON

controlled by Lady Bird JOHNSON, without the knowledge of
her husband, LYNDON JOHNSON.

     Major DeWITT C. ALFRED, Medical Corps, United
States Air Force, advised a Special Agent of the Federal
Bureau of Investigation on January 19, 1968 that DAVID
F. JENKINS entered the Andrews Air Force Base Hospital
on January 12, 1968. He has been diagnosed as having a
psychopathic mental illness and is classified as a schizo-
phrenic paranoiac. He is confined in Category 2 which
necessitates an orderly being in his company at all times
whenever he leaves the psychiatric ward, and on those
occasions when the President of the United States is on
the Andrews Air Force Base, he is placed in Category 1
which puts him under lock and key. JENKINS will be in
confinement at the hospital for a minimum of three months
and a maximum of six months at which time he will most
probably be transferred to a Veterans Administration
Hospital.

As conspiracy theories go, this one seems as plausible as anything Oliver Stone has committed to film. In fact, some CIA asset is probably pointing one of those nicotine rifles at Fidel Castro right now (and if the weapon didn't prove lethal, it would at least set his beard on fire).

2*

In the Fall of 1954, Berney first began to tell Miss Bock of his trip to the planet Venus. He told her he had made a trip to Venus and had gained the confidence of certain leading men on the planet. He narrated how he had traveled to the planet on a spaceship two miles long, stopping on the moon en route, and told of his travels on the planet, his tour of the major cities, some explanation of the governmental system on Venus, and about his return to Earth after two weeks on the planet.

In his fantastic narrations of life and culture on the planet, Berney stated that apartments and office buildings on Venus dwarfed the Washington Monument. He said that little crime or dishonesty was evident because when anyone was found guilty of committing a serious crime he was just picked up and dropped off on another planet. He also stated that gold was so plentiful that it was used in the manufacture of plumbing fixtures. He went on to say that he had gone to and returned from Venus on a flying saucer and in the time it took to get there from the earth the sun had come up twice. He said that the moon was a stopping place on the way to Venus to pick up articles of trade.

Returning to his original theme, Berney related the confidence the planet prince, "Uccelles," had in him, saying that he had been selected to supervise the manufacture on Earth of certain highly secret items which had been invented on Venus. The most important of these Berney referred to as a "modulator," a device which was designed to operate on energy obtained from the atmosphere and which would produce greater energy potential then any atomic device.

In a book Berney wrote, entitled "Two Weeks on Venus," he gave the following description of the "modulator": "It not only generates power for light and manufacturing, but manufactures of itself the product known as magnetic flux, that being a source of unlimited power to operate any type of machinery."

Allegedly, the modulator could softly lift and lower millions of tons in a fraction of a second and could propel planes and spaceships at about the speed of light or hold them motionless in the sky. A modulator-equipped plane, by means of the pull of its magnetic field, could, if desired, blow every fuse in a city, stop all motors and completely block communications.

Berney told Miss Bock that he was working in conjunction with a large corporation in the East to develop the "modulator" for use by this country. The project was so secret, he said, that the details were known only to the White House and certain top officials of the Government. For this reason, he swore her to secrecy but assured her that when the device was completed any money she had invested in it would be multiplied at least seven times.

- 2 -

Berney gave Pauline Bock certificates which he had signed and told her each certificate represented one share in the Telewand Corporation at $100 a share. He told her she was to take one certificate for each $100 she invested in the firm. He assured her that in order to make the stock certificates valid it was necessary only for her to add her signature as secretary-treasurer of the firm. This she was careful to do, and she believed in the project so completely that by September, 1956, she had entrusted to Berney between $38,000 and $40,000.

One transaction between the two involved a check for the sum of $10,000 which he claimed was necessary "to pay technicians for completing the modulator device ahead of schedule."

In addition, Berney had interested a man and his wife in his scheme to the extent that they had invested $20,000. During the period from 1954 to 1956, Berney was alleged to have made at least two trips to Venus aboard a spaceship as large as the Pentagon Building.

In the meantime, in November, 1956, it was reported that his wife and two children had received word that Berney had been killed in an explosion and that there would be no burial service. His personal effects had been sent to his wife. The package also contained a camera, billfold and contents including two or three hundred dollars and all Berney's credentials.

A letter which Mrs. Berney received, supposedly from Mr. "Uccelles" and written with a pen brush on parchment, advised her that her husband had died and that his body was lying in state on Venus. Mrs. Berney, who had not believed his tales of Venus, concluded that he had deserted her.

In February, 1957, the information regarding Berney's defrauding operations came to the attention of the FBI and investigation was started under the Fraud by Wire Section of the Interstate Transportation of Stolen Property Statute. In the furtherance of his scheme, Berney had frequently contacted Miss Bock by telephone or letter to have her send more money to him. The check for $10,000 had been sent to him through the mails and this he had converted to his own use.

When contacted by FBI Agents, Miss Bock instantly identified a photograph of Harold J. Berney as the individual who had defrauded her of her money. She said that the only things she had to show, in a material way, from Berney's schemes were a chair and a couch she got when the Telewand office was closed in 1955. She also had $800 from the sale of Telewand machinery.

- 3 -

After the feds nabbed Harold Berney for the scheme described in this FBI memo, let's hope they seized his modulator, because that gizmo sounds like one hell of a "get out of jail free" card.

State of New York
County of Fulton
City of Johnstown

Johnstown Police Department
33-41 East Main Street
Johnstown, New York 12095

Deposition of Witness

Date 5/6/97 Time 305 PM Place Johnstown Police Dept

I, Earl S. Zea Age 34 having been born on 12/18/62

in the City of Gloversville state the following:

I think I had my Pants on when I Cut my Penis off. I had Everything on but my Shirt. I took my Shirt off because it hung out and was in the way, that Part I Remember. then after I took my Shirt off, that was when I did it. Right after that it was Right out the door.

Q: Earl, what happened to your Penis once you cut it off?
A: I flushed it.

Q: Earl, did you want us to know what happened?
A: I would say so. I didn't Try to hide Anything, or cover my Tracks.

Q: Earl, why did you cut your Penis off?
A: So he would Leave me Alone, because I don't want him Near me.

A false statement made herein is punishable as a Class "A" Misdemeanor pursuant to Section 210.45 of the Penal Law of the State of New York.

Sworn to before me this 6th
Earl S Zea

Day of May 19 97

Phone#

UNITED STATES DISTRICT COURT,

SOUTHERN DISTRICT OF NEW YORK.

--x
:
IN THE MATTER   :
:
-of the-   :
:
Petition of the OCEANIC STEAM NAVIGA-   :
TION COMPANY, LTD., for limitation of   :
liability as owner of the Steamship   :
"TITANIC".   :
:
--x

Come to think of it, when Leonardo DiCaprio was trying not to drown in those icy waters, wasn't he clinging to a life preserver that looked suspiciously like a wheel of Roquefort?

Now appears VINCENZO VICARIO, of Providence,
Rhode Island, and makes claim against the said Steamship
"Titanic", as follows:

Claimant was the owner of the following property,
of the kind and value hereinafter specified, which was aboard
the Steamship "Titanic" when she was sunk as a result of a
collision with an iceberg, in or about latitude 41.46 North,
longitude 50.14 West, on or about the 14th day of April,
1912, while the said Steamship "Titanic" was proceeding towards the port of New York, United States of America, from
Southampton, England. The character of the property and
its value .is set out in the following table:

Owner.	Shipment.	Value.
Vincenzo Vicario	40 cases Roquefort Cheese	$800.00

Claimant alleges that prior to April 14, 1912,
the above-mentioned goods had been duly shipped aboard the
Steamship "Titanic", for which bills of lading were duly
issued and are now in the possession of claimant.

On April 14, 1912, said Steamship "Titanic", with
all of the cargo hereinbefore specified on board, was sunk

IN THE HUNTINGTON CIRCUIT COURT
STATE OF INDIANA
199_9_ TERM

STATE OF INDIANA)
)
vs.)   Cause No.: 35C01-9902-CF-00004
)
EDWARD L. BODKIN)

INFORMATION FOR
PRACTICE OF MEDICINE WITHOUT A LICENSE
CLASS C FELONY
I.C. 25-22.5-8-1 and I.C. 25-22.5-8-2

The undersigned affiant, being duly sworn on his/her oath, says that he/she is informed and verily believes that:

On one or more occasions within five years prior to February 2, 1999, in Huntington County, Indiana, said Edward L. Bodkin did practice medicine without a license or permit to do so, to-wit: did perform an act or acts of surgery involving the removal of testicles from certain male persons.

All of which is contrary to the laws of the State of Indiana.

I swear or affirm, under the penalty of perjury as specified under IC 35-44.2-1, that the foregoing representations are true. (IC 35-34-1-2.4)

_____
Affiant

Reviewed this _8nt_ day of _February_ 199_9_.

_____
John F. Branham, Prosecuting Attorney, #3643-35

WITNESSES

Rod Jackson
Dave McElhaney
Janet E. Walters
Robert Jeffers
Tom Kolb
Christian Newton

> This Bodkin character has some balls trying to pull this illegal surgery stuff.

SPD CASE # 00200284   SGT ROETTGER
OCCURRED 011200 1420 HRS
REPORT MADE 011200 1535

BRUCE TRANSPORTED TO REGIONS HOSPITAL BY LAKEVIEW EMS AFTER
SEVERING HIS OWN PENIS. BRUCE TO BE HELD FOR PSYCH EVALUATION
AFTER TREATMENT FOR THE SEVERED PENIS.

RECEIVED A CALL TO THE ABOVE LOCATION FOR A MEDICAL ASSIST FOR A
MALE WHO STATED TO DISPATCH THAT HE HAD CUT OFF HIS PENIS. I
WAS CLEARING A MEDICAL AT STONE BRIDGE AND RESPONDED. UPON
ARRIVAL I COULD SEE THAT THE FIRE CHIEF KIM KALLISTEAD HAD
ARRIVED ON SCENE. HE DID NOT ENTER THE HOUSE UNTIL AFTER I
ARRIVED.

AS I APPROACHED THE HOUSE THERE WAS WHAT APPEARED TO BE BLOODY
FOOTPRINTS LEADING TO A VEHICLE PARKED OUTSIDE THE HOUSE AND
THEN BACK TO THE HOUSE. I WENT INTO THE HOUSE AND SAW ERVIN
BRUCE SITTING AT THE TABLE IN THE KITCHEN HOLDING A TOWEL OVER
HIS GROIN AREA. THERE WAS A SUBSTANTIAL AMOUNT OF BLOOD POOLED
UNDER THE CHAIR HE WAS SITTING IN AND IT HAD STARTED TO RUN TO
THE WEST.

I ASKED BRUCE WHAT HAD HAPPENED, AND HE STATED THAT HE CUT HIS
PENIS OFF. I THEN ASKED WHY HE DID THAT. HE STATED THAT WAS
FOR HIM TO KNOW. AFTER FURTHER QUESTIONS HE STATED THAT HE WAS
TIRED OF "IT" GETTING HIM IN TROUBLE SO "I CUT IT OFF." FIRE
AND AMBULANCE ADMINISTERED AID TO BRUCE. THE SEVERED PENIS WAS
TAKEN BY THE AMBULANCE TO THE HOSPITAL. BRUCE HAD TOLD
KALLISTEAD THAT HE USED A KNIFE IN THE BATHROOM. THAT HE HAD
PLACED DRY ICE ON THE PENIS AND FROZE IT SO IT WOULD NOT HURT
WHEN IT WAS SEVERED.

BRUCE CONTINUED TO STATE THAT HE WAS TIRED OF HIS PENIS GETTING
HIM IN TROUBLE, AND THAT WAS WHY HE CUT IT OFF. I ASKED WHAT
KIND OF TROUBLE HE HAD. BRUCE STATED THAT 9 YEARS AGO HE WAS
ACCUSED OF SOMETHING THAT HE DID NOT DO. I ASKED WHAT THAT WAS
AND HE SAID HE WAS ACCUSED OF HAVING SEX WITH HIS STEP
DAUGHTER. HE SAID THAT HE NEVER DID THAT. BRUCE IS A
████████████████████ AND HAS BEEN IN PRISON FOR THAT
OFFENSE.

THIS DEPARTMENT HAS HAD SOME COMPLAINTS ON BRUCE BEING A CROSS
DRESSER. THERE WERE WIGS, WOMEN'S CLOTHING, WOMEN'S
UNDERGARMENTS, FALSE BREASTS, AND UNDER GARMENTS DESIGNED TO
ENHANCE THE BUTTOCKS ALL IN PLAIN VIEW IN THE HOUSE.

THE HOUSE WAS PHOTOGRAPHED BY INVESTIGATOR SPENCER TO DOCUMENT
THE KNIFE THAT WAS USED. PHOTOGRAPHS WERE ALSO TAKEN ON THE
AREA IN THE KITCHEN WHERE BRUCE SAT, AND THE WOMEN'S CLOTHING
AND WIGS.

ROLLO stated that it took him approximately four weeks to build this guillotine. ROLLO stated that he has not shown this guillotine to anyone else. ROLLO stated that no one else helped him build this guillotine. ROLLO stated that no one else has used it at anytime.

ROLLO stated that he thought by cutting off his arm that this would enhance his masculinity and thus enhance his appearance. ROLLO stated that this is what he always wanted.

ROLLO stated that after he cut his arm off, he picked it up and put it into the refrigerator. ROLLO stated that he did this because he knew he would then be in the hospital for a couple of weeks and he had no where else to put it. ROLLO stated that after he cut his arm off that he immediately called for the ambulance and waited outside.

x   x

blood pool on the other side of the guillotine. Sergeant GACEK observed a blood trail which led from the guillotine to a refrigerator in the basement level. Sergeant GACEK stated that opened up the refrigerator door at which time he observed that the victim's arm was inside a Pick N' Save plastic bag. Sergeant GACEK

Next time Rollo wants to ratchet up the masculinity level, he might try splashing on some Old Spice or going to a monster truck show. Because you can get away with that arm amputation trick only a couple of times.

x
x
x
x
x
x x x x x x x x x x x x

5. That the factual predicate for Plaintiff's complaint is as follows:

a. That on or about March 11, 1996, Plaintiff went to the Gratiot and 12 Mile location of Defendant in the City of Roseville, County of Macomb, State of Michigan, in order to have a tattoo placed on him.

b. That John Doe, an employee of Defendant, applied a tattoo meant to spell "Villain" on the right forearm of Plaintiff.

c. That as a result of the incorrect spellling of the word "villain" the Plaintiff wound up with a tattoo spelled "Villian", the Plaintiff underwent plastic surgery resulting in extensive scarring.

> > > > > >
>
>
>
>

Don't obsess over clean needles. Forget about the license from the Department of Health. And don't fret about the pain. All you should worry about is whether your tattoo parlor has a dictionary.

AS THE WORM TURNS

6. That in addition to, and during, the afore described conduct and behavior of Defendant Rodman, the Defendant started rubbing the bald head of Plaintiff James Brasich, the Defendant further stroked and rubbed the chest of Mr. Brasich, even attempting to get inside of Plaintiff's shirt, and the Defendant furthermore, with the dice in his hand, rubbed his hand upon Plaintiff's groin; Defendant, a few minutes later, again rubbed Plaintiff in the groin with his hand, and moments later Defendant again, for the third time, rubbed Plaintiff in the groin with his hand; all the while Plaintiff was engaged in his duties as craps dealer in the game, and attempting to maintain his composure and

At approximately 1030 hours I spoke with Dr. Farol Tomson, Director of Animal Resources. I advised him of the meat that was recovered, and requested that he have David Cannon come by the Police Department to see me. Dr. Tomson said all of the meat from the pigs needs to be recovered and taken to the barn and burned.

David Cannon came by the University Police Department about 1300 hours and spoke with me. He said that he never told Kenny Atkins that Dr. Hauswirth said the meat was all right to eat. Cannon said everyone who works for Animal Resources knows the animals sent to the barn to be burned are not fit to eat.

On Friday, January, 19, 2000 at approximately 0930 hours Marvin Alligood was interviewed at his home North of Alachua by Investigator Burton Parker and me. Alligood said he saw a total of three pigs. He said he called Tom Crawford and Crawford told him the pigs were used for experiments and were not fit to be eaten. He said he wouldn't butcher them but Dave Washington did. He said that Washington is working in Union County and he would see him on Saturday and he would have him call me. Alligood said that James Horne had a pig and when he found out the meat was bad he buried the meat. Alligood gave us the directions to Horne's house, which is not far from Alligood's and is just off of County Road 241 just south of County Road 236.

At approximately 1030 hours Investigator Parker and I arrived at Willie James Horne's home. He advised that he had gotten the pork from Norman Blake on Friday, January 12, 2001. He said he found out from Marvin Alligood that the meat was poisoned and not fit to eat, so he buried it in his back yard. I advised James Horne that someone would be by later in the day to dig up the meat and haul it off.

We then went to James Horne's residence. Jesse Williams and Kenny Atkins followed us. Atkins dug up the pork in Horne's backyard and they took it back to the barn to be burned. I estimate there was about one hundred pounds of pork buried in Horne's backyard.

There's just something about the smell of rotting swine—and the accompanying maggot swarm—that kills your property value.

OFFICIAL CHANNELS

TOP SECRET

TOP SECRET

and

Most government dossiers are filled
with the kind of drab prose that
leaves many bureaucrats dozing at their desks
(that and the malt liquor lunches).
But every so often, a file coughs up a gem
that restores your faith in
Uncle Sam's civil service squadron.

Federal Bureau of Investigation
United States Department of Justice
Los Angeles, California.
July 17th, 1937.

To: The Director, Federal Bureau of Investigation, United
States Department of Justice, Washington, D. C.

From: Inspector   Special Agent in Charge J. H. Hanson

Subject: Report of Interview with Applicant   RICHARD M. NIXON
for appointment as Special Agent   2706 E. Whittier, Blvd.,
Whittier, Calif.

1. PERSONAL APPEARANCE:

A. PERSONAL APPEARANCE AND APPROACH: Excellent. Good. Fair. Poor.
B. DRESS: Neat. Flashy. Poor. Untidy.
C. FEATURES: Refined. Ordinary. Coarse. Dissipated.
D. PHYSICAL DEFECTS, if any: None

2. CONDUCT DURING INTERVIEW:

A. PERSONALITY: Excellent. Good. Fair. Average. Poor.
B. POISE: Well-poised. Steady. Temperamental. Average.
C. SPEECH: Average. Reticent. Talkative. Boastful.
D. ASSURANCE: Self-Confident. Fair. Over-Confident. Lacking.
E. NERVOUSNESS: None. Slight. Very nervous.
F. FOREIGN ACCENT: None. Slight. Noticeable.
G. TACT: Tactful. Average. Lacking.

3. GENERAL INTELLIGENCE:

A. Answers general questions definitely. Quickly. Vaguely.
B. Has Applicant studied Federal Procedure? No
C. Any investigative experience? If so, describe - None

D. Does the Applicant appear to be resourceful? Yes
E. Does the Applicant appear to have executive ability? Perhaps
F. Is he likely to develop? Yes

4. GENERAL INFORMATION:

A. What are the Applicant's plans for the future? Legal field if not
appointed.

B. What are his recreations and tastes? Handball, swimming, movies,
bridge, poker, dancing, reading.

5. HEALTH RECORD: Good

6. GENERAL IMPRESSIONS OF APPLICANT:

Applicant was born January 9, 1913 at Yorba Linda, California. He is
single and resides with his parents. His father is a grocer. He has
two brothers who are students. He has never been arrested or involved
in any kind of trouble, nor have any members of his family. He takes
an occasional social drink of liquor. He typewrites poorly with the
touch system. He has had no training or experience with firearms.
He drives an automobile. He has no relatives in the Government service.

Applicant attended public grammar school at Yorba Linda, California,
and high school at Fullerton and Whittier, California, graduating from
the latter school in 1930, thereafter entering the Whittier College where
he was awarded an AB Degree in 1934, having majored in history. He then
enrolled in the law school at Duke University, receiving an LL.B Degree
in June, 1937. He plans to take the California Bar examination commencing
on September 7, 1937.

Applicant's chief employment during his spare time from his studies and
during his vacations has been with his father who operates a grocery store.
He claims, however, that in the Summer of 1931 he worked part time for
the Whittier College, interviewing prospective students. (This work was
done under the supervision of the Acting President at that time, a Dr.
Herbert Harris. He claims that in the Summers of 1932 and 1933 he rented
from his father a gasoline filling station at 2706 East Whittier Blvd.,
which he operated on his own account, doing business with the Richfield
Oil Products Co.   In the Summers of 1934 and 1935 he assisted his father
in the latter's grocery store.   During the school year of 1935 and
Summer of 1936 he worked as assistant in the law library at Duke University.   Also during the school year of 1936 and 1937 he did research
work for the Dean of the Law School. He mentioned that at the time
he was awarded his Degree at Duke he was elected to membership in the
Order of Coif, Honorary Legal Fraternity. He also mentioned that he
made the football squad at Whittier, playing on it for four years but did
not receive a letter.

The applicant learned of this Bureau through a talk made by SAC J. A. Smith
at Duke University.   He is not acquainted with any Special Agents of the
Bureau nor employes of the Department of Justice.

x x x x x x x x

            Result of dictation test: Good. Fair. Poor.
            Bureau test rating   %.

7. Do you consider the Applicant qualified for the appointment he
    seeks and, if appointed, do you believe he would develop into
    better than an average employee? YES

                              J. H. HANSON, Special Agent in Charge.
                                    Inspec

x x

            x

x x   x x x x x

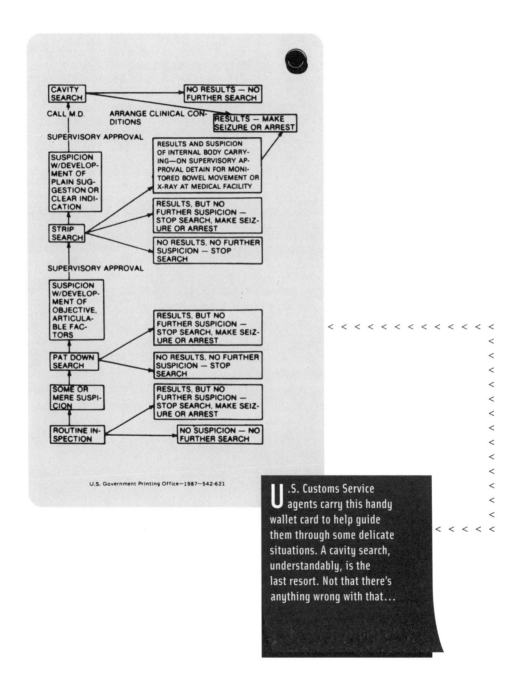

CAVITY SEARCH

NO RESULTS — NO FURTHER SEARCH

CALL M.D. ARRANGE CLINICAL CON-DITIONS

RESULTS — MAKE SEIZURE OR ARREST

SUPERVISORY APPROVAL

SUSPICION W/DEVELOP-MENT OF PLAIN SUG-GESTION OR CLEAR INDI-CATION

RESULTS AND SUSPICION OF INTERNAL BODY CARRY-ING—ON SUPERVISORY AP-PROVAL DETAIN FOR MONI-TORED BOWEL MOVEMENT OR X-RAY AT MEDICAL FACILITY

STRIP SEARCH

RESULTS, BUT NO FURTHER SUSPICION — STOP SEARCH, MAKE SEIZ-URE OR ARREST

NO RESULTS, NO FURTHER SUSPICION — STOP SEARCH

SUPERVISORY APPROVAL

SUSPICION W/DEVELOP-MENT OF OBJECTIVE, ARTICULA-BLE FAC-TORS

RESULTS, BUT NO FURTHER SUSPICION — STOP SEARCH, MAKE SEIZ-URE OR ARREST

PAT DOWN SEARCH

NO RESULTS, NO FURTHER SUSPICION — STOP SEARCH

SOME OR MERE SUSPI-CION

RESULTS, BUT NO FURTHER SUSPICION — STOP SEARCH, MAKE SEIZ-URE OR ARREST

ROUTINE IN-SPECTION

NO SUSPICION — NO FURTHER SEARCH

U.S. Government Printing Office—1987—542-621

U.S. Customs Service agents carry this handy wallet card to help guide them through some delicate situations. A cavity search, understandably, is the last resort. Not that there's anything wrong with that…

MONICA LEWINSKY

OBJECTIVE

- Seeking summer internship opportunity.
- Offering excellent skills in communication, writing, computer and research experience.
  Able to take direction, extremely enthusiastic, amiable and courteous

EDUCATION

- Lewis & Clark College - Presently attending
  Educational goal: Bachelor of Arts, Science. GPA 3.75
- Bel Air Prep School - Graduated 6/91 GPA 3.84

EXPERIENCE

> > >
>
>
>
>
>
>
>

Who would have guessed that an ability to file legal papers, the skill to "take direction," and expertise in "public affairs" would prove so useful during Lewinksy's Washington tenure?

- Practicum - Metropolitan Public Defender
  630 SW Fifth Street, Portland, Oregon
  Supervisor - Marcia Gruhler
  Duties include: assisting Legal Aid Office in counseling indigent clients, investigation, and filing of legal reports
  12/94 - Present
- Practicum - Southeast Mental Health Network
  2415 SE 43rd St., Portland, Oregon
  Supervisor - Chris Nielson
  Duties include: assisting staff in teaching socialization skills to clients in anticipation of their integration into society. Also assist in filing confidential reports, public affairs, liason to governmental office.
  1 94 - 6 94
- Knot Shop, Pioneer Place
  700 SW Fifth St., Portland, Oregon
  Position: Sales Associate
  Duties include: retail sales of upscale men's clothing, "key holder" with opening and closing responsibilities.
  Supervisor - Lisa Casey
  9 93 - Present

HONORS & AWARDS

Dean's List - Lewis and Clark 1993 and 1994
Class salutorian, Bel Air Prep School 1991
First Place - Southern California Shakespeare Festival (1990)
Third Place - Southern California Shakespeare Festival (1991)

RED_GUIDE_CONFIG
ABIG1
ACT239
ACT253
AC008
AC251
ADIOSMF
AENIUG
AGTWO
AINYS
AJAP
ALLA7777
AMAAL87
ANAL
ANUS
ANYS1
ARSE
AR251
AR529
ASOIFAM
ASPCA2
ASS
ASSHOLE
ASSH0LE
ASSOUL
ASS0UL
ASTUD
ASZKICR
ATTYSSUK
AVW4U2NV
AWCHIT
AWCH1T
AZZKICKR
AZZKICR
AZZKIKR
A69R
BACANAK
BADASS
BADBOX
BADB0X
BADSAI
BADSA1
BADSOB
BADS0B
BALL
BALLME
BALME
BANGAWAY
BANGN
BARB4
BARTAB
BASKET
BASTARD
BBBDD
BEERDOG
BICH

BIGANUS
BIGDICK
BIGD1CK
BIGLICK
BIGWANG
BITCH
BITEMEE
BITEMEEE
BLACKOPS
BLACOPS
BLO
BLOME
BLUBAHLZ
BLUBALLS
BLWME
BL0
BNL20
BNL21
BOOBIES
BOOBS
BOOSE
BOOZE
BOSSHOGS
BOXBIZ
BOXB1Z
BO0BS
BRA
BRDSHT
BRITE9
BRSTFEED
BTCHN
BTCHNRAM
BUCWHEAT
BUKNAKED
BULLSHT
BULSHIT
BULSH1T
BULSIT
BULS1T
BUSTANUT
BYEBYEMF
B0OBS
B0XBIZ
B0XB1Z
B00BS
B1GDICK
B1GD1CK
B1TCH
CABRON
CABR0N
CAFEBLU
CARNAL
CATSAZ
CHICHA
CHINGA
CHINK

CHOLD
CHULO
CH1NGA
CH1NK
CITY207
CIVAO81
CLIT
CLITORIS
CLSMST
CL1T
CMENDEZ
COC
COCAINE
COCK
COCKCA
COCKR
COCKY
COCKYB
COITUS
COK
COKE
COM
COMP113
COMP126
COMP200
COMP317
COMP74
COMP82
COMP85
COONASS
COP
COQ
COX
CO0NASS
CO1TUS
CRACK
CRAMIT
CRAM1T
CRAP
CTWID49
CULO
CUM
CUNT
CURLY69
CYOUNT
CY0UNT
C0C
C0CK
C0CKCA
C0CKR
C0CKY
C0CKYB
C0K
C0M
C0ONASS
C0P

C0Q
C0X
C00NASS
DA
DAGO
DAG0
DAMN
DAVEL123
DA12
DA15
DA25
DA27
DA32
DA33
DA35
DA40
DA42
DA54
DA55
DA62
DA7
DA8
DA9
DCJ19
DCJ29
DCJ35
DCJ4
DCJ44
DCJ45
DCJ48
DCJ5
DCJ53
DCJ55
DCJ58
DCUP
DEAL
DEPUTY
DGENARIT
DHJAP
DICKFACE
DICKHEAD
DIGSEX
DIK
DIKHD
DILDO
DILDOE
DILD0
DILD0E
DILIGAS
DILLIGAF
DJENRIT
DMSHT
DMV
DORK
DOUSWALO
DRSPEED

H ere's a page from the list of license plates banned by the New York State Department of Motor Vehicles. C'mon, did that guy really think he'd get the CO1TUS tags?

*
*
*
*
*
*
*
*
* * *

Tommy G. Thompson
Governor

Michael J. Sullivan
Secretary

**State of Wisconsin
Department of Corrections**

Mailing Address
3▓▓▓▓▓▓▓▓▓▓▓▓▓▓▓▓
Phone: ▓▓▓▓▓▓▓▓▓▓▓
Fax: ▓▓▓▓▓▓▓▓▓▓▓

June 11, 1997

Personalize Plates Dept.   File: ▓▓▓▓▓▓▓▓
Dept. of Transportation   D.O.B. ▓▓▓▓▓▓▓
Box 7911
Madison, WI 53707

RE: Recall Request

Dear DOT:

This is to request the recall of my parolee ▓▓▓▓▓▓▓▓▓▓▓'s specialized plates
"Mary Jn." Mr. ▓▓▓▓▓ has been convicted on at least 4 separate drug related
offenses since 1981. This exact record includes:

     5-22-81   Poss With Intent to Deliver - Heroin (4 yrs prison)
     12-06-90   Consp. to Deliver Controlled Substance (7 yrs prison)
     12-06-90   Del. Noncontrolled Sub as Controlled (2 yrs prison)
     12-95   Poss of Controlled Sub (1 yr prison)

Mary Jane or "Mary Jn" is a nickname for the substance marijuana. In lieu of Mr.
▓▓▓▓▓▓▓ convictions and drug related past, I feel it is inappropriate he continues
to drive a vehicle (Jaguar) with license plates promoting illegal substances.

Please consider my request. Feel free to contact me with any questions or concerns.

Sincerely,

▓▓▓▓▓▓▓▓▓▓▓▓▓▓▓▓▓▓▓
▓▓▓▓▓▓▓▓▓▓, #40508
Probation and Parole Agent

JPK:sm
cc: file

* * *
   *
   *
   *
   *
   *
   *
   *
   *
   *
   *
   *

Geez, the Wisconsin
fuzz have no sense of
humor.

(3 1997 JUN 12

SUGGESTED STATEMENTS

IN EVENT OF CREW FATALITIES

<u>The President</u>:

I have conveyed to the families of _____,

_____ and _____ the heart-

felt sympathy of both Mrs. _____ and myself.

Those they leave behind have suffered a grievous loss,

but mankind itself will be forever richer because these

gallant men dared accept the opportunity to undertake a

pioneering journey of great challenge and promise.

To those who follow, to those pioneers of heroic

courage and selfless dedication, the paths blazed by these

brave men will beckon through all the years.

#

(If at the time a longer statement on behalf of the Nation
is desired:)

I have conveyed to the families of _____ _ _____,

_____ and _____ the heart-

felt sympathy of a saddened Nation. The sense of loss felt

by Mrs. _____ and me is keen and personal. Count-

less millions of people at home and abroad must share this

sense of great loss, for these men sailed forth on the

seas of space on a mission of great interest and great

importance to all mankind. The families of these men

have suffered a grievous loss; may they find some comfort

in the thought, which so many share, that man's progress

has always been won, and still must be won, by brave men

who are ready to move out into the unknown without the

guarantee of a safe return, and who draw strength from

the knowledge that by their going they help to open the

way. They have followed a star, in the night of space,

and we for whom they went will not forget.

The Vice President:

The deaths of these three men will stand in the

annals of exploration as an everlasting example of

dedication, courage and the conviction that man's

intelligence will one day carry him safely to the stars.

\# \# \#

This "heartfelt" and "personal" script was prepared by NASA for the President to read in case of an Apollo space disaster. The nation would surely have been comforted to know that Mrs. _____'s husband would never be forgotten.

\#
\#

\# \# \# \# \#   \# \#

MEMORANDUM FOR:

SUBJECT: |Views on Trained Cats   / for
                       |Use

1.   Our final examination of trained cats

for |use in the |convinced

us that the program would not lend itself in a practical

sense to our highly specialized needs. Repeated checks .

on the state of training and equipment showed us that it

was indeed possible to train

locations; we were not able to visualize

          |use for this technique under conditions that

prevail |

2.   We have satisfied ourselves that j : is indeed

possible

                                   | This is in

itself a remarkable scientific achievement. Knowing that

cats can indeed be trained to move short distances

                    | we see no reason to believe

that a |cat can not be similarly trained to approach

RELEASED   SEP 1983   //1 P

                                   | Again,

however, the environmental and security factors in using

this technique in a real foreign situation force us to

conclude that, for our |purposes, it would not

be practical.

3.   The work done on this problem over the years

reflects great credit on the personnel who guided it,

particularly |whose energy and imagination

could be models for scientific pioneers.

UNITED STATES GOVERNMENT

Memorandum

TO : Mr. DeLoach

DATE: 8/14/63

FROM : M. A. Jones

SUBJECT: "THAT DARNED CAT"
PROPOSED MOTION PICTURE

BACKGROUND:

By previous memorandum it was noted that Walt Disney had recently contacted the Los Angeles Office to advise that he had purchased the rights to a new book written by Gordon Gordon and his wife entitled "Undercover Cat." Mr. Disney indicated his company planned to produce a motion picture based on this book. He stated that he was aware of Public Law 670 which he had discussed with his attorney and indicated that his treatment of the FBI in his proposed movie would be in good taste. Inasmuch as galley proofs were not available in Los Angeles regarding this book, arrangements were made to obtain a copy of the book through our New York Office.

It is noted that Gordon Gordon is a former FBI Agent who has collaborated with his wife Mildred on a number of books since leaving the Bureau. In their writings, they have capitalized considerably on the former FBI affiliation of Gordon Gordon. It is noted that the Los Angeles Office has been advised to follow this proposed movie closely and keep the Bureau advised.

REVIEW OF BOOK:

Captioned story is written in a lighthearted vein and concerns a large cat who is known as "D. C." (short for "Damn Cat"). The plot concerns a bank robbery perpetrated by two individuals who kidnaped a female teller to insure a clean getaway. "D. C." enters the actual investigation of the case when he returns to his home one night from a nocturnal prowl with the kidnaped teller's wrist watch around his neck. When this fact is reported to the local FBI office, Agents set up a surveillance of "D. C." with the hope that he will return to the place where the teller placed the wrist watch on his neck. The story then comically portrays the steps the FBI takes in setting up the surveillance of this cat. These steps included the painting of the cat's tail with phosphorescent paint and putting a small bell on the cat by which they could follow him at a distance through the use of a "sound cone."

On the first night the Agents are following "D. C.", a neighbor takes a shot at the cat. The reason for this, according to the plot, is that the cat had previously stolen a favorite duck. On subsequent nights while the Agents are following "D. C.", the Agents are led on the nightly rounds of garbage cans and crawling under parked cars. Eventually "D. C." returns to the apartment where the two robbers and their kidnaped victim are living, and the robbers are subsequently apprehended by the FBI and the victim is freed.

1 - Mr. Sullivan
1 - Mr. DeLoach   RLR:mas

EX 104   REC 46 94-4-4667-41

SEP 20 1963

11 SEP 20 1963
CRIME RESEARCH

Speaking of pussies, this Disney feline got on the FBI's nerves. Writer Gordon Gordon's screenplay left the bureau really pissed pissed.

FD-302 (Rev. 4-15-64)

FEDERAL BUREAU OF INVESTIGATION

Date _____11/6/68_____

67C

On November 1, 1968, SA's ███████████ and ███████████
███████ attended the midnight showing of the motion picture, "Lonesome
Cowboys," at the San Francisco International Film Festival held at
Masonic Auditorium, San Francisco, California.

The film was introduced by ALBERT JOHNSON, an official
of the Film Festival, and was represented by JOHNSON to be an
ANDY WARHOL production made in Arizona. TAYLOR MEAD and two
other individuals were introduced as actors in this production.
The actress in the film, VIVA, and ANDY WARHOL were not introduced.
The explanation given for WARHOL's absence was that he was ill.

MEAD spoke to the audience for a few minutes in a sense-
less monologue and said something about not knowing whether to
put the beginning of the movie at the end or vice versa.

There were no title or credits flashed on the screen.
The film was in color and an attempt had been made to synchronize
sound with the action.

The characters in the film were a woman, played by VIVA;
her male nurse, played by TAYLOR MEAD; a sheriff who resided in
a small Arizona town---population, three; and a group of about
five cowboys with an additional new member called "Boy Julian."
All of the males in the cast displayed homosexual tendencies and
conducted themselves toward one another in an effeminate manner.
Many of the cast portrayed their parts as if in a stupor from
marijuana, drugs or alcohol.

It appeared that there was no script for the film but
rather the actors were given a basic idea for a plot and then
instructed to act and speak as they felt.

The movie opened with the woman and her male nurse on
a street in the town. Five or six cowboys then entered the town
and there was evidence of hostility between the two groups. One
of the cowboys practiced his ballet and a conversation ensued
regarding the misuse of mascara by one of the other cowboys. At

< > < > < > <

On __11/1/68__ at San Francisco, California File # ___SF-145-653___
                                                    ___PX-145-230___

SA's ████████████████████████

by _____████████████ 67C_____ Date dictated ___11/4/68___

This document contains neither recommendations nor conclusions of the FBI. It is the property of the FBI and is l
your agency; it and its contents are not to be distributed outside your agency.

-5-

> <

times it was difficult to understand the words being spoken, due
to the poor audio of the film and the pronunciation by the actors.
The film also skips from scene to scene without continuity.

As the movie progressed, one of the actors ran down a
hill. The next scene showed a man wearing only an unbuttoned silk
cowboy shirt getting up from the ground. His privates were exposed
and another cowboy was lying on the ground in a position with his
head facing the genitals of the cowboy who had just stood up. A
jealous argument ensued between the cowboy who was observed running down the hill and the one wearing the silk shirt. The man
in the silk shirt was then seen urinating; however, his privates
were not exposed due to the camera angle.

Later in the movie the cowboys went out to the ranch
owned by the woman. On their arrival, they took her from her
horse, removed her clothes and sexually assaulted her. During
this time her private parts were exposed to the audience. She
was on her back with her clothes removed and an actor was on his
knees near her shoulders with his face in the vicinity of her genitals
but a second actor with his back to the camera blocked the view.
The position of the male and female suggested an act of cunnilingus;
however, the act was not portrayed in full view of the camera.

At the end of this scene the woman sat up and said,
"Now look---you have embarrassed those children." There were no
children in the movie.

There are other parts in the film in which the private
parts of the woman were visible on the screen and there were also
scenes in which men were revealed in total nudity. The sheriff in
one scene was shown dressing in woman's clothing and later being
held on the lap of another cowboy. Also, the male nurse was
pictured in the arms of the sheriff. In one scene where VIVA
was attempting to persuade one of the cowboys to take off his
clothes and join her in her nudity, the discussion was centered
around the Catholic Church's liturgical songs. She finally
persuaded him to remove all of his clothes and he then fondled
her breasts and rolled on top of her naked body. There were movements and gyrations; however, at no time did the camera show
penetration or a position for insertion.

Another scene depicted a cowboy fondling the nipples of
another cowboy.

There were suggestive dances done by the male actors with
each other. These dances were conducted while they were clothed
and suggested love-making between two males.

There was no plot to the film and no development of characters throughout. It was rather a remotely-connected series of
scenes which depicted situations of sexual relationships of hom-
sexual and heterosexual nature.

Obscene words, phrases and gestures were used throughout the film.

ACTIVITIES OF PAT HUTTON

ON

FRIDAY, NOVEMBER 22, 1963

I came back from lunch, and went to the O.B.-Gynocology section where I was working. At approximately 12:30 P.M., the triage nurse called us to bring a cart out to the entrance. We took said cart out the door, and it was then that I realized who was in the car.

Several people helped put the President on the cart, and we then proceeded to the Major Surgery Section of the Emergency Room to Trauma Room # 1. Mr. Kennedy was bleeding profusely from a wound on the back of his head, and was lying there unresponsive.

As soon as we reached the room, a doctor placed an endotracheal tube, and prepared for a tracheostomy. Within a few minutes, there were numerous doctors in the room starting I.V.'s, placing chest tubes and anesthesia with O_2. A doctor asked me to place a pressure dressing on the head wound. This was of no use, however, because of the massive opening on the back of the head.

Blood was pumped in along with the I.V.'s running. After a period of handing instruments and equipment to the doctors as needed, it was announced that the President had expired. We then removed the tubes and I.V.'s from him. Mrs. Kennedy came in with a priest, and last rites were performed. When Mrs. Kennedy left, we removed all of the equipment from the room, and I then left at the request of the supervisor to get a plastic cover to line the coffin. I returned with it, and Mr. Kennedy was placed in the coffin to await orders to move him by ambulance. After that, I stood outside the door with Mrs. Nelson until the body was removed. When the area was clear, another nurse and I went up to the dining room for coffee. We returned to the Emergency Room where I changed clothes, and left at approximately 4:00 P.M. for home.

SATURDAY, NOVEMBER 23, 1963

I arrived for work at 9:30 A.M., and was told that our names had been released, and to check with administration before talking with anyone.

I was not asked any questions by anyone, and spent an uneventful 8 hours on dut

Patricia B. Hutton, R.N.

PBH:bwh

Price X-21

PRICE EXHIBIT No. 21

(3) *Posture and Gait*

If you have round shoulders, a strong "figure eight" cord, crossed in the back, will serve as a reminder to throw out your chest and stand up straight. Put your arms through it and slip it over your head. If you *want* round shoulders, cross it in front. Tying your suspenders together high up in the back will do the same thing to a lesser extent.

Try the old trick of buttoning your pants to your vest to acquire a stoop. Another way to keep hunched over is to use a strip of adhesive plaster stuck from just above the navel up to the hair on the chest. It should be applied while slouched over. Then try to straighten up!

Basically, posture and gait must fit the type of man you are portraying, his age, upbringing, physical condition, degree of ambition, and his whole outlook on life. Even without making a clothes change, a student can assume a completely different cover merely by changing his gait and switching to the exact opposite of the tempo used in the first cover.

Start now to observe how men of different classes of society and age sit, stand and walk. One section of the crowd will move with a purpose, preoccupied with their own important little lives. Another group will slouch or waddle along, like dully curious animals. Any little object catches their interest for a fleeting moment. They have no goal in life and every movement and line of their body show it.

Building up the inside of one shoe-heel will give a "short-leg" limp. With the same device it is easy to assume the walk of someone who has been paralyzed on one side. Build up, say, your left heel about an inch and a half, crook your right arm into a useless set, drop the right shoulder down and *swing* the right half-dead leg forward. Be sure your face has that drooped, dull, set expression of one who has had a stroke. The eyes are usually all that move, with a bewildered, anxious expression as though the person does not quite know what has happened to him. This cover, if not overplayed, has a good psychological angle because one's natural impulse is to look away from such cripples.

A small stone or other hard object in one sock heel will produce a convincing limp. Slightly larger ones in the arch of each foot will produce a "flat foot" walk. Detachable rubber pencil erasers or other firm but pliable articles are best for this because they do not bruise the foot so much over a period of time. Putting them inside the sock helps keep them in place. The last-mentioned device also aids in maintaining an "old age" gait. Try also a tight bandage around the calf of your leg with something under it to hurt the muscle as the weight is put on that foot.

Try the "lost arm", which is best done when wearing a double-breasted coat. Take the left arm from the coat sleeve. Tuck the empty sleeve in the coat pocket. Hold the elbow close to the waist at the side front and put your forearm around your waist with the left hand resting on the right hip. If you can button your vest around your arm, it will keep it even flatter, but you may want your arm more readily available. The other arrangement can be very convincing provided your coat is not too tight.

9

Here are a few pages from a 1944 disguise manual prepared by the Office of Strategic Services, the CIA's predecessor agency. Forget the cloaks and the daggers. Who knew that a small stone and a pencil eraser were such crucial elements in a spook's bag of tricks?

While many of the suggestions outlined in this volume are applicable to both men and women students, the following section is written solely for the women.

A change of hair style is one of the most simple and effective aids in changing a woman's appearance. If the usual style, for instance, is a "long bob", the hair should be done up, or slicked straight back into either a knot or a roll. The position of the part should be altered or eliminated altogether. If the hair is usually worn closely set, brushing it out frizzy and adding a ribbon bow will create a different effect immediately. The advisability of taking along a switch, either to add more hair or to use as a braid, should be considered. The style chosen should be one that a woman can arrange herself, naturally, without recourse to a beauty parlor. An important point to remember is that the most unbecoming hair style will probably change the wearer's appearance more than any other.

It should be borne in mind that in many parts of the world women do not get or use much make-up. If lipstick is used, however, making a different lip line will alter the appearance greatly, as will changing the shape of the eyebrows.

If a woman does not want to be noticed, she should strive to look mousy or old or dumpy. If the work calls for glamour, an expert on make-up should be consulted.

A woman who normally chooses bright and colorful clothes should change to something darker, say a grey dress or suit. The point is to achieve a complete contrast from the clothes usually worn.

A woman of between thirty and forty years of age can easily add ten to fifteen years to her apparent age after a little instruction. She should clean off all make-up, wrinkle up her face, and with a very sharp Factor's brown eyebrow pencil lightly line all of the creases. Rub these down to the point where they are only soft shadows. A very thin application of the brown pencil mixed with Factor's No. 6 blue-grey liner, close to the bridge of the nose and accentuating the circles under the eyes, will add to the effect. Next, a light-colored make-up should be used on all the high spots — the cheek bones, nose, chin and the tops of all wrinkles, care being taken to blend all edges out to nothing. Patting the face lightly all over will help do this. Remember, it is shadows and highlights which are being added, and they must be soft so as to look completely natural. A fairly light powder should be applied, patted well in first, then brushed off as much as possible. Next a damp cloth should be used to remove all the excess powder. If any lipstick is used at all, it should be thin and light-colored and blotted off. Next, the lips should be puckered and powder added on top of the lipstick.

If the student wears dental plates or removable bridges, she should take them out. The neck and hands must not be overlooked; all must tie in together. A little hair white should be combed in at the temples or streaked through the whole head and the hair done up in an older style. When the make-up is all finished, the details should be checked. If she looks made-up at all, the job has been overdone. The materials were probably used too thick or not blended enough. Students will find that a little practice before a mirror will produce excellent results.

13

Chapter III

Permanent Disguise

Permanent disguise requires the services of a plastic surgeon. It is mentioned in order that attention may be called to some of the changes that have been accomplished by facial surgery. Its use has been successfully employed in individual cases where a valuable man who had a particularly noticeable feature, such as a prominent nose, ears that stick far out, or an easily remembered scar, might have been recognized on returning to the field.

Surgery has been used to alter the racial characteristics of Jewish students before they enter the field. Broken, bulbous and sharp Roman noses have also been successfully changed to shapes less eye-catching. Nose operations usually require about a week to ten days' hospital care, but a month must be counted upon before all swelling has gone down and the resulting "black eyes" have disappeared. One advantage is that there are no outside scars.

Prominent ears are dealt with by pinning them back. This leaves a small inconspicuous scar where the skin joins the ear to the head. Two to three weeks should be allowed for this.

Scars that show are definite and dangerous marks of identification which should always be eliminated if possible. They can be removed surgically by a specialist without requiring hospitalization. An operation lasting two to three hours and removal of stitches after seven to ten days are all that are necessary.

Tattoo marks are extremely difficult to remove. The process is long and painful and is not recommended. A more satisfactory treatment is re-tattooing with a larger and more elaborate design. Skillful blending can achieve very satisfactory results. It has the advantage of speed and there is much less discomfort to the subject.

AS THE WORM TURNS

10.

As of January 14, 1993, Defendant Rodman knew that he was infected with the herpes simplex virus and that he was capable of transmitting the disease to a sexual partner through intimate contact. Defendant Rodman did not inform Ms. Judd of the fact that he was infected with the herpes simplex virus at any time during the course of their relationship.

Judd v. Rodman, U.S. District Court, Northern District of Georgia, 1994

Subjects

Seven female military volunteer subjects were asked to participate in the cockpit compatibility portion of this study. The Cockpit Integration Laboratory, Armstrong Laboratory, Brooks AFB, TX was used for the USAF F-15, F-16, and A-10 fighter cockpits. Four centrifuge subjects were asked to evaluate the devices (for comfort only) while experiencing a high Gz centrifuge ride.

Following demonstration of compatibility within the laboratory, all currently deployed female fighter pilots were asked to evaluate these pieces of equipment, in conjunction with a 1.5-2.0 inch zipper extension.

Materials

The materials consisted of several bladder relief devices: the Freshette[a] by Sanifem, the Lady J adapter[b] ordered from Sporty's Pilot Shop, Hollister's Female Urinary Pouch (9840), Boss Product's Gal's Tote a Potty, Convenience Bag (for vomit and urine collection) from Sporty's Pilot Shop, Foley catheter, and diapers. The collection bag used is the standard issue "Piddle Pack" (bag, pilot relief, male, NSN 8105-00-922-9469)[c] . Also a male condom catheter and a connector tube was used with the Lady J adapter. The flight suits were modified with an extended midline zipper[d] of 1.5-2.0 inches.

Methods

All devices were discussed with a group of women pilots before testing began. Most of the devices were excluded from further testing for various reasons. Boss Product's Gal's Tote a Potty was excluded due to its large size, 8in x 4.5in x 18in. The device was too large for use in the fighter cockpit and was not inconspicuous. The Hollister Female Urinary Pouch was also eliminated before cockpit testing due to the shaving requirement and its sticky application to the female genital area. The Convenience Bag was excluded due to its shape and its incompatibility with the flight suit. The Foley catheter was not acceptable because pilots were unwilling to be catheterized before every flight and the USAF medical community was concerned about potential bladder infections and the subsequent short term removal

---

[a] Freshette: International Sani-fem, PO Box 4117, Downey, CA 90241, (310) 928-3435
[b] Lady J Adapter: Sporty's Pilot Shop, Clermont County Airport, Batavia, OH 45103-9747, 1-800-LIFTOFF (543-8633)
[c] "Piddle Pack": Lighthouse Industries, Long Island City, NY 11101
[d] Zippers: Scovill Fasteners Inc, PO Box 44, Clarkesville, GA 30523, 1-800-756-4734

Sure, you're an airborne female killing machine, protecting the good old U.S. of A. from the cockpit of your fighter jet. But what do you do when nature calls and you're stuck in that F-15? Thanks to this Air Force report, relief is at hand, so to speak.

Observations

The cockpit testing showed that both the Freshette and the Lady J Adapter were acceptable devices for bladder relief in-flight. Out of the eleven trials, only two had some leakage. Both times the leakage occurred with the Lady J Adapter in the F-16 cockpit; one was 100% leakage and the other was 50% leakage. The Lady J Adapter was used in the F-16 cockpit three other times with only negligible leakage. One problem is that the F-16 seat tilts back 30 degrees - both devices work by gravity flow. The other problem with the Lady J Adapter is that the condom catheter, which attaches the tubing, can kink, restricting the flow of urine. The Freshette was the most effective of the two devices with only minor leakage.

The centrifuge testing was very positive. All four women did a gradual Gz onset run up to 9 Gz plus multiple rapid onset 5-9 Gz runs during the centrifuge ride. Out of the four subjects, only one experienced some discomfort. The discomfort was only minor; it was not enough to interfere with the ride. Since the devices are made of hard plastic they have a tendency to rub against the skin. Two of the women felt the devices were more comfortable at higher Gz and that the devices were not noticeable during the centrifuge ride.

The most important observations were from the actual female fighter pilots. Both devices were given to 64%(7/11) of the currently active female fighter pilots who were asked whether these devices were acceptable and if they would use them. These pilots were given modified flight suits and one each of the two urine collection devices. They received a briefing on our findings which included our recommendations. The response was encouraging: all of the female pilots approached readily approved of and accepted these urine collection devices. One F-16 pilot used the Freshette on a 1.5 hour cross country flight and found it to work great in the cockpit without leaks. She said this was far superior to "holding it" for four to five hours as she had done while flying over Bosnia a few months earlier.

SECRET

Theatre.- He very rarely went to the theatre.

Vaudeville.- He likes vaudeville.

Circus.- He loves the circus. The thrill of under-paid performers risking their lives is a real pleasure to him. He is particularly pleased with tight rope acts and trapeze artists. After his imprisonment in Landsberg he came to lunch at Dr. Sedgwick's house in 1925 and when Dr. Sedgwick was called to the telephone he said to Mrs. Sedgwick: "Now we'll have to try all over again, but this time you can be certain that I won't fall from the tight rope!"

During the summer of 1933 he went several times to the circus and on the next day he would send flowers and chocolates to the value of several hundred marks to the girls, who had performed dangerous feats before him. He remembered the names of these people and in the event of an accident to one of them would concern himself with what happened to them or to their surviving relatives. Upon one occasion after reading the account in a newspaper he sent a message of sympathy to the family of a trapeze artist who was killed during her act. (Nb. The appeal of the non-bourgeois - "the gypsy milieu of circus artists.")

He does not care much for wild animals acts, unless there is a woman in danger.

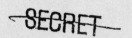

SECRET

UK/BM-170 TRANSLATION

Torture Methods: Secret agents use two methods of torture:

A. Physical torture.   B. Psychological torture

A.   Method of Physical Torture:
 1.   Blindfolding and stripping of clothes.
 2.   Hanging by the hands.
 3.   Hanging by the feet [upside down].
 4.   Beating with sticks and electrical wires.
 5.   Whipping and beating with sticks and twisted rubber belts.
 6.   Forcing the brother to stand naked for long periods of time.
 7.   Pouring cold water on the brother's head.
 8.   Putting out lighted cigarettes on the brother's skin.
 9.   Shocking with an electrical current.
10.   Kicking and punching.
11.   Attacking the brother with vicious dogs.
12.   Making the brother sit on a stake.
13.   Throwing in a septic tank.
14.   Pulling out the nails and hair.
15.   Dragging.
16.   Tying the hands and feet from behind.
17.   Utilizing sharp objects, such as a pocketknife or piece of glass.
18.   Burning with fire.
19.   Sleeping on a bare marble floor without a cover and flooding the cell with sewer water.
20.   Standing on toes and against a wall pressing with the fingers for long hours. The brother may be denied sleep, food, drink, and medicine.
21.   Beating on cuts and sore parts of the body.
22.   Giving the brother a lot of water or very watery fruits, such as watermelon, after denying him

----

food and drink. After the brother drinks or eats the fruit, his hands and penis will be tied so the brother will not be able to urinate.
23.   Placing drugs and narcotics in the brother's food to weaken his will power.
24.   Placing the brother in solitary confinement where the cells are made of a special kind of cement that gets extremely hot in the summer and cold in winter.
25.   Hitting the brother's genitals with a stick or squeezing them by hand.
26.   Dragging the brother over barb wires and fragments of glass and metal.

In a terrorist how-to handbook used by followers of Saudi madman Osama bin Laden, jihad members learn what to expect when you're expecting (to be tortured).

Ah, the old "imaginary Cuban leader" trick! Hard to believe those gullible Commies didn't fall for this one, just another in a long line of harebrained U.S. government schemes aimed at destabilizing Fidel Castro's regime.

SUBJECT: Future Cuban Leadership

INTRODUCTION

      Following is a proposal for the creation of an imaginary Cuban leader. This proposal is presented primarily to fill gaps existing in the present policy study. It will become obvious that this proposal can be utilized in conjunction with current programs as well as many of those programs proposed for the future. It may be necessary to address this proposal or a similar proposal separately and in advance of the policy study; however, in the event no pressing requirement exists, it is suggested that this proposal be considered in conjunction with the policy study and handled on a closely held basis.

REASON FOR PROPOSAL

      Following are listed a number of indications that the leadership question will be addressed in the near future:

      a. With the termination of U.S. support to the Cuban Revolutionary Council (CRC) a vacuum has been created. Various exile groups in the U.S. and elsewhere will be vying for recognition and support in an attempt to fill this void.

      b. There has been constant pressure on the U.S. and on other Latin American countries to recognize a government in exile. This proposal could serve to lessen or eliminate much of this political and psychological pressure.

      c. This proposal could serve to reduce the bickering among exile groups and may serve to resolve some of the problems of Cuban exile unification.

EXCLUDED FROM AUTOMATIC REGRADING
DOD DIR 5200.10 DOES NOT APPLY

      d. The proposal could emphasize the development of a native "David" in opposition to Castro, the Cuban "Goliath." This could serve the U.S. image by making Castro the "Goliath" rather than the "David" who opposes the "North American Giant."

      e. This proposal could serve to prevent the U.S. from making premature commitments to a leader or a particular exile group and could be used as a device to test exile response.

      f. This proposal could retain for the U.S. the ability to control future selections of leaders or groups (timing and political ideologies).

      g. This proposal could permit the U.S. on a progressive basis to influence the idealogies of the resistance and thus to influence the platform of a future Cuban Government.

      h. The publicity associated with the prolonged existence of a resistance in Cuba can serve to delay the furtherance of the de facto recognition of the present Cuban Regime.

OBJECTIVE

      To create an imaginary leader or image of resistance in Cuba. This image would serve as a focal point for resistance directed against Castro by Cubans or Latin Americans.

DEVELOPMENT

      An imaginary name of a resistance leader could be developed utilizing a popular name from Cuban history, a name associated with resistance in Cuba or a newly devised name. The name selected should typify a person who is friendly to the Cuban people, is anti-communist, is willing to fight against the Regime, and is little-but tough. There is no requirement for a detailed staff study in order

to determine this name. "The Little Bull," "The Little Worm," "The Friendly Worm," "The Fighting Friend," "The Tough Peasant, or any such name which is acceptable and meaningful in Spanish could suffice. Over a period of several months the name could be "dropped" or leaked through U.S. officialdom, in diplomatic channels, in intelligence channels or within the Cuban exile community. Specific acts against the Regime could be credited to this individual or members of his group. Communications could be arranged between this individual and his subordinates to be picked up either by Castro's censors or by radio intercept in Cuba or in the U.S.

After a period of time, all unexplained incidents and actions for which credit has not been seized by some other exile group would automatically be ascribed to our imaginary friend. At some point in time it could be leaked that the U.S. is, in fact, supporting this imaginary person. Similarly, other Latin American countries may, without inducement, publicly follow the U.S. pattern.

During the course of this operation it is quite possible that the Castro Regime could indicate that the activities of this individual were terminated, that the individual was captured, that he was being pursued, or that he was an imaginary faker or fraud. Such action would only serve to further publicize the actions of the individual and so long as resistance in general continued the fame of our "Cuban Kilroy" would spread. Humorous antics could be credited to our imaginary friend and rumors of his exploits of bravery (ala Zoro) could be circulated.

At some point in time it may be wise to indicate what this individual stands for. (It will become obvious that he is opposed to the Regime in Cuba.) It could be possible to indicate little-by-little his political platform in very general terms -- realizing that the mistique and the "generalness" connected with his operation is, in fact, the power behind the operation. Ultimately, Cubans and others may demand that he proclaim his complete political views or even that he present himself physically. Since this is not desirable,

3

arrangements could be made to have selected individuals meet with his appointed representative. His instructions and words could be relayed to the public by many means.

As his political platform becomes more apparent within the exile groups, it may be possible to determine those willing to follow his leadership (to gain Cuban independence under his terms) or those who are unwilling to accept his leadership. The lines of controversy among exiles can be drawn more clearly. Undesirable leaders and exile groups can be eliminated from the competition through his disavowals.

Eventually, a member of the resistance in Cuba may gain sufficient stature to assume or to be given the title of this imaginary leader. This, of course, will depend in large measure on individual leadership ability and the ability to "fill the boots" of this anti-Castro image.

While this scheme is replete with gimmickery, its implementation could be undertaken in a relatively short period of time. Sensitivity of this scheme is such that the knowledge should be held on the tightest basis and if implemented, those proposing should not be informed. In the event the scheme is compromised, (unless knowledge is widespread) there is little need for plausible deniability; however, once used and compromised the scheme can hardly be reinstated. A major advantage is that this image can be created over a long period of time or developed rapidly without a political or economic commitment on the part of the U.S. There may be a point at which the U.S. could no longer disavow collaboration with this imaginary person. This point, however, is so distant that during any point in the intervening period it would be possible for the U.S. to disengage easily without suffering embarrassment or loss of prestige.

4

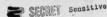

CONCLUSION

Based on a consideration of factors indicated above, it appears that the U.S. should immediately undertake to implement this proposal, determining at 30 to 60 day future intervals what additional action should be taken to improve, reduce, or change the image during the subsequent 30 or 60 day period.

James K. Patchell
James K. Patchell
Lt Colonel,   USA

This anti-Castro plot was included in a once Top Secret U.S. Army memo detailing a dozen other wacky operations envisioned by Uncle Sam.

11. Operation GOOD TIMES:

a. Objective: To disillusion the Cuban population with Castro image by distribution of fake photographic material.

b. Concept: Prepare a desired photograph, such as an obese Castro with two beauties in any situation desired, ostensibly within a room in the Castro residence, lavishly furnished, and a table briming over with the most delectable Cuban food with an underlying caption (appropriately Cuban) such as !!My ration is different." Make as many prints as desired on sterile paper and then distribute over the countryside by air drops or agents. This should put even a Commie Dictator in the proper perspective with the underprivileged masses.

ART GALLERY

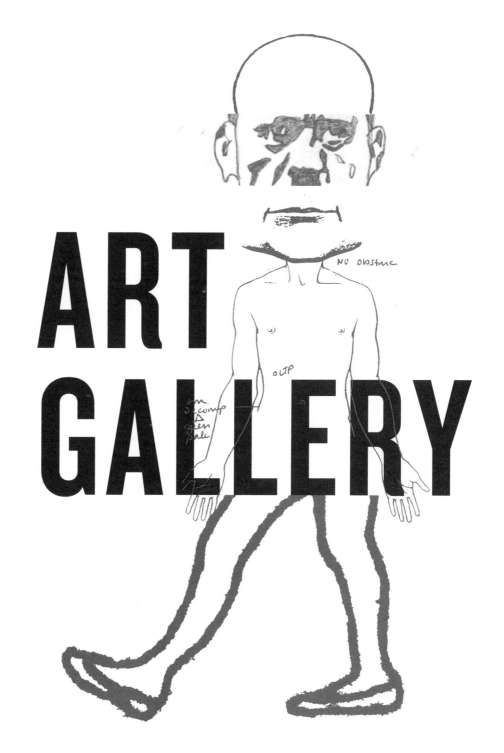

Frankly, words are pretty overrated.

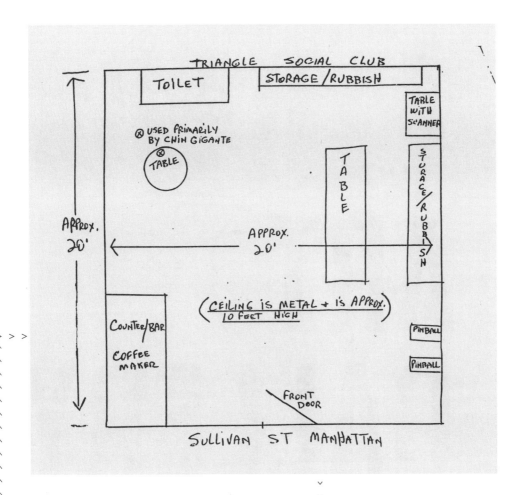

TRIANGLE SOCIAL CLUB

TOILET

STORAGE/RUBBISH

TABLE WITH SCANNER

⊗ USED PRIMARILY BY CHIN GIGANTE

⊗ TABLE

TABLE

STORAGE/RUBBISH

APPROX. 20'

APPROX. 20'

(CEILING IS METAL + IS APPROX. 10 FEET HIGH)

COUNTER/BAR

COFFEE MAKER

PINBALL

PINBALL

FRONT DOOR

SULLIVAN ST MANHATTAN

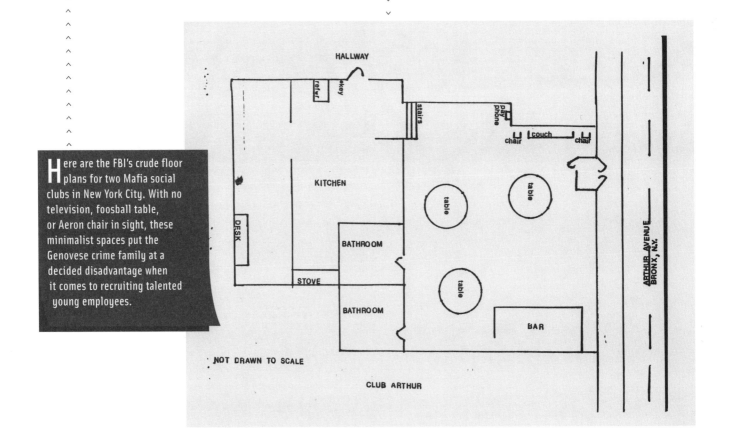

HALLWAY

refer

key

stairs

pay phone

chair couch chair

KITCHEN

table

table

DESK

BATHROOM

table

STOVE

BATHROOM

BAR

ARTHUR AVENUE BRONX, N.Y.

NOT DRAWN TO SCALE

CLUB ARTHUR

Here are the FBI's crude floor plans for two Mafia social clubs in New York City. With no television, foosball table, or Aeron chair in sight, these minimalist spaces put the Genovese crime family at a decided disadvantage when it comes to recruiting talented young employees.

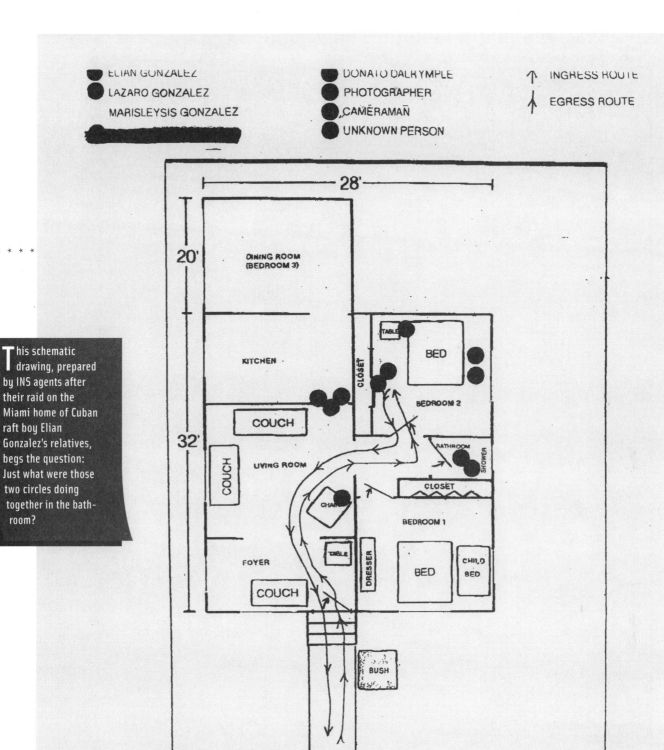

ELIAN GONZALEZ
LAZARO GONZALEZ
MARISLEYSIS GONZALEZ

DONATO DALRYMPLE
PHOTOGRAPHER
CAMERAMAN
UNKNOWN PERSON

↑ INGRESS ROUTE
↑ EGRESS ROUTE

This schematic drawing, prepared by INS agents after their raid on the Miami home of Cuban raft boy Elian Gonzalez's relatives, begs the question: Just what were those two circles doing together in the bathroom?

28'

20'

32'

DINING ROOM (BEDROOM 3)

KITCHEN

COUCH

COUCH

LIVING ROOM

FOYER

COUCH

CLOSET

TABLE

BED

BEDROOM 2

BATHROOM

SHOWER

CLOSET

BEDROOM 1

CHAIR

TABLE

DRESSER

BED

CHILD BED

BUSH

TEAM MEMBER 3 PATH OF TRAVEL

20

WD WN cm looks age, no trauma
EKG pads on upper torso, L hip,
Livor anterior + Both sides of face + torso; Rt also dorsal. Fixed. Rigor minimal. Thin brown liquid at nares & mouth

00-03532
HUGHES. MARK REYNOLD
NATURAL   1 3

Tanned except bikini area

No obstruc

dk brn, short wavy. mild temp. bald'g

Ø beard/must.

OLTP

sm decomp Δ
green pale

Circ

No scars

OK

W/to SS

3/16"
sm
Abr

pale band of skin
Lt ring
male

Faint blue
C ~ ½"

No NPW seen
No tracks
No tattoos

Own teeth, good condit.
Eyes: Brn, PER, congested, Ø PH

Sm ant pubic hair shaved at base of penis.
NO genital trauma

Schemm   M.D.
5/23/00   Deputy Medical Examiner

P5.93

If this coroner's report is any indication, then the vitamin products that Herbalife founder Mark Hughes touted will do little to prevent hair loss. Worse yet, you'll expire with merely an "OK" ass.

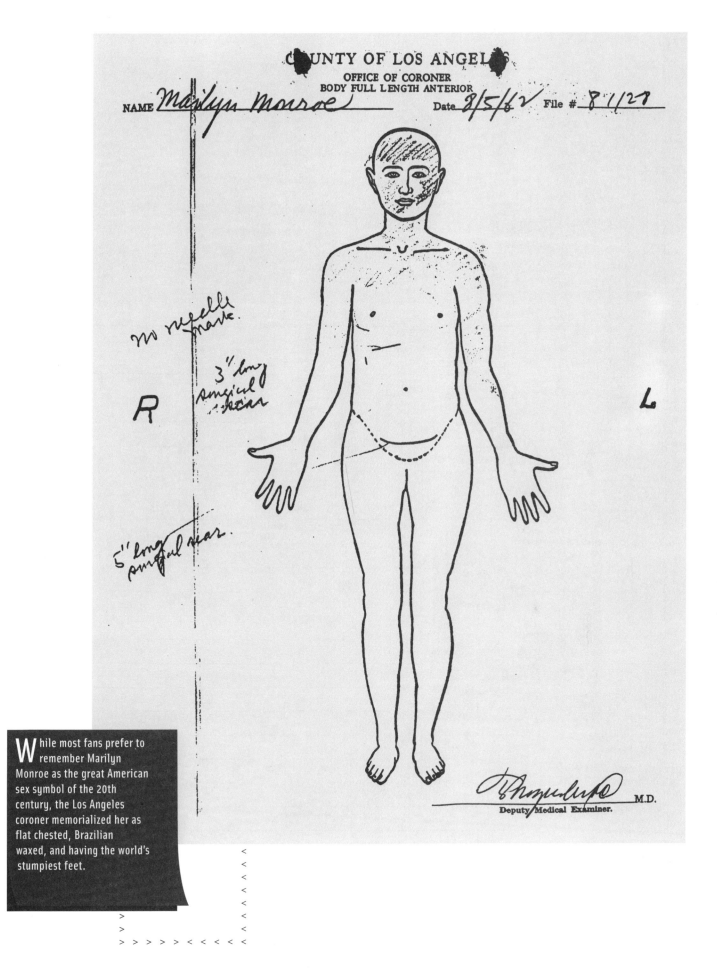

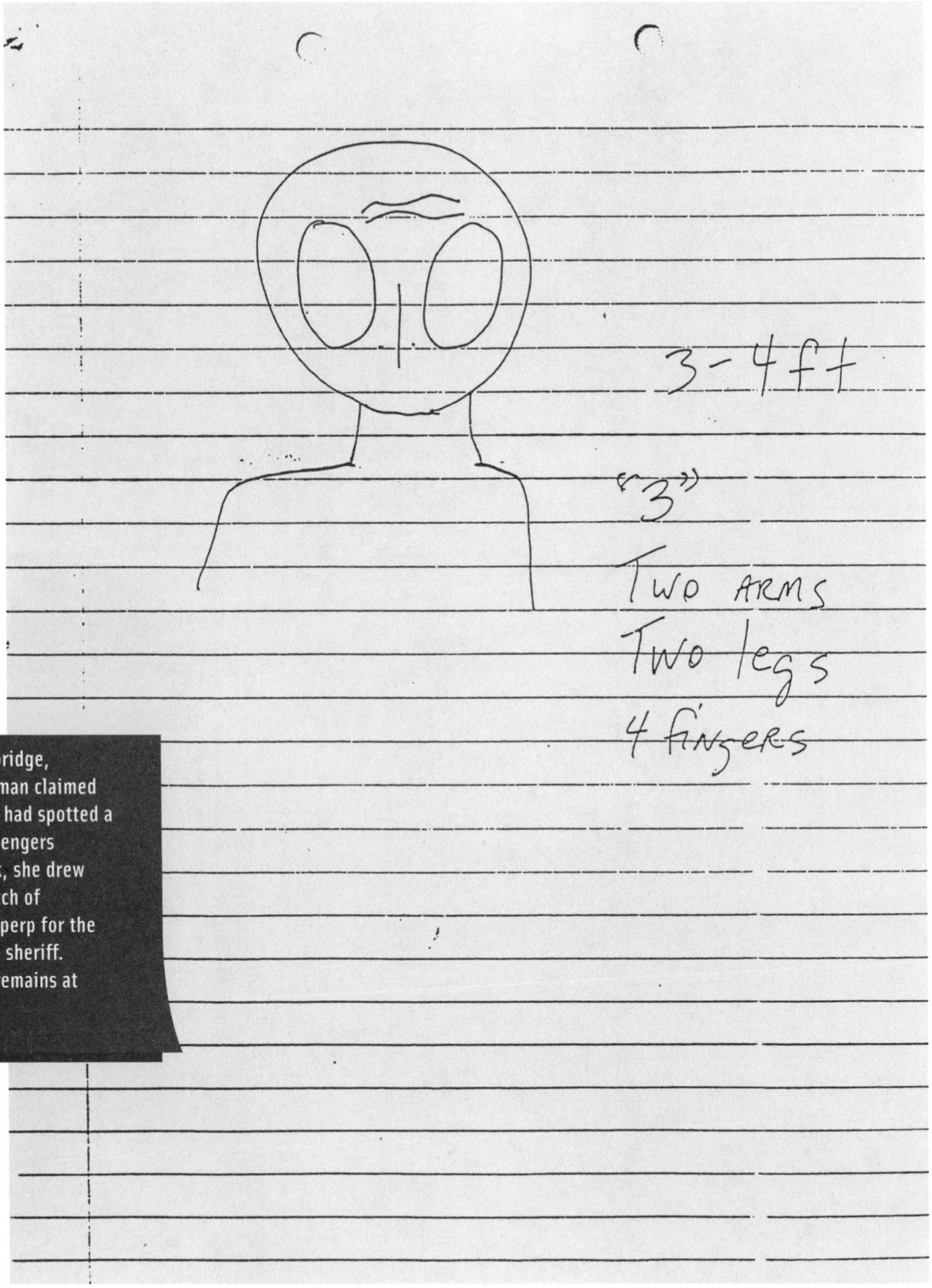

3-4 ft

"3"

Two Arms
Two legs
4 fingers

After a Woodbridge, Virginia, woman claimed in 1999 that she had spotted a UFO and its passengers near a local park, she drew this helpful sketch of one little green perp for the Fauquier County sheriff. To date, the ET remains at large.

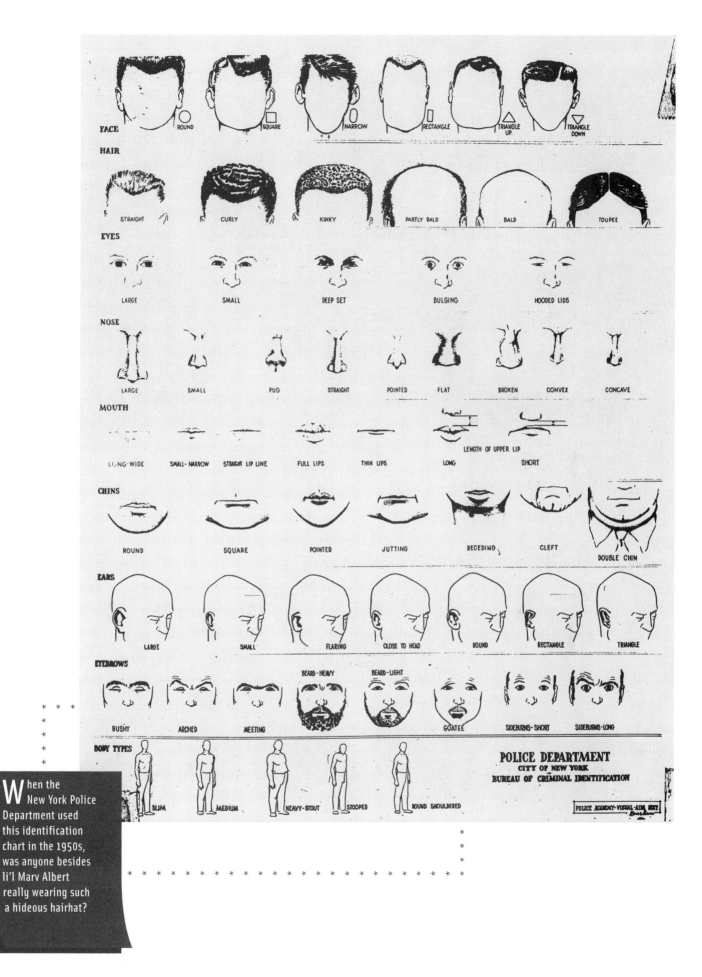

When the New York Police Department used this identification chart in the 1950s, was anyone besides li'l Marv Albert really wearing such a hideous hairhat?

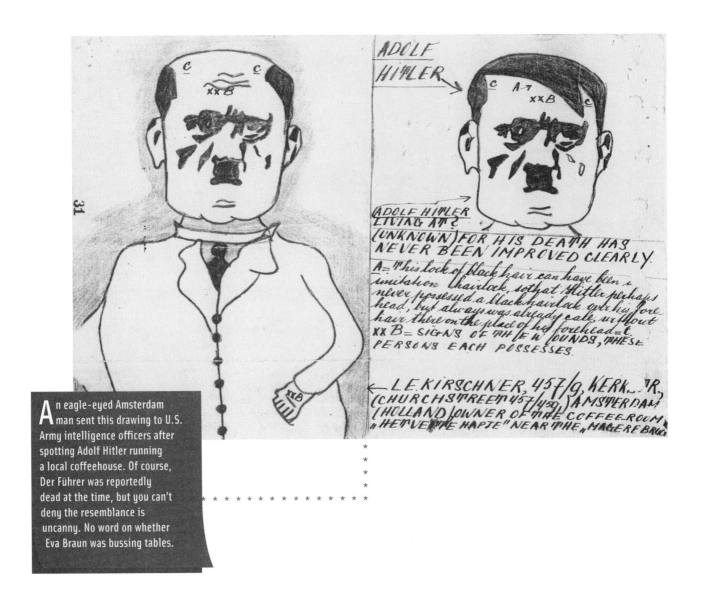

An eagle-eyed Amsterdam man sent this drawing to U.S. Army intelligence officers after spotting Adolf Hitler running a local coffeehouse. Of course, Der Führer was reportedly dead at the time, but you can't deny the resemblance is uncanny. No word on whether Eva Braun was bussing tables.

AS THE WORM TURNS

4.   That on October 11, 1998, while the Plaintiff was inside the Las Vegas Hilton working as a security officer, the Defendant, without cause, consent, or provocation, sexually assaulted the Plaintiff by physically grabbing her breast and shaking it.

WANTED By This Department

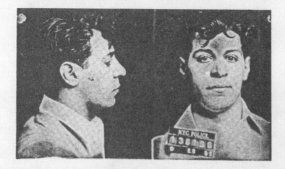

FRANK BELLONE

for MURDER

ALIAS: James Bellone, "Tanky."

P.D. Number: B 136196.

Fingerprint Classification:

5	O	29	W	IIO	16
	I	18	R	OII	

CIRCUMSTANCES OF CASE

Bellone is sought for the murder of Michael Macagnone of 1013 Willoughby Street, Brooklyn, on July 19, 1935. The victim left a female friend at 415 East 13th Street at 8:30 P.M. and was walking east when he was shot down by two men in a passing sedan who fired a volley of shots at him. He suffered three gunshot wounds and died two hours later in Bellevue Hospital.

BACKGROUND INFORMATION:

The ~~victim~~, 22 years old, refused to give information. ~~had~~ been in the fruit business and had been ~~in~~ 1934. He had one arrest for robbery. On ~~7~~, 1935, Joseph "Piney" Armore, 441 East ~~Street~~, was arrested for acting in concert with ~~Armore~~ was sentenced to 2½ to 5 years.

~~DESCRIP~~TION:

~~He~~ is now 48 years old; height, 5'7"; weight ~~brown~~ eyes, black hair. A restaurant worker, ~~known~~ to frequent cafeterias in the vicinity of ~~Street~~, Manhattan. Last known address (1935), ~~5~~th Street, Manhattan.

> A picture is worth a thousand words. Or, in the case of the photograph at far right, probably a thousand days in jail.

WANTED FOR ASSAULT AND ROBBERY

26th Sqd. 61# 5948, Det. Carroll

CIRCUMSTANCES OF CRIME:

At 7:40 P.M. on Tuesday, Nov. 6, 1962, this unidentified male entered the premises of photographer Vincent Armas, 437 W. 125th St., professing to be a customer. He posed for two photos and then struck proprietor on the head with a glass jar and took $249 from his person and a notary public stamp.

DESCRIPTION:

Male, Negro, in his early twenties.
5'11", about 170 lbs.
Wearing glasses and a small goatee, grey checked three-quarter length coat, blue dungarees, tan straw hat, khaki shirt, military boots.

Mount Sinai Medical Center
Departments of Psychiatry and Radiology
Positron Emission Tomography with ^{18}F deoxyglucose

Scan date: May 7 '97

0 gigantevi	1 gigantevi	2 gigantevi	3 gigantevi
FDG Gigante Vincent	FDG Gigante Vincent	FDG Gigante Vincent	FDG Gigante Vincent
4 gigantevi	5 gigantevi	6 gigantevi	7 gigantevi
igante Vincent	FDG Gigante Vincent	FDG Gigante Vincent	FDG Gigante Vincent
tevi	9 gigantevi	10 gigantevi	11 gigantevi
FDG Gigante Vincent	FDG Gigante Vincent	FDG Gigante Vincent	FDG Gigante Vincent
12 gigantevi	13 gigantevi	14 gigantevi	15 gigantevi
FDG Gigante Vincent	FDG Gigante Vincent	FDG Gigante Vincent	FDG Gigante Vincent
16 gigantevi	17 gigantevi	18 gigantevi	19 gigantevi
FDG Gigante Vincent	FDG Gigante Vincent	FDG Gigante Vincent	FDG Gigante Vincent

Ever wonder what's inside the head of a legendary gangster like Vincent "Chin" Gigante? Well, as these brain scans clearly show, it's puffy cumulus clouds.

B L Diamonds

Manufacturers of fine Jewelry

Date: December 27, 1995   INVOICE #8794

NAME: MARION SUGE KNIGHT
      10900 WILSHIRE BLVD, 12TH FLOOR
      LOS ANGELES, CA 90024

1X 18K Y/GOLD PAVE HEART NECKLACE, 5.90CT T.W. *Suges mother* $ 7,600.00

1X 18K ROLEX BRACELET PAVE DIAMONDS,9.65CT T.W. *Suge* $ 13,450.00

1X 18K ROLEX RING PAVE DIAMONDS, 5.51CT T.W.   *Tupac* $ 4,890.00

1X CUSTOM Y/GOLD DIAMOND 34" NECKLACE, PAVE
   SET BR CUT DIAMONDS,29.52CT T.W. PLUS 219   *Suge* $ 32,300.00
   GRAMS IN WEIGHT

1X 14K YELLOW GOLD DIAMOND PAVE SET PENDANT,   " $ 7,780.00
   CUSTOM MADE, 7.20CT T.W.

10X 14K Y/GOLD #1 MOM DIAMOND PENDANTS, @$280.00 $ 2,800.00

10X 14K Y/GOLD 3.5MM ROPE CHAINS   @$185.00 $ 1,850.00

                                       SUB TOTAL: $ 70,670.00
                                          S/TAX: $ 5,830.00

                                     BALANCE DUE: $ 76,500.00

Those "#1 Mom" diamond pendants again prove the unmatched generosity of Death Row Records executives. Imagine what they lavished on all their bitches and hos!

631 SOUTH OLIVE STREET, SUITE 570 • LOS ANGELES, CALIFORNIA 90014 • (213) 622-3221 • FAX (213) 627-6320

UNSAFE USING
'THINGS NOT TO DO!"

1. Smoking from a pipe or stem that doesn't have a rubber covered mouth piece.

2. Smoking from a hot pipe.

3. Smoking form a cracked pipe.

4. Not wiping the stem pipe when you share.

5. Giving or receiving "shotguns."

6. Using plastic bottles as pipe without changing tin foil or keeping fresh ashes.

7. Smoking with cracked lips

8. Having sex without latex condoms or dental dams, especially when on a binge.

9. Having oral sex with cracked lips.

Sex

Try to negotiate out of vaginal and anal sex, or get your customer off some other way. Charging a lot more for vaginal or anal sex may discourage cheap johns. If not, use a well lubricated male or female condom from beginning to end.
It is wiser to give, than to get. This goes for bondage, spankings, water sports, oral sex, and rimming. It is never a good idea to allow a stranger to tie you up or spank you. Whether you are engaging in S & M or not, always be in charge or on top.

Setting

Pick your own parking spots and hotels. Stay alert and in control of the date. When in a car or in a room, keep an eye on the exit at all times and do not let the customer block your access to it. Trust your instincts and be willing to turn customers down.

These pamphlets, distributed by a New York public health group, offer handy tips for prostitutes and crack smokers, although some of the advice should be heeded by civilians as well. For example, do not allow a stranger to spank you and be sure to wipe the mouthpiece before sharing the pipe—it's only polite.

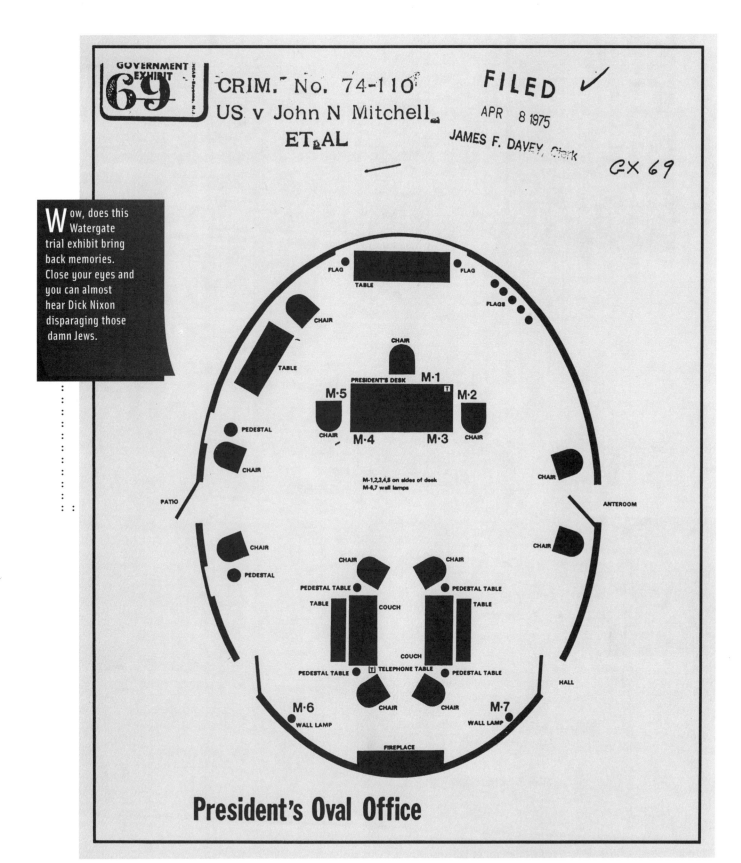

GOVERNMENT EXHIBIT 69

CRIM. No. 74-110
US v John N Mitchell
ET AL

FILED ✓
APR 8 1975
JAMES F. DAVEY, Clerk

GX 69

FLAG   FLAG

TABLE

FLAGS

CHAIR

TABLE

CHAIR

M·1

PRESIDENT'S DESK

M·5   T   M·2

CHAIR   CHAIR

M·4   M·3

PEDESTAL   CHAIR

CHAIR   CHAIR

M-1,2,3,4,5 on sides of desk
M-6,7 wall lamps

PATIO   ANTEROOM

CHAIR   CHAIR

PEDESTAL

CHAIR   CHAIR

PEDESTAL TABLE   PEDESTAL TABLE

TABLE   COUCH   TABLE

COUCH

PEDESTAL TABLE   T   TELEPHONE TABLE   PEDESTAL TABLE

HALL

M·6   M·7

WALL LAMP   WALL LAMP

CHAIR   CHAIR

FIREPLACE

President's Oval Office

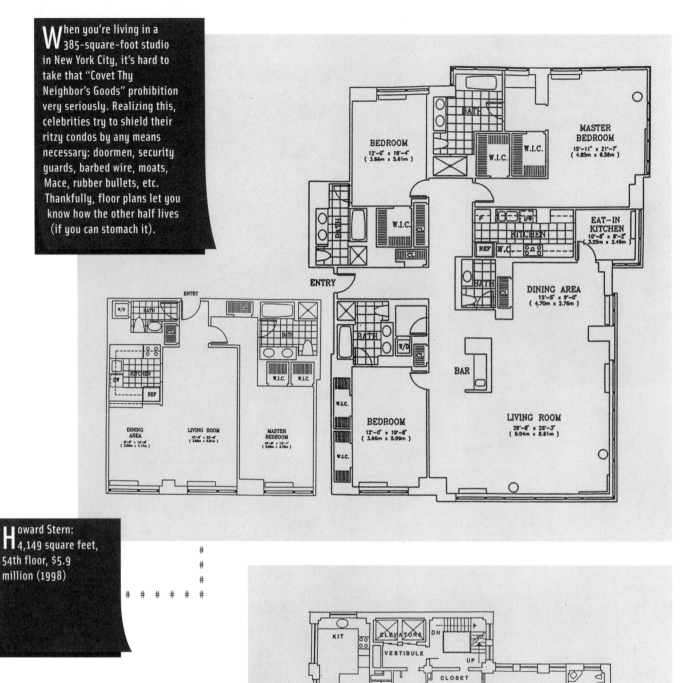

When you're living in a 385-square-foot studio in New York City, it's hard to take that "Covet Thy Neighbor's Goods" prohibition very seriously. Realizing this, celebrities try to shield their ritzy condos by any means necessary: doormen, security guards, barbed wire, moats, Mace, rubber bullets, etc. Thankfully, floor plans let you know how the other half lives (if you can stomach it).

Howard Stern: 4,149 square feet, 54th floor, $5.9 million (1998)

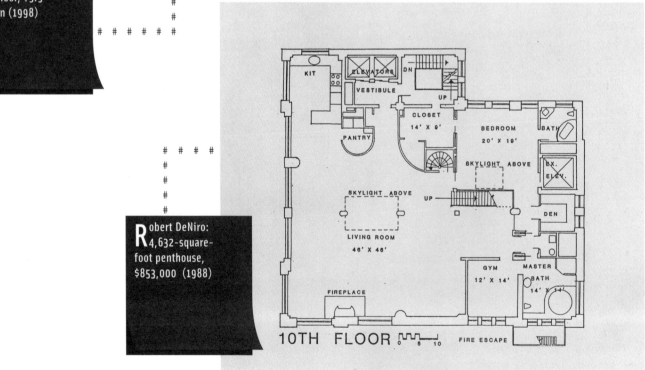

Robert DeNiro: 4,632-square-foot penthouse, $853,000 (1988)

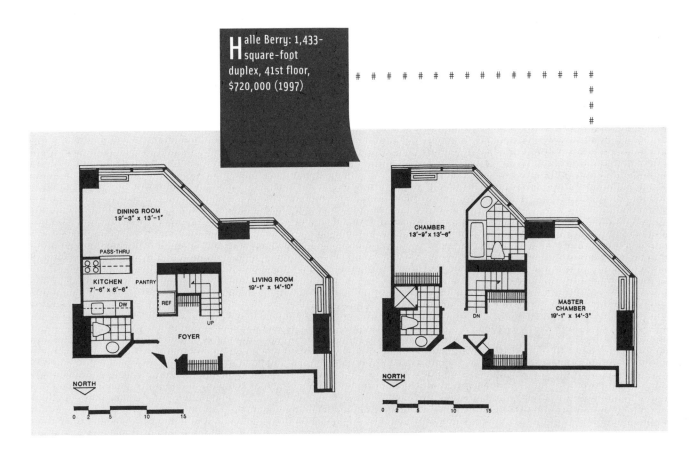

Halle Berry: 1,433-square-foot duplex, 41st floor, $720,000 (1997)

DINING ROOM
19'-3" x 13'-1"

PASS-THRU

KITCHEN
7'-6" x 6'-6"

PANTRY

REF

UP

LIVING ROOM
19'-1" x 14'-10"

DW

FOYER

NORTH

0   2   5   10   15

CHAMBER
13'-9" x 13'-6"

DN

MASTER CHAMBER
19'-1" x 14'-3"

NORTH

0   2   5   10   15

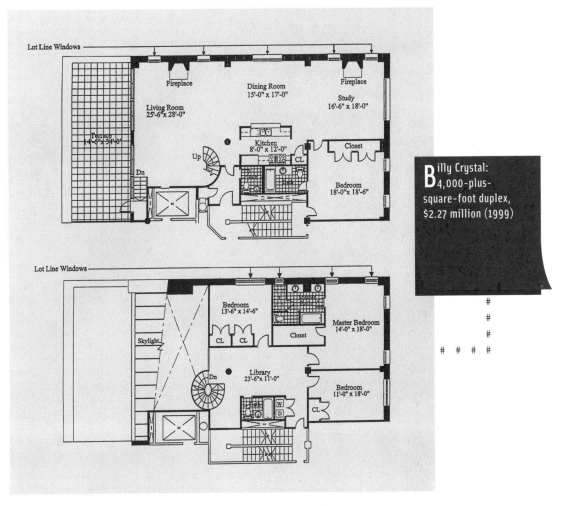

Lot Line Windows

Fireplace

Dining Room
15'-0" x 17'-0"

Fireplace

Living Room
25'-6"x 28'-0"

Study
16'-6" x 18'-0"

Terrace
14'-6"x 34'-0"

Kitchen
8'-0" x 12'-0"

Closet

CL

Up

Dn

Bedroom
18'-0"x 18'-6"

Billy Crystal: 4,000-plus-square-foot duplex, $2.27 million (1999)

Lot Line Windows

Bedroom
13'-6" x 14'-6"

Master Bedroom
14'-0" x 18'-0"

Skylight

CL   CL

Closet

Dn

Library
23'-6"x 11'-0"

Bedroom
11'-0" x 18'-0"

CL

שמע ישראל יהוה אלהינו
HEAR O ISRAEL THE LORD OUR GOD
יהוה אחד
THE LORD IS ONE

CERTIFICATE OF CONVERSION

This is to record that _[signature]_

having sought to join the household of Israel by accepting
the religion of Israel and promising to live by its principles
and practices was received into the Jewish Faith

on _July 1, 1956_

corresponding to the Hebrew date _22nd Tammuz, 5716_

at _Lewisboro, New York_

Rabbi Robert E. Goldburg
SIGNATURE

[signature] miller
SIGNATURE

[signature]
SIGNATURE

Arthur Miller

THY PEOPLE SHALL BE MY PEOPLE AND THY GOD MY GOD
BOOK OF RUTH

Two days after her marriage to Arthur Miller, Marilyn Monroe signed this certificate recording her conversion to Judaism. With Marilyn becoming a member of the tribe, Lauren Bacall dropped to second on the list of Hottest Jews in Hollywood.

(NO COCA COLA)

(No Red Delicious)

(NO Chrysanthemums, Lilies, Carnations or Daises)

(No HYDROGENATED OILS)

Must not contain Canola Oil

NO PRESERVATIVES PLEASE

NO squirt bottles, please.

NO BROWN

No less than six (6) bottles of water (NOT EVIAN)

M&M'S

No pre-made sandwiches or pressed meats

no Iceberg lettuce, please

ABSOLUTELY NO COLD CUTS

(NO PLASTIC or PAPER)

(no paper plates, cups, or saucers of any kind)

(no Styrofoam)

not more than 1 week old

NO ANIMALS

Not Pepsi and no diet

(no seafood, shellfish or mushrooms)

(not formal wear)

(NO SUBSTITUTES)

Van Halen once contractually required concert promoters to
remove all the brown M&M's from the dressing room candy bowl.
It seems that when you're a famous performer, you and
your lawyers must obsess over the smallest backstage details
(you know, when the music doesn't get in the way).

AIN'T DOWN, INC. RIDER

DEBBIE REYNOLDS's dressing room is to contain the following, no later than two (2) hours prior to show time:

> Six (6) 12 oz. Classic Cokes
> Four (4) quart bottles spring water (non-sparkling)
> Four (4) water glasses (NO PLASTIC or PAPER)
> One (1) pound of clean ice
> Two (2) boxes of Kleenex tissues

Note: Musical Director, singer/dancers, and production staff refreshments may be combined in a Green Room area, when available.

Ice down all drinks in a large plastic bus tray or ice chests. <u>Trash cans are not acceptable.</u>

Meals are to be provided for PRODUCER's two (2) person road crew as follows:

> (A) Load In Call (Check with PRODUCER's Production Manager)
> Cold Cuts: Ham, Roast Beef, and Turkey
> Bread: Rye, Whole Wheat and White
> Lettuce, pickles, tomatoes, onion
> Drinks: Coffee, Milk, Classic Coke, Diet Coke
> Condiments
> Knives, forks, spoons, plates
> Glasses, bowls, napkins, cups, etc.
> No pre-made sandwiches or pressed meats (i.e.
> Spam, turkey roll, etc.)
> (B) Dinner (When artists, staff, and crew cannot return to
> hotel after sound check. Check with PRODUCER's
> Production Manager)
> Soup
> Salad with choice of three (3) dressings
> Hot Entree (from a regular restaurant menu...NOT
> from any fast food chain!)
> Two (2) hot vegetables
> Bread and Butter
> Desserts
> Drinks: Coffee, Milk, Classic Coke, Diet Coke
> Condiments
> Knives, forks, spoons, plates
> Glasses, bowls, napkins, cups, etc.

THIS AGREEMENT CANNOT BE AMENDED, SUPPLEMENTED, OR VARIED EXCEPT BY A INSTRUMENT IN WRITING SIGNED BY DEBBIE REYNOLDS FOR AIN'T DOWN, INC.
Page 18

DRESSING ROOM - CHRISTINA AGUILERA (To be ready by 3:00 p.m.)

- Ten (10) Bottles of room temperature bottled water (Not Evian)
- Full coffee and tea set-up to include
    - Real Coffee Mugs
    - Honey
    - Variety of Teas/herbal
    - Sugar
    - Spoons
- One (1) 6 pack of COKE (Not Pepsi and no diet)
- Four (4) Packs of Carnation Instant Breakfast "Original Malt Flavor"
- One (1) Small container of "Nesquick" Chocolate Flavor
- One (1) Pint of Organic Whole Milk (Health Food Store)   (Health Food Store)
- One (1) Liter Full Fat Vanilla Soy Milk (Must not contain Canola Oil, Barley, Oats or malt of any kind   (Preferably Eden Soy Eden Blend Rice & Sot   (Health Food Store)
- One (1) Package of "Soya Kaas" Soy Cheese Full Fat Mozzarella or Cheddar(Health Food Store)
- One (1) Bottle of Echinacea Capsules   (Health Food Store)
- One (1) Small Fruit Platter of Raspberries, Blueberries, Strawberries, Plums and Whole Bananas (All must be Organic)   (Health Food Store)
- One (1) Small Tray of Fresh Roasted Turkey, Chicken & Roast Beef Deli Only (No pressed or processed meats)   (Health Food Store)
- One (1) Small Veggie Tray with Carrots, Cherry Tomatoes, Red Peppers, Cauliflower, Celery, and Jhicama   (All must Be Organic)   (Health Food Store)
- Assorted Raw Almonds, Banana Chips, Dried Cranberries   (Health Food Store)
- Assortment of Power bars, Cliff Bars and Balance bars   (Health Food Store)
- One (1) Small Bottle of "Flintstones" Vitamins with Extra Vitamin C
- One (1) Small Bottle of Chewable Vitamin "C" Tablets   (Health Food Store)
- One (1) Small Cheese Platter with Cheddar, Jack, Gouda and Swiss
- Platter Assortment of Gums and Mints
- One (1) Roll of APS Film/ 200 Speed Exposure
- One (6) Clean Large Bath Towels
- Display of Fork, Knives, Spoons, Plates (Not Plastic)
- One (1) ½ Pint of Fat Free Small Curd Cottage Cheese ("Knudsen or Clover Only")
- One (1) Container of "Coffee Mate Non-dairy Creamer
- Twelve (12) Solo cups
- Four (4) votive candles with matches
- Two (2) chicken or turkey club sandwiches (white bread with bacon, lettuce and tomato)
- No less than six (6) bottles of water (NOT EVIAN)
- Chocolate chip or Oreo cooks

Please place all perishable items <u>ON ICE</u> or keep refrigerated.

DRESSING ROOM – DANCERS – 4 MALES

- Twelve (12) bottles of cold water
- Eight (8) bottles of Starbucks or other brand of ice coffee
- Eight (8) cans of "Red Bull."
- Two (2) six packs of assorted soda and ice teas
- Fresh made deli sandwiches: assorted turkey, roast beef or chicken
- Fresh fruit
- Cookies

Please place all perishable items <u>ON ICE</u> or keep refrigerated.

PRODUCTION OFFICE (To be ready by 9:00 a.m.)

- Six (6) bottles of Spring water (33.8 fl. ounce size)
- Two (2) six packs of Perrier
- One (1) six-pack diet Coke
- Ten (10) bars of Ivory soap

TSG-**0093**   NO BROWN M&M'S

LYNYRD SKYNYRD
DRESSING ROOMS
(REVISION AUGUST 1 ,1997)

ALL OF THE FOLLOWING ITEMS SHOULD BE ATTRACTIVELY,AND CLEANLY LAID OUT IN THE DRESSING ROOM. AN AMPLE SUPPLY OF "SOLO" CUPS, ICE , AND ALL UTENSILS REQUIRED SHALL BE AVAILABLE. ALL COLD DRINKS SHALL BE, AND REMAIN COLD/ICED, AND ALL HOT BEVERAGES SHALL REMAIN HOT. PORCELAIN CROCKERY AND METAL CUTLERY ARE ESSENTIAL.

A. LYNYRD SKYNYRD DRESSING ROOM.(SPLIT BETWEEN 2 ROOMS-TBA)
    COFFEE SET UP
    TEA SET UP W/ ASSORTED HERBAL TEAS (HONEY,4 LEMONS,4 LIMES)
    48- 16OZ BOTTLES EVIAN WATER (ROOM TEMPERATURE- UNDER TABLE)
    24- 7OZ BOTTLES OF COCA COLA
    12- 7OZ BOTTLES OF DIET COKE
     6 GINGER ALE
     6 ROOT BEER
     8 8OZ CARTONS OF CHOCOLATE MILK
     1 QUART OF ORANGE JUICE OR 4 INDIVIDUAL SIZES
     2 INDIVIDUAL SIZE GRAPE GATERAID
    12 INDIVIDUAL SIZE ASSORTED FRUIT JUICES(OCEAN SPRAY ETC.)

    POT OF HOMEMADE VEGETABLE SOUP (TOMATO BASED)W/BEEF, CHICKEN
    OR HAM WITH LOTS OF BROTH.
    FRUIT TRAY(FRESH FRUIT IN SEASON W/PLENTY OF WATERMELON)
    10 DESSERTS FROM CATERING
    FINGER FOODS (CHOOSE ONE --DISCUSS DURING ADVANCE/OR DAY OF SHOW
       a- KFC CRISPY STRIPS; b-CHILLED SHRIMP; c-JALAPENO POPPERS;d-DELI

    CLEAN ICE / SCOOP
    12 CERAMIC CUPS FOR COFFEE AND TEA
    SOUP BOWLS, SPOONS,AND LADLE
    16 OZ SOLO CUPS
    NAPKINS, PAPER TOWELS,KLEENEX,SALT,PEPPER,SOUP CRACKERS ETC.
    ASHTRAYS,FULL-LENGHT MIRRORS,TRASH CANS,CLOTHES RACKS,FANS
    2 DOZEN BLACK HAND TOWELS.
    6-8 EMPTY BOXES (PLACED UNDER TABLE)

The following meal will be chosen by the ARTIST'S representative, in as far as what will be served and at what time. Some guidelines to be followed:
Hot meal to be determined by Production Manager.

Quality deli tray (Unless another meal has been chosen and AGREED upon by ARTIST'S representative.)
One (1) bowl tuna salad
One (1) bowl egg salad
Hot soup (i.e. ham and bean, chili, not soup that is only broth)
One (1) loaf white bread
One (1) loaf wheat bread
Milk - two (2) gallons
Iced tea
Lemonade
Diet soda -1/2 case
Spring water - two (2) gallons
Hawaiian punch - 1/2 case individuals
Perrier - !/2 case
Gatorade - four (4) quarts
Condiments - mayonnaise, Heinz ketchup, mustard, Tabasco sauce, plates, napkins, etc..

D. BAND HOSPITALITY ROOM - from one half hour prior to sound check through the end of the performance.

FOOD: for twelve (12) (confirm with artist rep)

Assorted cheese tray
Fresh vegetable tray consisting of: broccoli, cauliflower, celery, carrots, ripe avocados
Fresh fruit tray consisting of: red seedless grapes, white seedless grapes, oranges, bananas, honey dew melon, berries, apples, water melon etc.(fruits to be clean, unpeeled and uncut)
One box quality chocolates
Pretzels and Chips(also low-fat)
Asst. Cereals
Asst. Yogurts - six (6)

Lemons, Tabasco sauce, salt and pepper.

E: SHANIA Dressing room food: (confirm with prod mgr)
Fruits and vegetables.. (we carry a juicer)
6 lemons, 3 papayas, 3 mangoes, 18 apples, 6 bananas, 1 pineapple, 1 cantalope, 1 honeydew melon, 1 small watermelon, 10 pounds carrots, 3 medium beets, 2 bunches celery, 3 heads broccoli, quarter pound ginger root.

kettle for boiling water

In light of Shania Twain's carrot scarfing, you'd think the Grammy winner would have X-ray vision by now. Or the complexion of Garfield.

=
+
= + = + = + = + = +

DIONNE WARWICK - DRESSING ROOM REQUIREMENTS - *ONE NITER ONLY*

Purchaser is to provide the following items for Ms. Dionne Warwick's dressing room at no cost to Artist:

all platters should be able to feed eight (8) to ten (10) people.

1.   Hot hors d'oeuvres (no seafood, shellfish or mushrooms) chicken wings, bar-b-que ribs, little franks, meatballs and egg rolls.

       A.   Cold hors d'oeuvres: ham, sliced turkey, roast beef salami, Swiss cheese and American cheese.

       B.   Fresh fruit platter: slices pineapples, green seedless grapes, slices watermelon, sliced honeydew melon, sliced cantaloupe melon and bananas. If any of the above fresh fruit is not in season, please contact World Celebrity, Inc.

2.   Television (21" color)
3.   Telephone
4.   Two (2) bath towels; two (2) face towels; two (2) hand towels
5.   Six (6) wooden hangers
6.   Makeup mirror with lights
7.   Full length mirror
8.   Fruit juices: apple, pineapple, tomato and grapefruit
9.   Assorted sodas: Pepsi, Lipton Iced Tea (cans), 7-up, Orange Slice (NO COCA COLA)
10.   One (1) platter assorted cheeses and crackers
11.   Coffee and tea (with cream, lemon and sugar)
12.   Six (6) glass ash trays
13.   Cups, saucers, plates and silverware (**no paper plates, cups, or saucers of any kind**)
14.   Heater in winter months
15.   Two (2) bottles of <u>Cristal</u> Champagne per concert. **(NO SUBSTITUTES)**
16.   Security for Ms. Warwick and dressing room
17.   Private Toilet

Please be advised that Purchasers failure to provide any of the above mentioned items in Ms. Warwick's dressing room, without prior written approval of World Celebrity, Inc. shall be deemed a material breach of the contract and in the event of such breach, producer reserves the right to cancel the engagement and retain any monies there to fore paid by Purchaser.

By: _____
      Purchaser

The music biz's dirtiest secret? Artists as varied as Dionne Warwick and ZZ Top need a little weenie now and then.

BAND DRESSING ROOM

Set up at least one hour prior to start of show, unless told otherwise by production staff, and to remain until one hour after ZZ TOP performance is concluded. All persons entering into the band dressing room will need to be escorted in and out by authorized ZZ TOP personnel. Always provide and outfit dressing room with high quality utensils, service, cups, table cloths, etc. Be certain to create a clean , pleasing environment. All drinks and ice service requested below is to be checked and replenished as required.

Small coffee set up & condiments - **BFG**
Hot tea set up and herbal tea, artificial sweetener - **BFG**
1 case Diet Coke/Pepsi mix - **BFG**
2 cases small bottles Evian water
1 case large bottles Evian water
1 six pack TAB cola - **FB**
1 six pack diet IBC Root Beer - **DH**
1 large bag plain M&Ms
1 large bag peanut M&Ms
1 large bag Baby Reeses Peanut Butter Cups
1 jar jalapeno peppers - **BFG**
1 loaf wheat bread - **BFG**
Fresh fruit assortment in serving bowls to include : strawberries, pineapple, and bananas
1 liter fresh squeezed orange juice
3 Limes
1 six pack V8 juice
1 crock pot of home made cream of tomato soup, bowls & spoons -**BFG**
1 bottle tobasco sauce
1 medium serving bowl coctail franks in special sauce. (consult with production assistant for the recipe and preparation instructions.) - **FB & BFG**

All dressing room food and drinks are to be split equally between 3 band members in their respective dressing rooms, unless initialed. (Initialed items are requested for that particular band member only.) For example items marked BFG are intended for Billy F Gibbons only and it is not necessary to supply other rooms with these items.

> > > > > > > >

> > > > > > > >

TTT INC _____   3   PROMOTER _____

6. One (1) <u>BAND LOUNGE.</u> This room should be immediately adjacent to the dressing rooms and decorated with appropriate ambiance. It should contain an area for a large catering set-up for up to 60 people. This room also uses a large amount of power and should contain at least 100 amps and three (3) separate services.

The BAND LOUNGE should also contain the following:

a. One (1) full size Snooker table, <u>not</u> a pool table, with a full set of cues, bridges, chalk and racks. <u>Tour will provide their own snooker balls.</u>

b. Five (5) video type games to include: a motor or driving type game, a pinball machine, a combat game, a virtual reality game and a game suitable for families and small children.

c. A ping pong table and accessories, if space allows.

7. One (1) <u>WARDROBE & MAKE-UP ROOM</u> six (6) hanging racks, ironing board with iron, ample lighting and outlets and four (4) six foot tables. This room should be large enough to accommodate wardrobe, make-up and personnel as well as a traveling make-up station.

8. We will need a <u>TOUR MANAGEMENT OFFICE</u> in close proximity to the dressing room compound.   This room should contain two (2) phone lines and one (1) fax line. It should also contain two (2) 8' banquet tables, four (4) chairs, clean trash receptacles and proper heating/air conditioning.

9. There should be an <u>HOSPITALITY AREA/TENT</u> for approx. 30 guests. (In certain markets this may be increased to hold 200-250 people) This area may be near the dressing room compound but should not have any direct access to the dressing rooms themselves. This room may also contain various cold drinks but will not have a proper catering set-up. The need for this area will be confirmed in advance with the Rolling Stone's Production Manager.

10. <u>MEET & GREET ROOM</u>. We will require the use of one well lit, carpeted room for band meet and greet prior to the performance. This room should comfortably hold 24 people.

9

Video games suitable for families and small children? A snooker table? Ping-fucking-Pong!? What happened to the days when the Rolling Stones' "band lounge" was caked with Keith's vomit and the floor was littered with hypodermic needles?

must be completely draped by 12 noon on the day of the show. This should be carpeted and furnished with:

1	Six Foot Sofa
1	Love Seat
2	Easy Chairs
2	Chairs
2	Table Lamps
2	Floor Standing Lamps
1	Coffee Table
2	Six Foot Banquet Tables (covered with white linen table cloths)
4	Large Green Plants
1	Large Arrangement Of Colored Flowers (NO Chrysanthemums, Lilies, Carnations or Daises)

In addition, this room should be supplied with the following catering:

4	Large San Pellegrino bottled water or 12 Small Bottles
4	Large Evian or 18 Small Bottles of Water
8	Diet Coke (MUST BE IN CANS)
4	Diet 7-UP / Diet Sprite
1	Pint of Fresh Squeezed Orange Juice
1	Pint of Fresh 2% Milk
1	Hot Water Kettle
1	Assortment of Teas, Coffee, Sugar, Uncut Fresh Lemons To Include English Breakfast Tea. Equal (Brand) Sweetener

---

NB - Please be aware all drinks in all rooms need to be iced down, we will use approx. 40 kilos of ice on a show day.

THE ROOM SHOULD BE SET UP FOR FOUR PEOPLE

Fresh fruit basket (the fruit left whole)

ABSOLUTELY NO COLD CUTS

6	Cups, saucers, plates (stoneware)
	Knives, forks, spoons (no plastic)
12	Drinking Glasses (no plastic)
24	Large plastic cups
2	Lined Trash Cans
2	Bottle Openers

CONTINUED ON NEXT PAGE

What do you think Sir Elton would do if someone snuck an offending chrysanthemum in that flower arrangement? They'd probably never be heard from again—kinda like Kiki Dee.

* * * * * * * * * * *
*

33.1 COLD DRINKS

1 (One) case Coca -Cola
1 (One) case Pepsi Cola
1.5 (One-half) case 7-Up
1.5 (One-half) case Diet Soda (Diet Pepsi, Diet Coke, etc.)
2 (Two) bottles Plain Seltzer (750 ml) . . . No salt
1 (One) case natural non-alcoholic fruit Cooler drinks, *Cranberry, Kiwi, Lime*, <u>Naturally carbonated</u>
1 (One) quart Low-Fat Milk
1 (One) quarts *fresh-squeezed* Orange Juice (bottles w/tops)
1 (One) six-pack small disposable 'juice box' Pink Grapefruit
1 (One) six-pack small disposable 'juice box' Apple
1 (One) six-pack small disposable 'juice box' Cranberry
1 (One) six-pack small disposable 'juice box' White/Regular Grape
30 (Thirty) litres Evian or other 'designer' water (30 x 1 litre or 20 x 1.5 litre)
2 (Two) gallons distilled water
1 (One) case Sharps non-alcoholic beer (must be in cans)
One-Half (1/2) case <u>regular</u> local beer (in cans)
One-Half (1/2) case Premium Beer (Grolsch, Pilsner Urquell, Corona)
One (1) pint Jack Daniels (Black Label)
One (1) pint Absolut Vodka or substitute with Finlandia or Stolichnaya.
One (1) 750 ml. Bacardi Anejo Rum (Bacardi 'Dark' if not available) - not Black.
Two (2) bottles white wine, top quality/may vary with dinner, pl. consult with Road Manager.
One (1) bottle red wine, top quality
One (1) 750 ml. Tequila - the best you've got! Gold variety. <u>Upon request.</u>
Choices as follows:
A. Chinaco
B. Tesoro de San Felipe Muy Anejo
C. Tesoro de San Felipe
D. Herradura Anejo
E. Herradura Repasada
F. Gueros 1800
Small bottles of Grand Marnier, Cointreau.
Ingredients for Bloody Mary's.
**Six (6) whole limes and Margarita salt and 4 shot glasses.
**Please furnish a 'Blender' for Margarita's

Note: Please put *only half* of the 'non-perishable' beverages (milk, orange juice *are* perishable) *on ice in shallow containers*, e.g. 'Bus Trays'. Containers should be on tables and spare drinks not yet on ice should be *under* tables. Soft drinks and regular local beer should be in cans. Premium beers should be in bottles. Ice must be replenished as required. This entire catering set-up (including food) usually requires 3 x 8' banquet tables.

33.2 DELI TRAY (4 people)

Assorted fresh-cut cold meats, including <u>Turkey (not pressed)</u>, Ham, Salami, Roast Beef ...1/3 (One Third) pound each
Cole Slaw*
Potato Salad*
Macaroni Salad*
<u>*Note: Dry. Not much Mayonnaise. Served in seperate bowls, with serving spoons. 1 (One) pint each.*</u>
When possible . . . substitute the above for local favorite Sandwiches.

Van Halen Rider, Initial _____

28

i) 2 quarts Rice Dream (1 Vanilla, 1 Original)
j) Plenty of Solo cups, wine glasses, openers, ice, etc....

FOOD: *Should be purchased at health food store and organic!*

a) 1 Moderate size Deli tray w/ Smoked Turkey, and Swiss and Brie Cheese
b) 2 types bread (pita and regular whole wheat)
c) 1 Moderate size Fresh Vegetable Platter w/ Broccoli, Cauliflower, Red & Yellow Peppers, Asparagus, Radish, Carrots, Celery, etc..
d) 2 Tubs of Hummus
e) 1 Small bag of fresh Sunflower Sprouts
f) Mixed leafy greens w/ Balsamic Vinegar & Olive Oil dressing (*no Iceberg lettuce, please*)
g) A large assortment of fresh seasonal fruit: apples (No Red Delicious), Oranges, Tangerines, Pineapple, Bananas, Kiwi, Mangoes, Papayas, Red Cherries (1lb.) and Grapes
h) Cereals: 2 or more of the following: Barbara's Puffins, Barbara's Shredded Oats, Natures Path Corn Flakes (Big Box), Bran Flakes.
i) Box of Granola
j) 2 large bags Tortilla Chips (No HYDROGENATED OILS) Blue Corn, Garden of Eden, Red Hot Blues.
k) Salsa: 1 Container of fresh tomato salsa med. or med. hot
        1 Container of fresh Verde (Green) Salsa (Tomatillo)
        NO PRESERVATIVES PLEASE
l) 1 Small box of Carr's table water crackers (any variety)
m) 2 Cans tuna in Spring Water (Starkist/Bumblebee) UNOPENED
n) 1 small jar Peanut Butter
o) 1/2 pound fresh gourmet coffee beans (dark roast), coffee machine, w/ filters, sugar, etc...
p) 2 packs Winston Lights box & 2 packs Marlboro Lights
q) 10 lb. bag of ice
r) Cups, Openers, Plates, Bowls, Glasses, Table cloths, etc....

f) Stage Drinks: To be placed 1/2 hour before show time in Ice and coolers:

a) 10 bottles Mineral Water (Evian, Sparkletts, etc)
b) 4 bottles Gatorade
c) 6 Import beers
d) Solo Cups

g) FOH Drinks: To be placed 1/2 hour before show time in Ice and coolers:

a) 6 bottles of Mineral Water
b) 6 Asst. Soda
c) 6 Asst. Beer
d) Solo Cups

You know The Wallflowers are health nuts when they even shop for their Marlboros at the organic food mart.

FOOD REQUIREMENTS/BAND (Continued)

VEGETABLE TRAY
One small fresh cut organic vegetable platter to include but not limited to, carrots, celery, cucumbers, tomatoes, broccoli and cauliflower with one dip.

SEPERATE PLATE
One sliced AVOCADO
One small package of alfalfa sprouts

FRUIT TRAY
ONE (1) Dozen (12) Bananas (A MUST)
Organic Fresh fruit platter to include but not limited to, apples, oranges, kiwis, grapes, Bing cherries, pears, melons, etc. (All fruit should be left whole and not sliced.)

Two (2) sharp knives   One (1) cutting board

MUNCHIES

Three	(3)	Assorted Dannon Fruit Yogurt
One	(1)	large bowl of boiled and peeled high quality shrimp (25 pieces) with cocktail sauce and lemon slices
Three	(3)	1/2 lb. size bags 2 Plain, 1 Peanut M&M's
One	(1)	large bag ridged potato chips
One	(1)	jumbo pack Freedent Spearmint Gum
One	(1)	**small** bag of Werthers Original candy (a few rolls are okay)
One	(1)	small bowl mixed nuts
One	(1)	small bowl white (no red) pistachio nuts
One	(1/2)	chaffing dish hot hors d'oeuvres (To be selected by Production Manager) e.g., Chicken or Beef Satay, Mini Chicken or Beef Kebobs, Chicken Wings, Pot Stickers, Anything Cool or local specialty, etc.
One	(1/2)	chaffing dish vegetarian hors d'oeuvres (To be selected by Production Manager) e.g., Mini Vegetable Quiches, Pigs in Blankets Fried Shrimp, Egg Rolls, Potato Skins, Anything Cool or local specialty, etc.

NOTE: All items to be placed in bowls/containers which artist may take with them.

SUPPLIES
1. The following non-food items are to be placed in BAND HOSPITALITY ROOM at the same time as the food and drinks.

Forty eight	(48)	large CLEAN cloth <u>BATH SIZE</u> towels (No bar towels)
Sixteen	(16)	CLEAN cloth <u>HAND SIZE</u> towels (8 dark color, 8 white) (bar and cut up towels not acceptable)
Eight	(8)	CLEAN TERRY CLOTH WASH CLOTHS
One hundred fifty	(150)	16 oz. Plastic cups (for cold drinks: Solo brand Party Cups preferred cups should be colored, not see through or clear; not waxed paper or clear plastic)
Fifty	(50)	10 oz. hot cups - paper with handles (no Styrofoam)
Thirty	(30)	China dinner plates (no paper or plastic)
Thirty	(30)	each forks, knives, and spoons (silverware not plastic)
One hundred	(100)	paper napkins
Two	(2)	rolls VIVA (brand name) paper towels (MUST BE VERY SOFT)
Ten	(10)	ash trays
Ten	(10)	books of matches
Four	(4)	large trash cans with plastic liners
One	(1)	carton of Marlboro Lights **soft pack** Cigarettes (NOT 100's, not in a box) This is an ESSENTIAL ITEM!!!
Three	(3)	BIC type large lighters (preferably without child guards) NOT GREEN!
Three	(3)	Cans of Copenhagen LONG CUT Dip (not more than 1 week old) SEE DATE ON BOTTOM OF CAN!!
Two	(2)	bottle openers
One	(1)	50 foot roll saran wrap
Twenty Four	(24)	takes out food containers or 100 high quality paper plates
One	(1)	box (3 bag, 3..5 oz) Betty Crocker HOME STYLE Microwave Pop Corn (sprinkled with salt made with butter)

Linen table clothes for all catered tables
Clean and fresh ice cubes for drinks
Serving utensils for all food dishes

29

Is there a more demanding oldies act than the Beach Boys? Viva paper towels. Betty Crocker popcorn. A deep muscle masseuse. Bic lighters (but not green ones). Who says Brian Wilson was the only crazy one?

AFTER SHOW HOSPITALITY ROOM

To be advised by Company Production Manager regarding after show requirements on day of show, if any.

Be prepared to supply 2 cases assorted sodas and 2 cases of beer.

DOCTOR

Purchaser agrees to arrange for the services of a licensed physician, qualified in internal medicine who can be available as needed throughout Artist's stay in the city, and who has admission privileges at a first-rate hospital in the vicinity. Purchaser should have physician's phone number, pager number and service number readily at hand in anticipation of immediate need. (it is not necessary for physician to be on 24 hours stand-by call for Artist, but to be available for consultation and care of members of the entourage in the event of an emergency situation).

MASSEUSE/MASSEUR

Purchaser agrees to arrange for the availability of the services of a licensed masseuse or masseur, qualified in either Swedish or Oriental deep muscle massage, who can be available on the day of the engagement or on a day off Artist may have in the city. At the time of advancing the show the name and telephone number of the masseuse or masseur should be given to Company's Tour Manager. This person should be available in the morning so a time and place may be arranged for massage if needed. Company will be responsible for compensating masseuse/masseur In the event that services are actually engaged.

LAUNDRY

In order to facilitate the cleaning of stage costumes, Purchaser will instruct runner and production manager to determine the nearest laundromat and dry cleaners. The responsible person should determine the hours of operation for a location that provides a same day wash and fold laundry service and a dry cleaner with a same day service, which is open and accepting laundry on the day of engagement. The laundromat should be made aware that laundry may be coming and that it must be returned washed and be available for pick up on that day. Any expense incurred by the inability of runner to get the laundry prior to the laundromat closing will be paid by Purchaser. The actual cost of the laundry is a Company expense.

RIDER ATTACHMENTS

The Agreement, Addendum 'A' and this Rider set forth the entire Agreement between the parties hereto and all prior Agreements whether oral or written are merged herein. This Rider, the Addendum 'A' and the Agreement and the terms thereof may not be amended, changed, modified, waived discharged or altered except by an instrument in writing signed by the parties hereto. ANY proposed additional terms and conditions which may be affixed to this rider and the Agreement by Purchaser shall not become part of the Agreement until signed by Company.

SPECIFIC ADDITIONAL PROVISIONS

Intentionally deleted.

DEF LEPP INC. 2000 "FAIR RIDER"

DONATED TO A FOOD CENTER FOR THE HOMELESS OR SIMILAR
INSTITUTION.
DEF LEPPARD DRESSING ROOM CATERING REQUIREMENTS

**DEF LEPPARD requests that a photocopy or facsimile of this document be
delivered directly to the caterer for this date. DO NOT REWRITE OR
RETYPE THIS DOCUMENT FOR DISTRIBUTION. Instead use only this
original for distribution to the caterer of this date. It is our experience that
translating this document causes problems easily avoidable if this original is
used.**

All dressing room catering is to be set up by 1:00 PM. The catering in this room
should be prepared for six (6) people. Please provide the following items
remembering sizes and BRAND NAMES are important to us. Also please use low
fat or fat free items whenever possible.

BEVERAGES

Please place drinks in coolers. The beer and wine are to go in a separate cooler.

One (1) cooler of clean drinking ice (Def Leppard will provide the cooler).
Eight (8) cans Diet Coke
Eight (8) cans Diet 7-UP
Thirty-Six (36) one-liter bottles of Evian served at room temperature LITER
BOTTLES ONLY!!!
One (1) half-gallon of 2% milk
Three (3) liters of Vanilla 1% Soy Milk (West soy when available, must be vanilla
and 1%) (You can find this at a health food store)
One (1) quart of **fresh squeezed** NON-PASTEURIZED Orange Juice (Health
Food store, this can't come in a carton please no Tropicana or Minute Maid) !!
This is very important to the band !!
One (1) quart (48 oz) of Ocean Spray Cranberry Juice
Four (4) quart size bottles Lemon-Lime Gatorade
Two (2) quart size bottles Orange Gatorade
One (1) gallon of distilled water served at room temperature
Forty-Eight (48) 12 oz cans of Heineken Beer (Must be in CANS, please)
Six (6) bottles of Non-Alcoholic Beer (Coors Cutter or O'Douls Amber)

Some groups are preoccupied with sound checks. Some are concerned about choreography. Def Leppard cares deeply about orange juice, which is "very important to the band!!"

o x x x x x x x x
x
x

ALABAMA
Artist of the Decade

PRODUCTIONS

CATERING RIDER 1998
(Updated 6-5-98)

We are looking forward to working with you on this year's show. The meals should be economical and nutritious. Because we are trying to be more aware of the fat content in our meals we would appreciate the use of low-fat products when possible. (We prefer steamed vegetables and would like to limit the use of butter.) Your suggestions are welcomed, but substitutions may only be made with the approval of Brent Barrett. WE REQUEST THAT, (WHEN PRACTICAL) SUPPLIES USED ARE FRIENDLY TO THE ENVIRONMENT. *In most cases 1st quality plastic and paper ware will be fine, however, if the entree selected for lunch or dinner requires intense cutting, (and it is economical), please use stainless steel silverware and china or hard plastic plates.

Your contact on the day of the show is Brent Barrett and only he is authorized to make changes or additions on show day. When catering is an ALABAMA expense, the total catering cost should be quoted to Brent at least 10 days prior to the show and the bill should be given to Brent at the breakfast meal on show day. Any additional costs during the day should be on a separate bill.

We will need to have someone from your staff available from the time of the first service until at least 45 minutes after the show has ended. Brent must know the location of this person at all times during the day. At the end of the day, all non-perishable food and drinks left over from the meals and dressing rooms should be placed in a location determined by Brent, for after show use.
All bottled waters needs to be screw top. NO squirt bottles, please.
Catering needs to located in the backstage area. When possible it needs to be in the same location for all meals. It isn't practical to have catering in an off premise location.
We have no strict vegetarians traveling with us.
This is a guideline for a full production evening show. In situations where adjustments may need to be made Brent Barrett will be happy to listen to your suggestions.
We need for the caterer or the building to provide 3 dozen bath towels and 1 1/2 dozen white hand towels for ALABAMA and 1 dozen bath towels per front act, unless otherwise requested.

PLEASE BE ADVISED THAT NO ANIMALS ARE ALLOWED IN THE BACKSTAGE AREA AT *ANYTIME* DURING THE DAY. (IF THERE IS AN ANIMAL BACKSTAGE, ALABAMA WILL NOT PERFORM.)

If you have any questions, please call Brent Barrett or ~~Vivian McAllister~~ at (256) 845-6004.
Thank you,

Brent Barrett
ALABAMA Production Mgr.

RECYCLED PAPER   101 GLENN BLVD. S.W. • FORT PAYNE, AL 35967-4963 • PH: (205) 845-6004

Frank Sinatra
Dressing Room Contents

Color TV (with second input for in-house video feed)
Upright Piano
Private Telephone with dedicated line, direct dial out
1 Bottle each: Absolute or Stoli
                     Jack Daniels
                     Chivas Regal
                     Courvoisier
                     Beefeater Gin
                     White Wine-premium
                     Red Wine-premium
                     Bottled Spring Water
                     Perrier-large
Soda   Diet Coke-twenty-four (24)
                     Regular Coke-twelve (12)
                     Club Soda
                     Assorted Mixers
1 Fruit Platter of sliced fresh fruit(to include watermelon when available)
1 Cheese Tray (incl. Brie) with assorted crackers
1 Dijon Mustard
Sandwiches(Two (2) of each)
                            Egg Salad
                            Chicken Salad
                            Sliced Turkey
Twenty-four (24) chilled jumbo shrimp
1 Platter of Nova Scotia Salmon & Hor D'oueres
3 cans Campbell's Chicken & Rice Soup
12 Rolls Cherry Lifesavers
12 Rolls Assorted Lifesavers
12 Boxes Ludens Cough Drops-Cherry, Honey, etc.
1 Bag Miniature Tootsie Rolls
1 Bowl Pretzels and Chips
Salt And Pepper
Tea Bags-Lipton or Teatly
Honey...Lemon...Limes
Sugar & Sweet'n Low
6 Bottles of Evian Spring Water
12 Water Glasses

3

While the Chairman of the Board was washing down his Tootsie Rolls with a fifth of Beefeater, Frank the Younger made do with some fruit juice and Diet Coke. Looks like the apple fell far from the tree, baby.

12 Wine Glasses
6 Rocks Glasses (8-10 ounce size)
4 Porcelain Soup Bowls with knives, forks, spoons
1 Double Burner Hot Plate
1 Tea Kettle with spring water
1 Crock Pot for soup with ladle
1 Coffee Pot Set-up with milk, cups, saucers
6 Linen Napkins
6 White Bath Towels
6 Hand Towels
2 Bars of Ivory soap
6 Boxes Kleenex tissues
1 Carton Camel Cigarettes (no filter)
1 Bucket of Ice Cubes

*Note:*All Soda all rooms to be 75% Diet. Contact Prod. Mgr. for alternatives when performing outside the U.S.

DRESSING ROOM REQUIREMENTS

FS, Jr.
ASSORTED SODAS (REGULAR & DIET - ESPECIALLY DIET COKE)
BOTTLED WATER
FRUIT JUICES
BAR SET UP
ICE
GLASSES
SNACKS & SANDWICH TRAYS
UTENSILS & NAPKINS
WELL LIT FULL LENGTH MIRROR
TOWELS
CLOTHES RACK
KLEENEX
TELEPHONE LINE

DRESSING ROOMS (MALE & FEMALE)
ASSORTED SODAS (REGULAR & DIET)
BOTTLED WATER
FRUIT JUICES
ICE
GLASSES
COFFEE & TEA, CREAM, SUGAR, ETC.
FRESH FRUIT OR VEGETABLE TRAY
UTENSILS & NAPKINS
WELL LIT FULL LENGTH MIRRORS
TOWELS
CLOTHES RACKS

XVIII. VALET REQIREMENTS/DRY CLEANING

Michael Bolton wears designer suits and clothing that will require special dry cleaning treatment. The fabrics are very delicate, and cannot be machine pressed. THEY MUST BE HAND PRESSED WITH A COVERED IRON ONLY. Name and numbers of local dry cleaners that can accommodate these requirements must be supplied to the Production or Tour Manager in advance of the day of performance so we may plan ahead for dry cleaning days.

XIX. GOSPEL CHOIR

Producer will require the services of the best (African American or ethnics/mixed) gospel choir available in your market. Use the following guide lines in locating a choir.

    Choir shall consist of sixteen (16) voices (Ten (10)
        female and Six (6) male).
    Choir will perform two songs during the show.
    Choir must be available to rehearse on day of performance at
    the Venue no later than three (3) hours prior to   showtime.
    Choir will have some choreography to learn
    Producer will provide audio cassette of choir parts.
    The choir must wear black clothing (not formal wear),
        Producer will supply additional items of stage
        clothing.

Purchaser will provide Artist's Production Manager and Ms. Pat Bawk with the names and telephone numbers of choir directors. Purchaser will ensure that all local union requirements for choir are fulfilled to ensure their performance and inform Artist's representative of same.

ACCEPTED AND AGREED TO: ACCEPTED AND AGREED TO:

PURCHASER: PRODUCER:

_____   MBO TOURS INC.

By:_____   By:_____

Print Name:_____   Print Name:_____

                                  Title:_____

_____   Date:_____

                                  35

Before Michael Bolton clipped his golden tresses, those covered irons were also likely used to permanently press his mullet into place.

: :X

picked up a sword obtained a personal

hair stylist imitated the Clint Eastwood character

and expose a bra filled with

balloons that he was wearing while

decorating his home with Christmas lights.

I GRABBED THE HAMMER wrapped

in some type of canvas, waiting in

a back hoe **threw up** on CW noted an abnormal

odor in the room hitting EBOLI in the head

with her shopping bag get a cucumber, paint

it black, sit around, drink a beer and

watch NASCAR **to be shot between bites of salami**

sandwiches found dead in the microwave oven.

CRIME TIME

According to the FBI's annual Uniform Crime Report, felonious behavior is
at its lowest level in two decades. Geez, that's too bad.

STATE OF WISCONSIN   CIRCUIT COURT   DODGE COUNTY

STATE OF WISCONSIN

           Plaintiff,   **CRIMINAL COMPLAINT**

     vs.

                            Case No.

TROY W. GASSNER, DOB: 12/3/69,
222 Buchanan St., #B
Mayville, WI 53050,

           Defendant.   DA: BJP

The next time Troy and his buddies get together for some beer and a Clint Eastwood flick, maybe they should rent *Every Which Way But Loose*. Monkeys are far safer than Magnums.

Gassner indicated that he, Justin Ruckel, Adam Mueller and Jeffrey Breselow sat around his apartment eating pizza and watching a Clint Eastwood movie, Dirty Harry. At some point during the early morning hours, Gassner indicated he went into his bedroom, retrieved his Smith and Wesson .44 magnum revolver, and came back to the living room with the others present. When he came back to the living room, Gassner indicated he sat down on the couch with the gun and showed it to his friend, Breselow, and that Breselow took the gun in turn and unloaded it before giving it back to Gassner.

After eating pizza, drinking beer and watching the Clint Eastwood movie, Gassner indicated he "just got stupid and careless with the gun" and loaded it with various shells. After loading it, Gassner indicated he cocked the hammer back on the revolver approximately one-half dozen times during a short span of time. Gassner also stated that each time he would spin the cylinder after loading a different number of shells into the weapon and that he would then cock the hammer and point the weapon directly at Justin Ruckel.

Gassner indicated that he then "sort of" imitated the Clint Eastwood character in the movie, Dirty Hairy, and said things to Justin Ruckel like, "Do you think it's loaded?" or "Do you feel lucky?" each time he pointed the loaded, cocked gun at Justin Ruckel. Gassner indicated that on one of these occasions while playing with the cocked gun, he picked the gun up from a living room table and brought the gun down to his lap with his left hand. According to Gassner, as the gun was cocked and lying on his lap or his right knee, the gun discharged and struck Justin Ruckel in the knee. Gassner stated he then went into shock as he could clearly see that Justin Ruckel's pants leg had been

split open and a bullet hole was in Justin's knee. Gassner further indicated that he immediately told Adam Mueller to pick up all the beer cans and throw them out of the house as Gassner and Mueller searched for a phone to call the police. Gassner indicated he also woke up his friend, Jeffrey Breselow, and told Breselow to take the gun and unload it.

Troy Gassner acknowledged to Detective Reed that he was very reckless with the gun throughout the evening and indicated he was very sorry for what he had done. Mr. Gassner also acknowledged that he had approximately six 12-ounce cans of Miller beer prior to shooting Justin Ruckel in the knee and he wished he could take the whole evening and do it over again.

It should be noted that Troy Gassner was subsequently given a preliminary breath test which registered a .15 percent BAC reading.

Approved for filing and subscribed
and swom to before me on

2/22/99
William Bedker
(Asst.) District Attorney

[signature]
Complainant

Dodge Co. District Attorney
Administration Building
127 E. Oak St.
Juneau, WI 53039

NK 92-1193

Many of the neighbors plus the employees at the apartment complex know the subject through his reputation and would be literally terrified to cooperate with any law enforcement officials in furnishing information concerning EBOLI. Some time ago, one of EBOLI's neighbors, a middle aged woman who planned to take her dog for a walk, endeavored to board the elevator with EBOLI. Subject told the neighbor to take the dog down the service elevator and as a result of this demand, an argument ensued culminating with the woman hitting EBOLI in the head with her shopping bag. At this point subject became so enraged that he struck the woman in the jaw with a right upper cut. As a result of this altercation, the police were summoned and the lady's husband got in the act, threatening EBOLI with jail, a law suit, plus a physical beating. At this point, the neighbor of subject, was informed of EBOLI's identity, at which time the neighbor turned to his wife, and severly admonished her for percipitating the argument, instructed her to take the dog down the service elevator in the future, apoligized to EBOLI for the inconvenience informed the police that he did not wish to press any charges and then shoved his wife back into the apartment and locked the door.

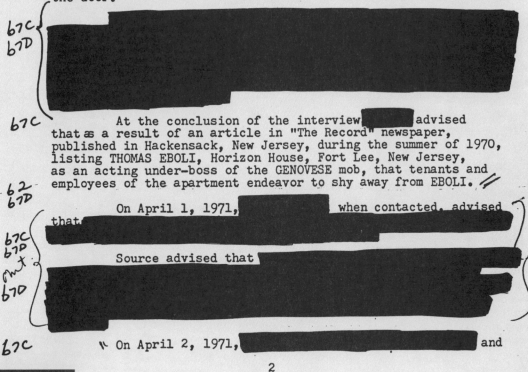

At the conclusion of the interview ▮▮▮▮ advised that as a result of an article in "The Record" newspaper, published in Hackensack, New Jersey, during the summer of 1970, listing THOMAS EBOLI, Horizon House, Fort Lee, New Jersey, as an acting under-boss of the GENOVESE mob, that tenants and employees of the apartment endeavor to shy away from EBOLI.

On April 1, 1971, ▮▮▮▮ when contacted, advised that ▮▮▮▮

Source advised that ▮▮▮▮

On April 2, 1971, ▮▮▮▮ and

2

J02 (Rev. 3-10-82)

FEDERAL BUREAU OF INVESTIGATION

Date of transcription _____3/29/93_____

JOSEPH M. RUSSO, 1713 77th Street, Brooklyn, NY, appeared in Judge Hurley's courtroom in the Eastern District of New York with his attorney, Michael Ross.

While waiting for his case to be called RUSSO initiated a conversation with SA CHRISTOPHER M. FAVO by asking how JOSEPH AMBROSINO was doing. SA FAVO responded that AMBROSINO was doing well.

RUSSO asked if AMBROSINO was in "My Blue Heaven" which SA FAVO interpreted as a reference to the movie "My Blue Heaven" in which STEVE MARTIN portrayed a government witness in the Witness Protection Program. SA FAVO responded that RUSSO was correct.

RUSSO asked whether SA FAVO had obtained a personal hair stylist for AMBROSINO because AMBROSINO was always concerned about how his hair appeared. SA FAVO responded that AMBROSINO had never asked for a hair stylist but if RUSSO wants one when he enters the program SA FAVO would find one for him.

x x x x x
x
x
x
x
x
x
x
x x

The FBI is nothing but solicitous when trying to woo a Mafia snitch. Perhaps if the bureau threw in a Members Only wardrobe, then Russo might seriously consider switching sides.

281 A-NY-214955 sub K-11 · 14

see 1A1

FAVO av

Investigation on __3/26/93__ at __Brooklyn, NY__ File # __281A-NY-214955__

by __Christopher M. Favo/cmf__ Date dictated __3/29/93__

Federal Bureau of Investigation
United States Department of Justice
Washington, D. C.

IN REPLY, PLEASE REFER TO

FILE NUMBER _____

I. I. #540

·October 30, 1944

BODY IN RIVER IDENTIFIED
AS ESCAPED WAR PRISONER

On the night of July 3, 1944, Helmut Haeberlein, 31, escaped from a prisoner of war camp at Wilmington, North Carolina. He left a letter for the camp commanding officer in which he apologized for escaping. "According to the great philosopher Spinoza, every man has to seek happiness," Haeberlein also wrote. "Having not found it in this camp of war prisoners I·must go somewhere else."

He added that since the commanding officer of the camp was not in a position to grant him a furlough that he was assuming the initiative and taking one himself. He also said in his note that he had been told that two weeks in the United States as a free man would make him "never want to return home." He said he wanted to test that claim, promised he would not do anything to hurt the United States while he was at liberty and said he would return voluntarily if not caught.

Haeberlein was a corporal in the German Army and prior to the war he worked as a weaver.

The Federal Bureau of Investigation began looking for him immediately after his escape was reported and it was suspected that he might have gone to the New York metropolitan area.

On October 3, 1944, the Jersey City, New Jersey, Police Department recovered the body of an unknown man from the Hudson River at Jersey City. There was no evidence of foul play and the body was identified tentatively as Haeberlein. Fingerprints then were taken and were forwarded to the Identification Division of the FBI. As soon as the card arrived the prints of the dead man were compared with those of Haeberlein and a positive identification was established.

file in I.D. file Ben

RECORDED

62-23346-403

FEDERAL BUREAU OF INVESTIG·

INDEXED

DEC 22 1944

U. S. DEPARTMENT OF JUST·

282

55 JAN 3 1945

EX - 33

A POW whose escape note quoted Spinoza did not deserve to be dredged from the Hudson River. That's far too ordinary a way to check out.

x — — — — — — — — — — — — — — — — — — — x

CC019934.frm.js2
STATE OF WISCONSIN   CIRCUIT COURT   DANE COUNTY

CRIMINAL COMPLAINT

STATE OF WISCONSIN, PLAINTIFF

VS.

Sys. ID 91089868

CHAD M. ALVAREZ   DOB: 12/16/1975

Sex/Race:	M/W	
Height/Weight:	6'01/175	~~402 W DAYTON ST APT 304~~ 5822 Tree Line Dr.
Hair/Eyes:	BRO/GRN	MADISON, WI 53701

OFFENSE(S): Intentional Mistreatment of Animals resulting in Death
STATUTE(S): 951.02, 951.18(1)

DEFENDANT(S)

AGENCY & CASE NO: MAPD/99-45359   Court Case No: 99CF 1010
DA CASE NUMBER: 99-DA-006142

COMPLAINING WITNESS
Retelle/LaFrancois/Cator/Pharo

THE ABOVE-NAMED COMPLAINING WITNESS BEING FIRST DULY SWORN STATES THAT THE ABOVE NAMED-DEFENDANT IN DANE COUNTY, WISCONSIN, in the City of Madison, on May 4, 1999, did intentionally treat an animal in a cruel manner, resulting in the death of the animal, contrary to Sections 951.02 and 951.18(1) of the Wisconsin Statutes, a class E felony, and upon conviction may be fined not more than Ten Thousand Dollars ($10,000), imprisoned not more than two (2) years or both.

FACTS: City of Madison Police Department officer Tim Strassman reports that on 05/04/99 at approximately 11:34 p.m., he was dispatched to 221 Langdon Street, a fraternity house, in the City of Madison, Dane County, Wisconsin, regarding a dead pet. At that location, he contacted Nicolas Berg, who stated that he was visiting people at this location; that he went into the kitchen and noticed that the microwave was on, but no one was present. He also noted an abnormal odor in the room. He opened the microwave and saw a parrot that appeared dead. Berg stated that there were approximately 57 minutes

left on the microwave and it was running when he opened it, stopping it from running. Berg stated that he immediately went upstairs and contacted John Floss, a resident.

Officer Strassman reports that John Floss stated that after Berg notified him of what Berg had seen in the microwave, at about 10:00 p.m., he went to the microwave and saw a parrot, now dead, that he knew belonged to another resident of the house, Cory Greenfield. Floss stated that he removed the bird from the microwave and placed it in a shoe box. Floss stated that he took the shoe box to the basement, so that Cory Greenfield could do whatever he wanted with his dead pet. Det. Cory Nelson, MAPD, reports that Greenfield showed him the shoe box containing the parrot, and Det. Nelson took possession of it.

Officer Strassman reports that he spoke with Weston Struwe, who stated that during the evening of 05/04/99, he saw a person known to him from previous contact as Chad Alvarez, the defendant herein, at the house at the above location. Alvarez asked, "Is Cory here?" Alvarez returned a few minutes later with a master key, entered Cory Greenfield's room, grabbed Cory Greenfield's parrot and said something about taking the bird. He then left the room and ran down the hallway with the parrot. Struwe stated that there are several sets of master keys to rooms in the house.

Officer Strassman reports that he spoke with Baiers Heeren, a house resident, who stated that during the evening of 05/04/99, he saw a person known to him from previous contact as Chad Alvarez, the defendant herein, in Cory Greenfield's room. Alvarez said something about taking Cory's bird home and keeping it in the bathroom. Alvarez held the bird in his hand and locked Cory's door with the master key when he left, leaving with the bird. Heeren stated that he believed that Greenfield and Alvarez were friends, so he saw nothing particularly unusual about Alvarez's behavior. Heeren stated that about 30 minutes after Alvarez left with the bird, he learned that it had been found dead in the microwave oven.

Officer Strassman reports that he spoke with Jason Kaniss, a house resident, who stated that at around 8:30 to 8:45 in the evening on 05/04/99, a person known to him from previous contact as Chad Alvarez, the defendant herein, came to him and asked for the master key. Alvarez told Kaniss that he'd left a book in James Vickers' room and needed to retrieve it. Kaniss stated that he gave Alvarez the key and Alvarez returned it a short time later. Kaniss stated that at about 9:30 p.m. that date, he saw something that looked like Greenfield's parrot, in the microwave oven. It appeared dead.

Officer Strassman reports that he spoke with Matthew Emmerich, who stated that at about 12:30 p.m. on 05/05/99, he spoke by telephone with a person known to him from previous contact as Chad Alvarez, the defendant herein. Emmerich stated that Alvarez stated that he'd taken Cory Greenfield's bird and left with it in a rage; that he was angry about particular e-mails that he believed had been directed at him personally. Alvarez stated that he was angry at Greenfield and felt that the only way he could get back at Greenfield was to kill his bird.

2

Our culinary sources tell us that microwaved parrot smells just like chicken. And as for the apology Chad left on Alvie's machine, you can sense the remorse when he exclaims, "Please give me a fucking call, I fucking...fuck." That's poignant stuff.

Officer Strassman reports that on 05/05/99, he spoke with Cory Greenfield, a house resident, who stated that the bird found dead in the microwave oven was his pet; that it was a Quaker Parrot named Iago that he'd had for about one year. Greenfield stated that Alvarez used to live in the house, and roomed adjacent to him, but doesn't live at the house now. Greenfield stated that since his bird was killed, he had gotten telephone calls from Alvarez that had been recorded on his answering machine. Officer Strassman listened to the recorded message and transcribed it as follows:

> Greenfield, what's up, this is Alvie. I want to apologize to you; I'd like to sit down and talk with you. I honestly did not think that you were that attached; I've never had a pet. I honestly did not think that you would take it this hard as you obviously have. I wish I could speak with you. I understand that you are absolutely irate and don't want to, but give me a call please and if Nash or Weston, you get this message, tell Greenfield, I really want to talk to you. We're fucking friends, dude, we fucking lived together for fucking couple of years now and it doesn't need to be any fucking, any worse than you fucking me with a baseball bat on the head or something. Please give me a fucking call, I fucking. . . fuck.

> Greenfield, what's up? It's Alvie again. I just wanted to again fucking tell you I'm fucking sorry. I honestly, I don't know how else to say it. I -- if you don't want to see me, please call me. I don't wanna, just me and you, I . . I just want to again say sorry, dude, I honestly did not think about the repercussions of losing a friend and, and, and your attachment and I'm sorry. All right. Please give me a call.

Greenfield stated that he recognized the caller as Chad Alvarez. Officer Strassman reports that on 05/06/99, he spoke with Greenfield, who stated that on 05/05/99 at about 9:15 p.m., Chad Alvarez showed up at his door. Greenfield had not spoken to him. Greenfield stated that Alvarez came to apologize for killing his parrot. Greenfield stated that Alvarez started by saying something to the effect, "dude, we gotta talk. I'm sorry; I never had a pet; I didn't realize it was such a big deal." Greenfield stated that Alvarez continued to insist that he didn't think Greenfield would take it so hard and tried to minimize what had happened. Greenfield stated that he reminded Alvarez about a time last semester when Alvarez was in Greenfield's room; that Alvarez was holding the parrot and had thrown it at a wall. At that time Greenfield told Alvarez that he really cared for the bird and that Alvarez should not hurt it. Greenfield stated that when Alvarez was reminded of this incident, he stated, "yeah, I guess I forgot." Greenfield stated that Alvarez stated that he had taken the parrot from Greenfield's room to his apartment; that when he got there, he realized the bird would probably make a mess and he wasn't certain what to do with it. Alvarez stated that he called a friend and asked him what to do; that he was angry at Greenfield because of an e-mail message. Alvarez maintained that the friend told him that he could get back at Greenfield by killing his bird. Alvarez stated

3

that he wasn't certain how he would do that, but returned to the house with the bird and put it in the microwave and turned it on and walked away.

Officer Strassman reports that Greenfield stated that the e-mail that angered Alvarez was one that Greenfield had gotten from his parents and then forwarded to several members of the house, but not to Alvarez. Greenfield provided officer Strassman with a copy of the e-mail, which consists of humor relating to alcohol consumption, in the form of FDA-type "warnings". Greenfield stated one of these "warnings" in particular apparently angered Alvarez because he had recently gotten rug burns as a result of being intoxicated. The e-mail read as follows:

> WARNING: the consumption of alcohol is the leading cause of inexplicable rug burns on the forehead.

Your complainant is a detective with the City of Madison Police Department and believes the reports of officer Strassman and Det. Nelson are reliable because prepared in the course of official duties; the statements of citizens reliable because based on personal knowledge; those of the defendant against his penal interest.

Subscribed and sworn to before me and approved for filing this *13* day of May, 1999.

_____   _____
Assistant/Deputy District Attorney   Complainant
Dane County, Wisconsin

4

SUFFOLK POLICE

PUBLIC INFORMATION OFFICE
(516) 852-6308 or 6309
F.A.X. (516) 852-6524

POLICE DEPARTMENT, COUNTY OF SUFFOLK, N.Y.
30 YAPHANK AVENUE, YAPHANK, N.Y. 11980

NEWS RELEASE

For Immediate Release
October 16th, 1999

Incident: Woman Attacks Another Woman With a Sword

Location: 52 Winchester Road, Lake Ronkonkoma

Date/Time: October 16, 1999 at 12:17 A.M.

Suffolk County Police Fourth Squad Detectives are investigating an incident where a Lake Ronkonkoma woman came home and found her husband in bed with another woman. She then attacked that woman with a sword. Fourth Squad Detectives have arrested **Euadne Legrottaglie** for assaulting **Delores Andrews** with a sword cutting part of two finger tips off of her left hand.

On October 16th, 1999 at about 12:17 a.m., **Euadne Legrottaglie**, age 43, came home to her house located at 52 Winchester Road, Lake Ronkonkoma. Upon entering the house she went to a bedroom and found her husband Peter in bed with another woman. Euadne, picked up a sword which was in the house and confronted the two of them. During the confrontation **Delores Andrews**, age 32, of 275 Broadway, Huntington had two of her finger tips cut off. Euadne chased Andrews from the house naked where she was picked up by an awaiting car service and taken to Huntington Hospital. Andrews finger tips were recovered by Suffolk County Police and transported to Huntington Hospital and reattached. Andrews was released from Huntington Hospital. Andrews worked for Platinum Club Escort Service located at Veterans Highway, Islandia. Ms. Andrews stated this was the first time she had worked for this escort service. She was called to the house by **Peter Legrottaglie** for a massage and sex. Euadne Legrottaglie called the police to report the incident. Peter Legrottaglie left the house before the police arrived at the scene.

Euadne Legrottaglie was charged with Assault 2nd Degree and held at the 4th Precinct to be arraigned at First District Court, Central Islip this morning.

The investigation into this incident is continuing.

\# \# \#

Authority: D/Sgt. Matt Livingston   99-558594
                Fourth Squad Detectives   4058/0600

CASH FOR TIPS - CALL CRIME STOPPERS - 1 - 800-220-TIPS

PDCS-6119a   53-0319: 4/97cb

Well, what did you expect Euadne to do? Let that ho Delores off with a stern warning? A bitch like that's got to be dealt with. Euadne was fined $85 for her swordplay.

In this confession, New York City club kid Robert Riggs describes how he and pal Michael Alig settled a dispute with the aid of a hammer and some bathroom cleanser.

5:25 PM DEC. 2, 1996
PLACE OF INCIDENT: 560 W 43RD ST #3K

ON A SUNDAY IN MARCH OF 1996 I WAS AT HOME IN MY BEDROOM WITH A FRIEND. IN THE OTHER BEDROOM MICHAEL ALIG AND ANGEL MELENDEZ WERE LOUDLY ARGUEING. I, AT ONE POINT, HEARD A LITTLE CRASH LIKE GLASS BREAKING. THEN, I HEARD THE ARGUMENT PROGRESSING AND GETTING LOUDER. I OPENED THE DOOR TO THE ROOM AND STARTED FOR TOWARDS THE OTHER BEDROOM. I STOPPED JUST OUTSIDE THE BEDROOM DOOR AT WHICH POINT MICHAEL WAS YELLING "HELP ME!", "GET HIM OFF OF ME". ANGEL BRIEFLY TURNED AND SAID "STAY OUT". THEN HE GRABBED MICHAEL EITHER BY THE SHOULDER OR AROUND THE NECK AND STARTED SHAKING HIM VIOLENTLY AND BANGING HIM AGAINST THE WALL. HE WAS YELLING "YOU BETTER GET MY MONEY OR I'LL BREAK YOUR NECK" OR SOMETHING TO THAT EFFECT. I REMEMBER MICHAEL LOOKED RIGHT AT ME WITH A SORT OF PLEADING LOOK IN HIS EYES. I GRABBED THE HAMMER WHICH WAS IN THE CLOSET DIRECTLY TO MY LEFT. I STEPPED FORWARD AND HIT ANGEL OVER THE HEAD,

THE ACCUSED: *Your Honour, I'm only sorry I didn't call you a stupid fuckin' cunt though earlier.*

THE COURT: Would you please remove Mr. Fizell from the courtroom.

THE ACCUSED: *And lady, you wouldn't know the fuckin' truth if it fuckin' -- hit you in the face.*

THE COURT: Please remove Mr. Fizell from the courtroom.

Not surprisingly, Mr. Fizell was later found guilty of contempt of court for these outbursts before a Canadian judge.

TRYING TO GET HIM OFF OF MICHAEL AND
MAYBE KNOCK HIM UNCONCIOUS. I WAS
IN A PANIC AND VERY CONCERNED AT THE
LEVEL OF ANGER ANGEL WAS DISPLAYING.
AFTER THE FIRST BLOW, HE TURNED
AND GRABBED FOR THE HAMMER. HE MIGHT
HAVE GOTTEN HIS HANDS ON IT. I'M NOT SURE,
BUT I SNATCHED IT BACK AND HIT HIM
IN THE HEAD AGAIN. HE STARTED TO GO
DOWN, BUT HE WAS STILL PISSED OFF AND
HE STARTED GOING FOR MICHAEL AGAIN.
SO, I HIT HIM A THIRD TIME AND HE
WENT DOWN. AT THIS POINT, MICHAEL
GOT ONTO HIS CHEST AND WAS STRANGLING
HIM WITH HIS HANDS. I YELLED "WHAT
ARE YOU DOING?". MICHAEL SEEMED TO
BE VERY ANGRY AT THIS POINT AND
WAS CURSING AT ANGEL. HE THEN
TOOK A PILLOW AND PUT IT OVER
ANGEL'S FACE. I MADE HIM STOP BY
EITHER TELLING HIM TO STOP OR PUSHING
HIM OFF OF ANGEL. I THEN WALKED
INTO THE LIVINGROOM, AND POSSIBLY
TO THE BEDROOM. WHEN I RETURNED,
MICHAEL WAS BESIDE THE BODY AGAIN.
I NOTICED A BROKEN SYRINGE ON THE
FLOOR BY THE BODY, AND MICHAEL WAS
POURING SOMETHING FROM THE

BATHROOM, SOME CLEANER OR CHEMICAL, INTO
ANGEL'S MOUTH. I, AGAIN SCREAMED,
"WHAT ARE YOU DOING? WHAT IS YOUR PROBLEM?
HE'S OUT!" HE THEN STARTED WRAPPING
TAPE AROUND HIS MOUTH. HE ASKED FOR
THE DUCT TAPE FROM THE CLOSET AND
SAID "YOU HAVE TO HELP ME!". SO, I HELPED
HIM FINISH WRAPPING THE TAPE AROUND
ANGEL'S MOUTH. THEN I LEFT THE ROOM.
WHEN I CAME BACK ANGEL WAS UN-
DRESSED DOWN TO HIS UNDERWEAR, A PAIR
OF WHITE "FRUIT OF THE LOOM" TYPE UNDER-
WEAR. MICHAEL SAID "HELP ME PUT HIM
INTO THE TUB." SO WE CARRIED HIM TO
THE TUB, AND CLOSED THE BATHROOM DOOR.
ABOUT 5-7 DAYS LATER, MICHAEL
AND I DECIDED WE HAD TO DO SOMETHING
ABOUT THIS TERRIBLE MESS. IT WAS
DECIDED THAT I WOULD GO TO GET KNIVES
OR SOMETHING TO HELP DISPOSE OF THE BODY.
I WENT TO MACY'S AND BOUGHT 3 LARGE
KNIVES; 2 CHEF KNIVES AND 1 CLEAVER.
WHEN I GOT BACK MICHAEL TOLD
ME THAT IF I GAVE HIM 10
BAGS OF HEROIN HE WOULD TAKE CARE
OF THIS PART. SO I DID AND HE
WENT INTO THE BATHROOM ALONE, AND
CUT OFF BOTH OF ANGEL'S LEGS. THEN,

PAGE 4

WE PUT EACH LEG INTO PLASTIC BAGS, AND THEN A DUFFEL BAG AND SEPERATELY CARRIED THEM, ONE AT A TIME, TO THE RIVER AND ~~WE~~ THREW THEM IN. PROBABLY ABOUT THE NEXT DAY I WENT DOWNSTAIRS TO THE STORAGE AREA AND GOT A LARGE BOX. I BROUGHT IT UP TO THE APT. MICHAEL PUT THE REMAINDER OF THE BODY INTO A LARGE PLASTIC GARBAGE BAG. I GOT ANOTHER BAG AND PUT IT OVER THE FIRST ONE. I THINK BEFORE MICHAEL PUT IT INTO THE FIRST BAG, HE WRAPPED IT IN A SHEET. AFTER THE SECOND BAG I THINK I TAPED IT CLOSED. WE THEN PUT THE WHOLE BUNDLE INTO THE LARGE BOX. THE SMELL WAS SO UNBEARABLE THAT I PUT BAKING SODA IN TO ABSORB (HOPEFULLY) SOME OF THE ODOR. I ALSO STUCK ~~THE~~ A BROOM HANDLE INTO THE BOX FOR SUPPORT BECAUSE THE SHEER WEIGHT WAS MAKING THE BOX COLLAPSE. A FEW HOURS LATER WE TOOK THE BOX INTO THE ELEVATOR AND OUT THROUGH THE MAIN LOBBY INTO A YELLOW CAB THAT HAPPENED TO BE RIGHT OUTSIDE THE DOOR. THE DRIVER HELPED TO TIE THE TRUNK DOWN AND WE TOOK THE BODY TO THE ~~ROR~~ WESTSIDE HIGHWAY ~~AROUND~~ AROUND 25TH STREET. THE TAXI

RDR *I CUT THE VPC CODE OFF THE BOX* *RDR*

PAGE 5

DROVE OFF, AND WE THREW THE BOX INTO THE RIVER.

THIS STATEMENT WAS WRITTEN BY ME, ROBERT RIGGS, OF MY OWN FREE WILL, MY MIRANDA RIGHTS WERE ALSO READ TO ME, AT THIS LOCATION:
84 WOOSTER ST 7TH FL
N.Y., NY

Robert D. Riggs

INV. INT. Angel Flores 171
Sup. INV. Walter Alexander 338
DET Thomas Comisi 12259

STANISLAUS COUNTY SHERIFF'S OFFICE
NEWS RELEASE

Deputy Tammy Drew
209 525-7045

250 E. Hackett Road
Modesto, California 95358

LES WEIDMAN
Sheriff-Coroner

MAN ARRESTED AT COURTHOUSE WHILE IMPERSONATING A WOMAN

Modesto, CA – A Modesto man was arrested in the Superior Court Clerks Office after dressing in woman's clothing and allegedly impersonating his wife. A Court clerk notified deputies after the suspect submitted paperwork in his wife's behalf. The clerk had recognized the man from prior contact on the same matter.

Joshua Marete Mutuma, 32, came into the Stanislaus County Superior Court Clerk's Office Friday morning allegedly attempting to file documents under his wife's name. Mutuma was dressed in a flowery dress, black women's shoes, brown wig and was carrying a white purse containing his wife's California ID.

Mutuma tried to file documents under his wife's name allegedly signing the documents before submitting them to the clerk. Mutuma was allegedly trying to file a dismissal order on a case previously filed with the court by his wife. Two Superior Court clerks recognized Mutuma from previous contact on November 10. The clerks kept him occupied until Deputy Darren Gharat of Court Services arrived.

"Thanks to the alertness, quick action of the court clerks and the law enforcement presence in the courts the subject was arrested for a criminal act," said Court Services Lieutenant Jane Irwin. "The clerks did an excellent job in recognizing that this man was up to no good."

Mutuma was booked for 529.2 PC (felony) false personation of another. He is in custody at the Public Safety Center with $5,000 bail.

11/15/99

> **N**ice try, but the flowery dress and white clutch do nothing to offset the Adam's apple and the size 12 slingbacks. The charge against Mutuma was later dropped.

AS THE WORM TURNS

5.1.17   At approximately 9:30 am on June 21st, 1998 Rodman turned
           from the gaming table and grabbed Mrs. Chapa's breasts with his
           hands.

case narr/1048
INDEPENDENCE, MISSOURI POLICE DEPARTMENT
Case Narrative

Report # 2000-69310

Date: 07-25-2000

Narrative:

On 07-25-2000, at approximately 1607 hours, I was on patrol, stopped at the light westbound on Twenty-four Hwy. at Forest. I observed a female eastbound Twenty-four Hwy., also stopped at the light at Forest. She began frantically waving for me to come to her location. I pulled my patrol car in front of her vehicle and made contact with her. She began pointing at the vehicle next to hers, which was occupied by a white male, I observed the white male next to her to be driving 1994 blue F150 pickup with MO license 176BX0, 2001 expiration. The female advised that the male subject had been following her and rubbing himself. I had her and the male subject pull over into a parking lot in the northeast corner of the intersection.

As I was pulling in behind the pickup, I observed the male subject remove two balloons from underneath his shirt. He then removed a white bra, which he had been wearing. He threw the bra, which I later recovered, behind a dumpster. I later recovered the balloons as well. I told the subject to place his hands on the truck several times, and when he refused, I placed him in handcuffs. Officer Gietzen arrived to assist. I then identified the male subject as Norman E. Wisdom.

I recontacted the female and identified her as Piedad Salazar. She advised that prior to me stopping her, the male subject had been following her on Twenty-four Hwy. for several miles. She said that he continued to drive next to her and would stop next to her at stop lights. She said that every time she looked at him he would lift his shirt and expose a bra filled with balloons that he was wearing. She said that he would massage the bra and then would raise his crotch and rub it through the jeans. She advised that she found this contact as offensive and embarrassing. She then signed GOS number 6052311, for indecent exposure.

I had Sgt. Kuhler, radio 230, respond. Upon his arrival I took

TERMINATION REPORT
JUVENILE DIVERSION

NAME: Dylan Klebold   CASE NUMBER: 98JD337

DATE ACCEPTED: 3-25-98   STATUS: 12 month CA

TERMINATION DATE: 2-3-99   DCJ CRITERIA: YES

DIVERSION OFFICER:

STATUS: Successful Early Termination

TERMINATION REASON: Complete compliance with Diversion

PROGRAM PARTICIPATION: Dylan accepted Diversion on the presenting charges of 1st Deg. Criminal Trespass (F5), Theft (F4), and Criminal Mischief (M2). Dylan's Diversion contract included a Drug and Alcohol Evaluation, Ethics Class, CJ Class, Progress reports, Apology Letter, Community Service, Fees, Adult Legal Issues and Daytimer.
   Dylan did a very nice job on Diversion. He quickly completed the drug evaluation and no further tx. was recommended. He was able to attend the Discovery Class at ISAE although, he did not feel that it was of much use to him. Dylan's attitude while on Diversion was solid and he remained motivated even when I added the Adult Legal Issues Packet to the contract. As a result of the responsibility he displayed I removed the CJ Class from the contract in August. 45 hours of CSW were complete at various locations in the community and Dylan felt like this was the most effective piece of Diversion. He learned a lot from having to give up free time to work for no money. All fees and the two negative UA's provided while on Diversion were paid in a timely manner. Dylan had a tendency to struggle with motivation around school work so we focused on this area for some time. He was able to maintain a good grade point average after some confrontation and is set to graduate in the Spring 1999.

PROGNOSIS: Good Dylan is a bright young man who has a great deal of potential. If he is able to tap his potential and become self motivated he should do well in life.

RECOMMENDATIONS: Successful Termination
   Dylan has earned the right for an early termination. He needs to strive to self motivate himself so he can remain on a positive path. He is intelligent enough to make any dream a reality but he needs to understand hard work is part of it.

Just weeks before their Columbine High School rampage, teen gunmen Dylan Klebold and Eric Harris were portrayed in these probation reports as bright young men likely to succeed. The duo had previously pleaded guilty to breaking into an automobile.

TERMINATION REPORT
JUVENILE DIVERSION

NAME: Eric Harris

CASE NUMBER: 98JD336

DATE ACCEPTED: 3-25-98

STATUS: 12 Month CA

TERMINATION DATE: 2-3-99

DCJ CRITERIA: YES

DIVERSION OFFICER: ▓▓▓▓▓▓▓▓▓▓

STATUS: Successful Early Termination

TERMINATION REASON: Complete Compliance with Diversion

PROGRAM PARTICIPATION: Eric accepted Diversion on the presenting charges of 1st Deg. Criminal Trespass (F5), Theft (F4), and Criminal Mischief (M2). Eric's Diversion contract included a CJ Class, Progress reports, Apology Letter, 45 hours Community Service, Fees, Adult Legal Issues, Anger Mgmt, MADD Panel, Ind. Counseling.

Eric did a very nice job on Diversion. He remained focused on Diversion despite completing a few classes that he felt had not impact, such as the MADD Panel. He did enjoy completing the Anger Mgmt. at ISAE which seemed to fit nicely with the individual counseling he was involved with. Eric excelled in school and never had any problems in this area. All fees including the two negative urine scans were paid in a timely manner. Community Service was completed at the Link Rec. Center and the comments from the supervisor were very good. Eric completed the Adult Legal Issues Packet very quickly and stated that he thought that piece was interesting because he discovered things he did not know.

PROGNOSIS: Good Eric is a very bright young man who is likely to succeed in life. He is intelligent enough to achieve lofty goals as long as he stays on task and remains motivated.

RECOMMENDATIONS: Successful Termination

Eric should seek out more education at higher levels. He impressed me as being very articulate and intelligent. These are skills that he should grow and use as frequently as possible.

Arriving at the apartment house, all four men waited for OLIVERI to exit the building. Upon exiting the apartment house, BISACCIA shot OLIVERI, who was left dangling on a tree. CW stated that BISACCIA, who then was a "soldier" in "Captain" MICHAEL MANDAGLIO's crew, was selected as the shooter because he had "balls".

* * *

ACCETURRO's. CASSO stated that when the shooting was to occur, he wanted to be left alone with the ACCETURRO's, TESTA and SENTER. CASSO stated that he wanted the ACCETURRO's to be shot between bites of salami sandwiches. When the day came for the

* * *

When the "victim" arrived, SCARPA, Jr., SESSA, MELLI, GRANATO and PARLAGRECO took him to the bathroom area of the candy store where SESSA shot, and killed the "victim". SCARPA, Sr. or SCARPA, Jr. then took the revolver from SESSA, pulled down the gate closing the candy store, and locked SESSA; MELLI; GRANATO; and PARLAGRECO inside with the "victim". The "victim" was then taken to the basement of the candy store, and dumped in a hole, that unbeknownst to SESSA, had already been dug. SESSA; MELLI; GRANATO; and PARLAGRECO proceeded to bury the "victim".

* * *

PAGLIARULO'S gun was equipped with a silencer. CHIODO returned to the house and was informed by PAGLIARULO and CAREW that after PAGLIARULO shot MORRISSEY twice, his pistol jammed. CAREW then emptied his revolver on MORRISSEY which he had loaded with only four bullets. MORRISSEY was still alive saying that he was not a rat and to please finish him off because he was in too much pain. PAGLIARULO then unjammed his pistol and shot MORRISSEY one more time in the head. DESANTIS, who had been waiting in a back hoe heavy equipment machine also approached the house and PAGLIARULO and CAREW again recounted the story to him.

* * *

CW told PARUTA to get some coffee. After getting up, PARUTA grabbed a gun, a .380 caliber equipped with a silencer, from a cabinet, and shot DI BERNARDO twice in the head. GARAFOLA and CW placed DI BERNARDO's corpse in a body-bag, previously obtained from SCARPACI'S FUNERAL HOME. They cleaned up, locked the doors, and left the office.

These excerpts from FBI reports on organized crime activity are indispensable for both the aspiring hitman and the wannabe screenwriter.

          As AVELLINO and PAPPADIO approached the office area, AVELLINO
exclaimed to PAPPADIO, "Surprise! Look who's here!" Simultaneously,
D'ARCO assaulted PAPPADIO by striking him several times in the head
with the bludgeon. PAPPADIO put his hands up holding his head asking
why he was being hit and to stop hitting him. To everyone's surprise,
PAPPADIO remained standing. ZAPPOLA then reached for the .22 caliber
revolver and fired at PAPPADIO's head. The bullet must have
richocheted off of PAPPADIO's head because they later observed what
appeared to be a bullet hole through a door and into a wall. PAPPADIO
was still standing there holding his head. ZAPPOLA then reached for
what appeared to be a larger caliber snub nose revolver, which D'ARCO
did not know ZAPPOLA had, and shot PAPPADIO again in the head.

          Around 1988, VIC AMUSO came to CW and told him (CW) to kill
VISCONTE. AMUSO said VISCONTE was a disgrace because he had a
reputation of "sucking nigger pricks" while he (VISCONTE) was in jail.
AMUSO also called BRUNO FACCIOLA a "cornudo", meaning BRUNO, who knew
VISCONTE's background, still allowed his sister to live with VISCONTE
and was content with it. AMUSO instructed CW that when he killed
VISCONTE, he was to get a cucumber, paint it black, and shove it up
his (VISCONTE's) ass. There may have been some other underlying
reasons that AMUSO wanted VISCONTE killed, but CW was unaware of it at
the time.

          During December, 1991, ORENA faction member and COLOMBO
LCN Family Associate, VINCENT FUSARO, was murdered while
decorating his home with Christmas lights.

          On the day of the murder, the nephew, TOMMY SPERO, was
driving a car. Seated in the front passenger seat was JOE
COLUCCI. CW and a male named FRANKIE Last Name Unknown (LNU)
were seated in the back. CW shot COLUCCI twice in the back of the
head, with a .38 caliber weapon. SPERO continued to drive to
Rockaway Parkway where COLUCCI's body was then dumped out of the
car. CW then shot COLUCCI three more times.

On 06/14/00 at approximately 1:19 a.m., I was dispatched, along with PO W. Quast to 2201 Allied Dr. #4, reference a report of a male and female fighting with each other. While en route, Dispatch advised that the caller, later identified as **COLBERNET S. JACKSON**, was stating that her sister and her boyfriend were both naked and fighting with each other.

Upon arrival, PO Quast and I were able to hear sounds of a struggle, numerous persons screaming, thumping on the floor and sounds of a physical disturbance, as well as glass breaking, as we entered the lower level of the apartment complex. As PO Quast and I began going upstairs, we could also hear glass breaking and continued sounds of a struggle.

As PO Quast and I entered apartment #4, I observed a female/black, later identified as **JACQUESIA A. JACKSON**, on top of a male/black, later identified as **EMMIT Z. QUINN**, on the living room floor near a mattress. It should be noted that both Jackson and Quinn were nude at the time. After separating Quinn and Jackson from each other, I placed Quinn out in the hallway with PO Quast, while I stayed in the kitchen area with Jackson, along with Colbernet Jackson and **LILLIE N. BROWN**. The scene at that time, was very chaotic with numerous persons yelling and screaming. I also had to tell Jacquesia Jackson to be seated numerous times, as she continued to attempt to get up and walk out into the hallway.

I initially spoke to Colbernet Jackson, who was relatively calm and able to convey to me what had occurred. Colbernet stated that her sister, Jacquesia and Jacquesia's boyfriend, Emmit Quinn, had been arguing that evening over who was going to be on top while they were having sex. Colbernet stated that the argument had been going on for, what she estimated to be, approximately 2-hours. Colbernet stated that both were very intoxicated and had been arguing about who would be on top of the other during sex for sometime, while they were actually having sex. Colbernet stated that the two were not arguing about anything else, as far as she could tell. Colbernet stated that Jacquesia and Quinn began "wrestling" each other, each attempting to get on top of the other, while they were having sex.

Colbernet stated that, at one point, Quinn had gotten up and had gone toward her room and was wearing underwear, at that time. Colbernet stated that she had observed Jacquesia come toward Quinn and rip his underwear off of him. Colbernet stated that she could not recall exactly what Jacquesia had said at that time. Colbernet stated that she had called numerous relatives, asking each of them to come over and separate Jacquesia and Quinn from each other, although none would. Colbernet stated that she had warned Jacquesia numerous times that if the two did not stop that she would call police in order to separate them. Colbernet stated that she had a young child in the residence at the time and she and her child were being disturbed by the actions of Jacquesia and Quinn. Colbernet stated that she eventually did call police, due to the disturbance.

Colbernet stated that when police had arrived, that Jacquesia and Quinn were attempting to break each other's cell phones, because both were receiving calls from other people. It should be noted that only one cell phone was later found to be damaged, which did belong to Quinn. Colbernet stated that she did observe Jacquesia break Quinn's cell phone.

After speaking to Colbernet, I then spoke to Jacquesia. Jacquesia stated that she and Quinn have been together as boyfriend and girlfriend for approximately 2-years and have no children in common. Jacquesia stated that she and Quinn have resided together for approximately 1-year.

N aked bodies. Broken glass. A cell phone smashed to smithereens. Sounds like another night at Charlie Sheen's place, not some crib in Madison, Wisconsin.

Jacquesia stated that this evening she and Quinn were having sex, when they began arguing about who would be on top. Jacquesia stated that she and Quinn had started "wrestling" with each other in order to see who would be on top. Jacquesia stated that she had candles placed around the ground (it is not known whether these candles were lit) and that these were what had been broken while she and Quinn were "wrestling." Jacquesia also stated that Quinn's cell phone had gotten broken during the wrestling match, although she stated it was an accident. Initially when I spoke to Jacquesia, she did not make any mention of ripping Quinn's underwear. Although after I had spoken to him, I asked her if she had taken a knife and cut Quinn's underwear and she stated that she had not done so. Jacquesia stated that she had ripped off Quinn's underwear while he was in the hallway, near the back bedrooms because she had not achieved orgasm yet and did not want him walking away from her.

After speaking with Jacquesia, I then spoke with Quinn. Quinn stated that he and numerous other people were inside the apartment earlier playing cards. Quinn stated that after the card game and the others have gone home or Colbernet and Brown have gone to the back bedrooms, that he and Jacquesia had been lying on the mattress laid on the living room floor, having sex. Quinn stated that after he and Jacquesia have had sex that Jacquesia had wanted to have sex again, soon afterward. Quinn stated that he told her that he needed to "recuperate" and when he told her this, Jacquesia had gotten angry. Quinn state that Jacquesia had been lying on the mattress in the living room with covers over her and when he had gone to lay down next to her, and attempted to pull one of the covers on top of him that Jacquesia had pulled them off of him. Quinn stated that he had then gotten up and put on his underwear and had begun walking away from Jacquesia. Quinn stated that Jacquesia had gotten angry and had gotten up and gone to the kitchen and grabbed a steak knife. The steak knife was later taken as evidence and property tagged under Property Tag P64780, and placed into Locker #40, of the MPD Evidence Room. The steak knife was a black handled steak knife, approximately 10-12 inches in total length.

Quinn stated that Jacquesia had gone to the kitchen and had grabbed the steak knife described above and had returned to where he was standing. Quinn stated that Jacquesia had then grabbed the front of underwear and cut the elastic band around his underwear. Quinn stated that he did not believe that Jacquesia would have harmed him with the knife and she did not come very close to his skin, although, he was currently wearing the underwear when she cut them off of him. PO Quast, PO Sweeney and I later attempted to locate the underwear, although we were unable to do so.

Quinn stated that after Jacquesia had taken the knife and cut the elastic band of his underwear that she had told him "You're not going anywhere. Get back here." Quinn stated that, at that point, he had called out to Colbernet and Brown and asked them to separate Jacquesia from him, however they did not want to get involved.

Quinn stated that after he had again attempted to walk away and was attempting to get Colbernet and Brown to separate Jacquesia from him, that Jacquesia had gone back to the area near the television and mattress, where his cell phone was. Quinn stated that Jacquesia had then picked up his cell phone, a Nokia cell phone valued at approximately $89.00, and had thrown the cell phone onto the floor, breaking it. I did later observe pieces of the cell phone, which had been picked up and placed into the trash by Brown. Quinn stated that he had not given consent for Jacquesia to damage any of his property, specifically the Nokia cell phone. Quinn stated that shortly after Jacquesia had snatched the cell phone, was when police had

GRAND HAVEN PUBLIC SAFETY DEPARTMENT
NARRATIVE REPORT

CASE NUMBER	FILE CLASS	DESCRIPTION	DATE	PAGE
99-6737	0900	HOMICIDE	8-19-99	15

Danny stated that she was not into witchcraft to his knowledge at first, but once they got married she began to practice it regularly and got into it very heavy. She wanted him to take part in the rituals, which he refused to do, stating that he would prefer to sit around, drink a beer and watch NASCAR. This began the rocky relationship and made it difficult for him to live with her. Danny stated that he is not into fighting, so he felt the best thing to do was to move out.

Burmingham stated that he took a pillowcase and wrapped it around Proctor's neck to hide the marks that were left. Burmingham covered Proctor up with a comforter. When asked why he dd this, Burmingham stated that he wanted to give her some dignity if that was possible. Burmingham then told this officer that he went downstairs, smoked some bear root, which relaxes him and eventually fell asleep as he was very tired. When asked if he had sexual relations with Proctor that day, he replied that he did not. When asked if he had sexual relations with her after death, Burmingham stated that he did not.

Burmingham stated that he was awakened the next day by the cable guy knocking on the door. Burmingham told the cable guy that Proctor was not available. After the cable guy left, Burmingham stated that he went to the Manpower Office to pick up his check so that he could buy some cigarettes as he had smoked his last one last night. His check was not available so he left and went to his fathers house and called 911.

OFFICERS SIGNATURE	SERIAL NO	DATE
BULTHUIS	113	November 24, 1999
SUPERVISORS SIGNATURE	SERIAL NO	DATE
	101	12/8/99

FD-302 (REV. 11-27-70)

FEDERAL BUREAU OF INVESTIGATION

Date of transcription _____7/20/72_____

　　　　PETE DE FEO was interviewed at the corner of
Mulberry and Spring Streets, and furnished the following
information:

　　　　He knew TOMMY RYAN for many years but had not
talked to him or seen him for at least three years. He was
surprised over the murder of RYAN and has not heard why or
who was responsible for it.

　　　　He last saw TOMMY's brother, PATTY RYAN, approximately
six months ago near Mulberry Street. He asked PATTY how his
brother TOMMY was doing and PATTY said fine.

　　　　Mr. DE FEO last saw FRANK TIERI approximately three
weeks ago on the corner of Mulberry and Spring Streets.

　　　　When asked why he thought there currently was so
much violence, Mr. DE FEO stated things were getting like
Dodge City and he felt the violence on television contributed
to it.

　　　　Mr. DE FEO concluded stating in February, 1972,
he spent approximately three weeks in Fort Lauderdale, Florida.

> Long before Congress figured it out, this Mulberry Street sage knew exactly what was contributing to all the violence in America. Hint: It had nothing to do with DeFeo and his friends regularly shooting each other in the street.

Interviewed on___7/17/72___ at___Manhattan, New York___ File # ___NY 92-1569-1477___

SAS _____ and 67C

by_____ Date dictated___7/18/72___

D.D. 5 (Rev. 2-61)
SUPPLEMENTARY COMPLAINT REPORT (DO NOT FOLD THIS REPORT)

Complainant's Surname First Name Telephone No.

People

Complainant's Address Apt. No.

6. Date and Time Reported on U.F. 61	XX M. P.M.	14*	15*	19. Pct. 34	22. U.F. 61 No. 993
XX 2/21/65 3:10 PM					
11. Day, Date and Time of Occurrence	XX M. P.M.	16*	17* -	27. Pct. Post 29	30. C.C.D. No. 26815
Sunday, 2/21/65 3:10					
36. P.D. Code	39. Amt. Code Larceny Only	40*	41*	42. Pct. of Arrest	45. Arrest Nos.

FOLLOWING QUESTIONS PERTAIN TO THIS COMPLAINT REPORT	Answer Yes	No
Was this complaint previously cleared by an arrest?		
If yes, is this an additional arrest?		
Were identified persons wanted previously reported?		
Was any stolen property previously reported?		
Was this stolen property previously reported?		
Was any property recovered previously reported?		
Was this recovered property previously reported?		
Was complainant advised of action taken?		

NUMBER OF ARRESTS			ARRESTS MADE BY:	
	Male	Female	Uniformed Force	☐
Adults			Detective Div.	☐
Juveniles			Other Peace Off.	☐
			Civilian	☐

If an alarm is transmitted enter the following information:

Alarm Number	Date and Time Transmitted

Report of Investigating Officer: (LIST ALL LOST OR STOLEN PROPERTY ON REVERSE SIDE)

50. TYPE OF PROPERTY	51. Value of Property Stolen	57. Value of Property R
1. Autos Stolen or Recovered Locally		
2. Autos Recovered by Other Auth's.		
3. Autos Recovered F. O. A.		
THIS REPORT CONCERNS: (CHECK ONE) 4. Currency		
5. Jewelry		
6. Furs		
Lost Property ☐ 7. Clothing		
8. Firearms		
Stolen Property ☐ 9. Miscellaneous		

Crime or Offense as Classified on U.F. 61

Homicide Det. Sqd. Ser. 1022 -8

Crime or Offense Changed to Status of Case

Same **Active**

Copy of this report forwarded to Corr. Bur. for Communication. Signature of C.O. of Investigating Officer

YES ☐ NO ☐ Rank Name Command

Date of This Report 3/1/65

In these NYPD reports, Betty Shabazz and another witness give firsthand accounts of the 1965 murder of Malcolm X at New York's Audubon Ballroom.

Subject: **INTERVIEW OF ONE BETTY SHABAZZ.**

1. On March 1, 1965 Mrs. Betty Shabazz, alias Little, widow of Malcolm X was interviewed in the office of Percy Sutton, 135 W. 125th St. She refused to give her present address or where she was staying and indicated that xxx if we needed her, her lawyer, Mr. Sutton would contact her. She is not in fear of her life but would rather not make her address known to the police at this time.

2. On the date of occurrence when her husband was shot in the Audubon Ballroom, she entered said ballroom with her four children and seated herself in Box 4. Her husband was in the ballroom, apparently in the room off the stage. Malcolm X was then introduced by Benjamin 2X Goodman. He opened with the Muslim greeting to the audience who likewise responded. She suddenly heard a disturbance in a section about the 7th row center. She heard shots. She pushed the children under the chairs in the box and covered them with her body. She then heard someone say, "Oh my God, Oh my God". She immediately thought something must have happened to her husband. She indicated that she did not see the shooting and had no other information relative to the homicide that took place. She had no other direct or indirect information.

3. She was questioned as to an alleged list of names reportedxx in the press that Malcolm X had in his pocket as to the identity of the perpetrators. She had no knowledge of this other than what she read in the papers.

4. She was asked as to whether she removed any of his personal property wherein this alleged list might have been and had no knowledge in

*Entries by S.R.B. only

Investigating Officer's Name (Typed)	Investigating Officer's Signature
James Rusin	
Rank **Det** Shield No. **2244** Command **30**	

x

- 2 -

in this direction.

5. As to any information of what transpired between her and her husband as to any of the problems of the Muslim movement or trouble to be expected she indicated that at this time she would not make it known to anyone.

x x x x x x x x x x x

D.D. 5 (Rev. 8-62)

SUPPLEMENTARY COMPLAINT REPORT   (DO NOT FOLD THIS REPORT)

U.F. 61
File No.

Complainant's Surname	First Name	Telephone No.	6. Date and Time Reported on U.F. 61		14*	15*	19. Pct.	22. U.F. 61 No.
People			Feb. 21, 1965 3:10 A.M. P.M.				34	993

Complainant's Address	Apt. No.	11. Day, Date and Time of Occurrence		16*	17*	27. Pct. Post	30. C.C.D. No.
		Sun Feb. 21 1965 3:10 A.M. P.M.					26815

36. P.D. Code	39. Amt. Code Larceny Only	40*	41*	42. Pct. of Arrest	45. Arrest Nos.

FOLLOWING QUESTIONS PERTAIN TO THIS COMPLAINT REPORT

	Answer Yes	No
Was this complaint previously cleared by an arrest?		
If yes, is this an additional arrest?		
Were identified persons wanted previously reported?		
Was any stolen property previously reported?		
Was this stolen property previously reported?		
Was any property recovered previously reported?		
Was this recovered property previously reported?		
Was complainant advised of action taken?		

50. TYPE OF PROPERTY		51. Value of Property Stolen	57. Value of Stolen Property Recovered
1. Autos Stolen or Recovered Locally			
2. Autos Recovered by Other Auth's.			
3. Autos Recovered F. O. A.			
THIS REPORT CONCERNS: (Check One)	4. Currency		
	5. Jewelry		
	6. Furs		
Lost Property ☐	7. Clothing		
	8. Firearms		
Stolen Property ☐	9. Miscellaneous		

x x x x x x x x x x x

NUMBER OF ARRESTS

	Male	Female
Adults		
Juveniles		

ARRESTS MADE BY:
Uniformed Force ☐
Detective Div. ☐
Other Peace Off. ☐
Civilian ☐

If an alarm is transmitted enter the following information:
Alarm Number	Date and Time Transmitted

Crime or Offense as Classified on U.F. 61	Det. Sqd. Ser.
Homicide (Gun)	1022 154
Crime or Offense Changed to	Status of Case
Same As Above	

Copy of this report forwarded to Corr. Bur. for Communication.   Signature of C.O. of Investigating Officer

YES ☐   NO ☐   Rank   Name   Command

Report of Investigating Officer: (LIST ALL LOST OR STOLEN PROPERTY ON REVERSE SIDE)   Date of This Report **March 22, 1965**

Subject: INTERVIEWED ROBERT EDWARD:

1.   Robert Edwards of 1263 Grant Ave. Bx. apt. 3 #992 2919
D.O.B. 10-15-37 Employed as a paper cutter for 5 years
White Hill offset 71 5th Ave.

2.   I am a member of OAAU for 1 year, on February 21,1965 I
arrived at the ball room about 2:00 PM. I sat in booth 55 in the rear of the
ball room. I came there to be a usher. I reported to brother Abe, brother Benjamin
get up to speak , after he was finish, he then introduce Malcolm, at this time
I heard a disturbance in the middle in front of me, and Malcolm said hold your
seats, then I heard shot being fired, I saw Malcolm I held his chest, and felled
back. I   then got up off the floor, and ran out of the ball room into the street
of 166 st. between St Nicholas ave. and Bway. I then yelled to the Police
that was standing out side, dont'nt let any one out. I than notice a man coming
out of the front door, brother George "hitney was holding, and beating him, and
yelling this is one of them, I than went over, and kick the person that was on
the ground. Then the police came over, and took the man away from us after one the
police man shot into the air, and put him into the raidocar. I then went inside
the ball room, and went to the fron t of the rostrum, at this time I saw brother
Malcolm lying on the floor. I then help with the strecher to carry Malcolm over
to Medical Center. Then I stood on the out side of Medical Center for the word.

Case Active

*Entries by S.R.B. only

Investigating Officer's Name (Typed)	Investigating Officer's Signature
Winston W. De Vergee	
Rank Det. Shield No. 442 Command 24 Sqd.	

x
x
x
x
x
x x x x x x x x x x x x x

- 1 -

FEDERAL BUREAU OF INVESTIGATION

Date of transcription   6/4/92

A Cooperating Witness (CW) contacted a Special Agent of the Federal Bureau of Investigation who is known to him and provided the following information:

CW went to AMBROSINA's house to make his vig payment. While there AMBROSINA's baby threw up on CW.

AMBROSINA advised he still wants to have the meeting with JOSEPH BENFANTE but he has not been in his office and the Secretary has not called back to verify the meeting. AMBROSINA asked for CW's full name and date of birth to be provided to BENFANTE so that he can obtain CW's record. BENFANTE lives on Staten Island and a small possibility remains that the meeting may be on the island.

AMBROSINA told CW that he wanted more credit cards because he was setting up a business selling hats. AMBROSINA wants the fraudulent credit cards to use to purchase the hats and thereby make more profit on their sale.

No, loansharks do not reimburse you for dry cleaning expenses incurred during the repayment of your vig.

(telephonically)
·vestigation on 6/3/92   at Staten Island, NY   File # 183B-NY-214955

by Christopher M. Favo/cmf   Date dictated 6/4/92

b7c

RJL: Okay, you probably seen his picture but I'll show it
to you again, it's a picture of ███████████████, can you
identify that photograph?

TL: Yes, I believe this is the man who drove the camper
from Morro Bay to San Francisco and from San Francisco to
Seattle after my escape in September, 1970 . . .

RJL: When we first started talking about this and this
is the man who told you that he was active in the P.L.

TL: That's right.

RJL: And had acted as a sort of counselor or adviser to
the Weather people, that's in substance is the conversation
you had with him?

TL: Yes sir.

RJL: Okay, ██████████████████████

(BELOW STATEMENT OCCURRED IN MIDDLE OF AN INTERVIEW BUT IS
INCLUDED HERE FOR CLARITY).

TL: I'd like to discuss my motives, briefly in what I'm
doing. Number one, I want to get out of prison as quickly
as I can. And I believe that telling the total truth is the
best way to get out of prison. I don't want to continue in a
situation where hiding the truth is keeping me in prison.
That doesn't make any sense to me personally, or philosophically.
Secondly, I feel I have a great deal to contribute constructive,
ah, activities in the United States of America. I'd like to
use this as step number one, in seeing if I can work out a
collaborative and an intelligent, an honorable relationship
with different Government agencies and law enforcement agencies,
and educational agencies, so this does not just turn someone over to get out of prison, it's part of a longer range
plan of mine, I'm in full possession of my faculties, I
think I can contribute a great deal, I've learned a great
deal, and I intend to be extremely active in this country in
the next few years, however, the things turn out. I prefer
to work, I'm never going at it illegally ever again, but I
would prefer to work constructively and collaboratively with
intelligence and law enforcement people that are ready to
forget the past, and to use my, in the future, because I still
have a great deal to say in this country, I believe.

140

+
+
+
+
+
+ + + + + + + + + + + + + + + +

In a bid for leniency, jailed
counterculture guru Timothy
Leary once secretly agreed
to rat out his friends to the FBI.
In this transcript from a
debriefing session, Leary
pledges his allegiance to the
country's law enforcement
and intelligence community.
Yes, that sound you hear
is Abbie Hoffman rolling over
in his grave.

ASSAULT

Case No.
254-1961

Defendant NORMAN MAILER   **Age** 37   **Occupation** Writer

Presented by A.D.A. Fierro   **on** 1/21/61   **before** #3 January G.J.

Date, hour and place November 20, 1960, 5:00 a.m., 250 West 94th Street

Victim Adele Mailer   **Age** 35   **Occupation** Housewife

Extent of injuries Serious stab wounds of left lower chest and left lower back

Hospitalization Yes - University Hospital - entered November 20, discharged December 3

Nature of weapon Knife

Weapon recovered? Yes

Cause of assault Unknown

Relation of parties Husband and wife

On the evening of November 19, 1960, the defendant and his wife had a large party at their home, which lasted until 4:30 a.m. November 20, 1960. At that time, the nurse Nettie Bidle, stated that there were just a few people left in the apartment. Mrs. Mailer was heard to scream by the maid who said that she went out of the apartment to Mr. Humes in the building and asked Mr. Humes to go back for help. The maid stated that she did not go to inquire as to what happened to Mrs. Mailer and she did not think of calling the police. She said that she had seen Norman Mailer some minutes earlier in the apartment. Mrs. Mailer was then taken to the hospital by the maid in an ambulance and was treated there by Dr. Mackler. The complainant, Mrs. Mailer refused to sign a complaint in this case and in Felony Court and in the Grand Jury, denied knowledge of how she became stabbed.
(continued)

She stated that she had many drinks on the evening of the party and remembers being injured, but she does not know how! She did not whether her husband was in the apartment at the time she was injured. While Detective Burns could not testify to the following, he made his arrest because Mrs. Mailer on November 21, 1960, at about 8 p.m., told him that her husband had stabbed her with a pocket knife and that she did not want to see her husband or the knife again. Burns arrested the defendant at about 9:30 p.m. on November 21, 1960 at the hospital. At that time, Mailer stated that he was at the hospital because his wife was injured and when asked how she was injured, he did not give any answer or he said that she was injured. Mailer asked whether he could see his wife and Burns said she did not want to see him. Mailer said he could not understand why. Mailer refused to answer anymore of Burns' questions. Burns found on the person of Mailer, a pocket knife which Mailer admitted was his. Dr. Mackler testified in the Grand Jury that early in the morning of November 20, just prior to operating on Mrs. Mailer for stab wounds in the chest and back, the defendant came up to him and said that he was worried about his wife because he had stabbed her and he knew that he had gone in deep with the knife. This admission by Mailer was not brought out in Felony Court and was not known to us until made by the doctor in the Grand Jury. Mrs. Mailer stated that she could not recall ever talking to Detective Burns and telling him that she had been stabbed and that she did not want to see her husband or the knife. She repeatedly said she could not remember this. It should be noted that Dr. Mackler testified that he had never been a doctor for the Mailer family and Mrs. Mailer was his patient on November 20, 1960 for the purpose of surgery. There should be no problem with the doctor-patient privilege in so far as Mailer's admission is concerned because Mackler was not treating him and he was not his patient.

ARREST RECORD CARD

Name: BUSH, GEORGE W.

Address: P.O. Box 785 Midland, Texas 79702

D.O.B.: 07/06/76   Birthplace:

	Date	Charge	Arresting Officer	Case #
1	09/04/76	Operating Under the Influence	Bridges	2312

KENNEBUNKPORT POLICE DEPARTMENT — Kennebunkport, Maine

Here's the only documentary evidence of those so-called youthful indiscretions of George W. Bush (who was thirty at the time of this arrest).

AS THE WORM TURNS

7. Defendant, without warning, forcibly and aggressively grabbed Plaintiff's camera from her, slamming it to the ground.

8. Defendant committed an intentional and unprovoked battery by violently lifting Plaintiff off the floor, restraining Plaintiff by force, pinning her from being able to move, thereby, causing such fear of immediate bodily harm that the Plaintiff became so overcome by fear that she could not control her bodily functions.

Mardis v. Rodman, Clark County (Nev.) District Court, 1999
7 of 10

F U N WITH DOCUMENTS

Examine these psychiatric report excerpts and try to match each up with one of these five high-profile headcases.

A Mike Tyson
Former heavyweight champion, convicted rapist, and future WWF superstar.

B Vincent Gigante
Cuddly Mafioso charmed Greenwich Village neighbors with his quaint late-night strolls wearing a bathrobe and slippers.

C Izola Ware Curry
Plunged a letter opener into the chest of Martin Luther King, Jr., during 1958 attack.

D Ted Kaczynski
Montana nut once owned the scariest return address in America.

E Michael Lance Carvin
Spent six years in prison for threatening life of President Gerald Ford. Jailed again in 1998 for promising to kill Howard Stern.

1

Whereas I do not believe that the defendant has any conscious intention to harm anyone, unconscious influences and forces beyond his control cause him to be highly vulnerable to impaired judgment and insight when experiencing real and perceived stresses and he is more likely to act violently than the average person.

2

of 70.... Among the signs of disturbance are irrelevant answers, neologisms, extreme confusion, perseveration, etc. Projective material is almost entirely pathological with a heavy emphasis on the bizarre.... There is an undercurrent of hostile ideation and suspiciousness. The data are consistent with that seen in paranoid schizophrenia of long standing."

3

segment of the student body." He describes a number of incidents in his junior high and high school years, including a discussion of making a small pipe bomb in chemistry, which gained him some notoriety. He described himself as having "frustrated resentment towards school, parents, and the student body" which often was given outlet through "snotty behavior in the classroom which often took a sarcastic or crudely humorous turn."

4

have a censoring effect. Thus, although he reports being scared by the "bad things" he hears, when asked to elaborate, he responds, "God tells me not to say nothing." Even under repeated questioning, the most he will say is that the voices "call me bad names." Similarly, when asked later about his silent lip movements, he replies, "I'm talking to God." However, when asked why he doesn't speak aloud to God, he states, "He doesn't want nobody to hear."

5

Relative weaknesses were found in the areas of: attention/mental tracking; short-term memory/working memory; verbal learning and memory; executive functions on select measures, and bilateral motor speed/coordination. My observation of his performance also revealed mild difficulties with impulsivity and executive control.

Answer: 1-E, 2-C, 3-D, 4-B, 5-A

STANDING ON A PLASTIC BUCKET WITH HIS
PLACED HER HAND ON THE
inserting ping pong balls into her
placed her mouth over his
forcing her very large breasts into his
engaged in various simulated acts of
delivered a blow to the plaintiff's **NC-17**

September 22, 1999

To All Performers:

As a reminder the dildo camera will be up and running Monday morning... as mentioned before this **will** be a part of your job description.

The Labor and Industries, Industrial Hygiene Regional Supervisor was here this morning and gave us their seal of approval and okie dokie on using this devise.

For those of you who are continuing your employment with IEG if you have questions, please come talk with me

For those of you who have decided not to continue your employment here due to the dildo camera, Sunday will be your last day.

Here's an inter-office memo you don't see every day. IEG, by the way, is not an accounting firm. It's an online porn outfit.

PAGE 44 OF 51

Mason Police Department
Incident Report

Single Incident

INCIDENT LOCAL # PRIORITY ACC REP	ACTIVITY ADDRESS (JURISDICTION) DISPOSITION	OFFICER(S)	RECEIVED DISPATCHED ARRIVED CLEARED	DISPATCHER SUPERVISOR NATURE INCIDENT TYPE

Narrative(s):

Narr.   1: **PTL MICHAEL O. DOWNEY**   Division: **None**   Status: **Open**   **[I0007320]**
        Title: **NARRATIVE**   Entered: **PTL MICHAEL O. DOWNEY**
                                                Reviewed: **No officer**

On Tuesday July 17th, 2000 both suspects arrived at Kings Island at approximately 1030. They were walking through the park and noticed a portable photo booth on the ground at Kings Island. This booth is located right next to the children's portion of the park. Aaron Caudill casually mentioned to his girlfriend, Elizabeth Whitaker, that she could give him oral sex in this photo booth.

Later on this date at approximately 2000 hours they returned to this booth for the purpose of giving and receiving oral sex. They both entered this booth and secured the curtain. They placed their money in this booth and Aaron dropped his shorts to his ankles while still standing. After doing this, Elizabeth sat in the seat and placed her mouth over his penis performing oral sex. The pressed the button when Aaron approved of the pose which printed the picture.

An employee of Kings Island was at this location. There is a monitor screen that is located on the outside of this phot booth allowing anyone in the immediate vicinity to witness the photo that is taking place inside the booth. The Kings Island employee stated there were several patrons including children who were walking by and witnessed this sex act. The employee stated once Aaron knew this monitor was on the booth and people were watching, he an out and tried to cover the monitor with his hands. A security was called and they were taken to security.

I separated both Aaron and Elizabeth and read both of them their rights. I first interviewed Elizabeth. SHe stated they had seen the booth earlier and Aaron stated they should come back and perform fellatio. She stated that later in the day Aaron and her went back to the booth and she did perform oral sex on Aaron. She stated they had no idea the monitor was stationed outside of the booth, and they never would have done this if they knew that.

After reading Aaron his rights, he stated the same story as Elizabeth. Both were arrested for public indecency and transported to the Warren County Jail. Both were very cooperative.

This police incident report details one couple's shenanigans at an Ohio amusement park. No, this ride is not included in the pay-one-price admission fee.

While most guys carry the requisite wad of twenties to a strip club, these excerpts from two lawsuits indicate that packing a helmet and protective cup might also be advisable.

> > >
>
>
>
>
>
>
>
>
>
>
>
>
>
> > > > >

his neck on the back of the chair with his eyes closed, to be specially entertained by the star dancer. The Plaintiff, PAUL SHIMKONIS, complied with her request.

7.   The DIAMOND DOLLS' star dancer proceeded to dance in front of the Plaintiff, PAUL SHIMKONIS and then suddenly, without warning and without Plaintiff's consent, jumped on the Plaintiff forcing her very large breasts into his face causing his head to jerk backwards.

8.   That as a direct and proximate result of the conduct of the Defendant, DIAMOND DOLLS entertainer, as alleged above, Plaintiff, PAUL SHIMKONIS, was injured in and about his head, neck, body and limbs; and the Plaintiff has sustained the following past and future damages:

  (a) Bodily injury.

  (b) Disability.

  (c) Pain and suffering.

  (d) Disfigurement.

  (e) Mental anguish.

  (f) Loss of capacity for the enjoyment of life.

  (g) Medical and related expenses in seeking a cure for his injuries.

  (h) Loss or diminution of earnings or earning capacity.

  (i) Aggravation of pre-existing conditions or diseases.

WHEREFORE, the Plaintiff, PAUL SHIMKONIS, demands a trial by jury and judgment against Defendant, DIAMOND DOLL'S LIMITED, PANIC BROTHERS, INC. d/b/a BLOOPERS, for a sum within the

2

5.   On December 10, 1999 the plaintiff was acting as a designated driver for an office party. The plaintiff was driving a van for eight men. The last stop of the evening for the group was an exotic dance club in the City of Aylmer in the Province of Quebec. While at the club, one of the dancers, suddenly, without warning and without the plaintiff's consent, at a moment when the plaintiff was in no position to react, delivered a blow to the plaintiff's scrotum. The plaintiff experienced immediate, intense and throbbing pain. The plaintiff was unable to walk for a period of time, and it was uncomfortable to sit or drive.

6.   After completing his duties as designated driver, the plaintiff returned home. While getting ready for bed the plaintiff discovered bruising in his groin area, and that his right testicle had swollen to the size of a baseball. The plaintiff was worried and concerned enough to immediately attend the Emergency Room at the ████████████████████ Hospital ("Emergency Room").

7.   The plaintiff attended the Emergency Room in the early morning hours of December 11, 1999. The plaintiff was so embarrassed and upset about the circumstances of the injury. He described it as having occurred while horsing around with friends, but otherwise accurately describing the mechanics of the injury. The Emergency Room doctor ordered an ultrasound examination and blood test. Based on the results of the ultrasound the plaintiff was advised he had testicular cancer and was referred to Dr. ██████████ an urologist/surgeon for treatment for an appointment on December 17, 1999. The blood tests revealed no tumor markers to support a finding of testicular cancer.

8.   On December 16, 1999 the plaintiff underwent an abdominal ultrasound to determine whether the plaintiff's cancer has spread beyond his testicle. The plaintiff met Dr. ████ on December 17, 1999. Dr. ████ conducted a manual exam of the plaintiff. Dr. ████ confirmed the diagnosis, and told the plaintiff that:

    (a)   no biopsy was possible without removing the right testicle;

    (b)   that a second ultrasound would not change the diagnosis;

    (c)   the surgical removal of the right testicle (right radical orchidectomy) was the plaintiff's only option.

Dr. ████ never recommended, suggested or even mentioned any further examinations to confirm the diagnosis, nor did Dr. ████ discuss undergoing either a cat scan or CT scan. The plaintiff accepted Dr. ████'s opinion and consented to undergoing the procedure suggested.

9.   On December 22, 1999 Dr. ████ performed the surgery, removing the plaintiff's right testicle. Dr. ████ performed the surgery while the plaintiff was under general anesthetic. The pathology report performed on the plaintiff's right testicle demonstrated no malignancy. The report demonstrated that the area of concern on the plaintiff's right testicle was an area of hemorrhage with formation of a hematoma.

ENVIRONMENTAL HEALTH DEPARTMENT
Consumer Protection Division

November 13, 1995

TO: Richard Mitzelfelt, Manager, EHD-CPD

FROM: ▇▇▇▇▇▇▇ Env. Health Spec. II, EHD-CPD

SUBJECT: ICE HOUSE OBSERVATIONS

Contacted the Ice House at approximately 5:00 p.m. and was told that Stephanie Evans was to perform at 8:30 p.m. The Ice House informed me of the all you can eat pizza and all you can drink non-alcoholic beverage special. Arrived at the Ice House at approximately 8:20 p.m. on November 12, 1997. At 8:30 p.m. Stephanie Evans appeared on stage. Approximately 35 people gathered and stood around the stage area to view Ms. Evans on her back on stage inserting ping pong balls into her vagina. She then ejected the balls into the crowd where a small percentage of people attempted to catch the balls in their mouth. One person was successful. Others caught the balls with their hands. Ms. Evans then agreed to autograph the balls after the show. Approximately 15 ping pong balls were inserted and ejected into the crowd from Ms. Evans vagina. Ms. Evans then walked off stage and the first portion of the show ended at approximately 9:15 p.m.

Pizza was available at all times and people ate during and after the show. Unlimited drinks were offered and most patrons had drinks on their tables during the ping pong portion of the show. I observed no hot holding capabilities for the pizza. Pizza sat in the delivery boxes waiting to be served. Patrons could walk up to the bar and serve themselves or the wait staff would bring the pizza to the tables. I served myself and recieved a slice of pizza. Temperature of the pizza was around 80-degrees F.

At approximately 10:15 p.m. Ms. Evans re-appeared on stage. There were approximately 25 drink glasses on the counter that lined the stage from one end to the other being used by customers for drinking non-alcoholic beverages. There were no pizza slices on plates on this counter however there were people eating and half-eaten pizza slices on several tables directly in front and to the sides of the stage.

A large model of a champagne glass approximately four feet high made of a clear plastic of some kind was moved to the middle of the stage. It was allegedly filled with champagne but appeared to be water. Ms. Evans sat in the vessel then rose out of the vessel and ejected water from her vagina into the crowd. Aim did not appear to be a concern to Ms. Evans. Ms. Evans lowered herself back into the vessel and rose out again and repeated the act. After three or four water ejections she lowered herself into the water and jumped out of the vessel

and walked around the stage. It was obvious she had retained fluid in the oriface and was going to eject it somewhere. A customer was beckoned to move near her groin area. He moved to within five feet of her pelvic region. She violently ejected the fluid she had retained in her vagina directly in the customer's face then walked back to the vessel to secure additional fluid. In order to observe the event I had to be in rather close proximity to the act but by now Ms. Evans was ejecting water on almost everyone in the crowd and in order to avoid getting doused with her fluid I left the establishment.

In my judgment, the act of ejecting water from the vagina onto any food then consuming the food could create a health threat. Ms. Evans was forcing water from her vagina from the stage directly over numerous drink glasses that were being used by customers for drinking. Pizza was readily available for consumption and was being consumed during the show.

SUGGESTED COMPLIANCE ACTION:

1.) Require the Ice House to secure a reliable hot holding device to store pizza while it is not being eaten to maintain internal temperatures of 140-degrees F as required by the Food and Beverages Ordinance.

2.) Prohibit the serving of any food or drinks during any show that involves fluids being violently ejected from a vagina. This would minimize any cross contamination situation that may arise from food being in direct contact with vaginal fluids.

Feel free to contact me directly if you require any further details.

Yes, Stephanie Evans's performance may have technically constituted a "health threat." But had a blaze broken out at the Ice House, her unique skills would have been of invaluable help to the firefighters.

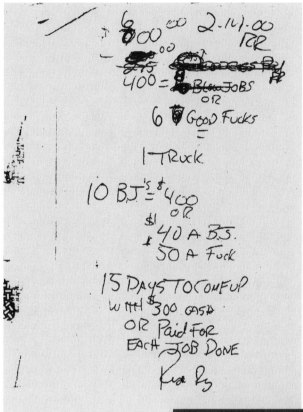

600^{00} 2.14.00 FOR

$400 =$ ~~BLOW JOBS~~
OR
6 GOOD FUCKS

1 TRUCK

10 B.J.'s = $400
OR
$140 A B.J.
$50 A Fuck

15 DAYS TO COME UP
WITH $300 CASH
OR Paid FOR
EACH JOB DONE

Kun Ry

4/CIGS = 100^{00}
2 #BJ's $80 00
$180 00

$700 00
- $180 00 CREDIT
$520 00 DUE
- CASH OR TRADE

Important Tax Return
Document Enclosed

143 LOCUST ST
AKRON OH 44302

$ $ $

$
$
$
$
$
$ $ $ $

$ $ $ $ $ $ $ $ $ $

$
$
$
$
$

When Rick Remmy sold his truck to Karen Kershaw, he came up with something much more creative than APR financing. According to this scribbled receipt—filed as part of an Ohio small claims lawsuit brought by Kershaw—Remmy wanted to trade his wheels for cash and other, um, valuable considerations.

CRIMINAL COURT OF THE STATE OF NEW YORK
PART APAR COUNTY OF QUEENS

THE PEOPLE OF THE STATE OF NEW YORK

V.

ANGEL GARCIA

DEFENDANT

STATE OF NEW YORK
COUNTY OF QUEENS

PEACE OFFICER JOSEPH MEYER OF THE NEW YORK RACING ASSOCIATION (NYRA), SHIELD #1846, BEING DULY SWORN, DEPOSES AND SAYS THAT ON OR ABOUT NOVEMBER 23, 1996 AT ABOUT 12:30 PM AT AQUEDUCT RACE TRACK BARN 2, COUNTY OF QUEENS, STATE OF NEW YORK,

THE DEFENDANT COMMITTED THE OFFENSE OF:
PL 130.20-3 SEXUAL MISCONDUCT

IN THAT THE DEFENDANT DID: ENGAGE IN SEXUAL CONDUCT WITH AN ANIMAL OR A DEAD HUMAN BODY;

THE SOURCE OF DEPONENT'S INFORMATION AND THE GROUNDS FOR DEPONENT'S BELIEF ARE AS FOLLOWS:

DEPONENT STATES THAT AT THE ABOVE-MENTIONED DATE, TIME, AND LOCATION OF OCCURRENCE, THAT WHILE PASSING BARN 2, HE OBSERVED THE DEFENDANT, ANGEL GARCIA, WITH HIS CLOTHES OFF, STANDING ON A PLASTIC BUCKET WITH HIS PENIS IN THE VAGINA OF A HORSE BY THE NAME OF "███████████." DEPONENT FURTHER STATES UPON ENTERING THE STABLE, THE DEFENDANT HAD FALLEN OFF OF THE BUCKET AND WAS LYING NAKED ON THE STABLE FLOOR AND THAT THE HORSE WAS FORCIBLY CHAINED TO THE FRONT OF THE STALL SO AS TO RESTRICT ITS MOVEMENT. THE DEPONENT FURTHER STATES THAT SAID HORSE WAS EXAMINED BY VETERANARIAN DOCTOR ISOMOTO AND THAT DOCTOR ISOMOTO INFORMED HIM THAT THE HORSE WAS INDEED PENETRATED IN THE VAGINA. DEPONENT FURTHER STATES THAT HE IS INFORMED THAT DOCTOR NEILSON, A VETERNARIAN, WILL BE CONDUCTING FURTHER TESTS ON SAID HORSE.

FALSE STATEMENTS MADE IN THIS DOCUMENT ARE PUNISHABLE AS A CLASS A MISDEMEANOR PURSUANT TO SECTION 210.45 OF THE PENAL LAW

11-23-96
DATE

Joseph O Meyer
SIGNATURE

SWORN TO BEFORE ME ON THE
DAY OF

COMPLAINT

STATE OF IOWA, COUNTY OF BLACK HAWK

STATE OF IOWA
Vs

Before (Judge, Magistrate):
Criminal Case No : AGCK095641 ctl
Waterloo Case #: 2000-90839

BHCSO #: _____

ROBERT ALLEN BRODERSON, DOB: **1/14/54**, SSN: ███████

The Defendant is accused of the crime of **Animal Abuse**, in that the defendant on or about **10/25/00**, at or about **08:04** in the City of Waterloo, in Black Hawk County, did Commit the crime charged by having sexual intercourse with a female ewe causing it pain and injury.

in violation of: **717.B2** Code of Iowa

STATE OF IOWA,
COUNTY OF BLACK HAWK, SS.

I, the undersigned, being first duly sworn and under oath, state that the following facts known by me or told to me by other reliable person form the basis for my belief that **Robert Allen Broderson**, the Defendant committed the crime charged:
On 102500 Officers were dispatched to The Hawkeye Tech. Farm located at 5503 Hammond Ave. on report of the Defendant being held by several students. Upon arrival Officers talked with the Farm Manager Rob Swinton. He said that at 0700 hrs when several of his students entered the livestock barn they found the Defendant hiding naked in a hay loft. They located a female ewe tied up in the corner. Next to the ewe was a blue nightgown. The ewe was tied with a halter rope around it's neck and legs and placed in a position that it's hindquarters were sticking up in the air. The area around the sex organs of the animal was swollen and red. It appeared to Swinton that the Defendant had engaged in sexual intercourse with the ewe. He said it was apparent that the ewe was injured from the assault. The Officers found that the Defendant had a strong odor of sheep urine on his person. The Defendant was taken into custody and transported to the BHC Jail.

Michael Wheaton

Subscribed and sworn to before me by the said, **Michael Wheaton**, on **102500**.
Complaint and Affidavit filed and probable cause found that the offense has been committed and that Defendant committed it.

Magistrate or Notary Public in the State of Iowa

Police_____   Prosecutor_____   Defendant_____

While Broderson was accused of a despicable crime, you have to give the guy credit: most booty callers wouldn't have been thoughtful enough to bring along a swell gift like a nightgown.

+ + + + + + + + + x

x x x x x x x x x x x x x x x x x x x x x x x x x x x x   x x x x x x x
                                                        x
                                                        x
                                                        x
                                                        x
                                                        x
                                                        x

FD-302 (REV. 11-27-70)

ME 145-233
2

FEDERAL BUREAU OF INVESTIGATION

1

Date of transcription ___11/4/75___

b7c

On October 31, 1975, SA ▮▮▮▮▮▮▮▮ and
SA ▮▮▮▮▮▮▮▮▮▮▮ paid the admission price of $3.00
each and viewed the film entitled "Penthouse Party Girls"
and another film which had no title or credits. These
films were playing at the Lamar Adult Theatre, 1716 Lamar
Avenue, Memphis, Tennessee. Two people were noted in
attendance. The first film commenced at approximately
4:10 p.m.

The opening scene of "Penthouse Party Girls" showed
a panoramic view of an unidentified city. The scene then
changed to the bedroom of a dwelling. A white female,
approximately 24 years of age with blonde hair wearing a
white nightgown was shown in bed. This character's name was
VALERIE in the film. She was shown in bed with a white
male, black hair, black mustache, stocky build, who played
the role of GEORGE, VALERIE's husband.

The scene showed a close up of the exposed female
genitals and showed the male actor perform cunnilingus on
VALERIE.

A second white male actor playing the role of
DONALD, the butler, enters the bedroom and advises GEORGE
that he must return to his place of business. VALERIE
pleads with GEORGE to remain as she has not had enough
sexual contact with him. DONALD leaves the scene and GEORGE
leaves the room to shower and prepare for work.

VALERIE, who is nude, rubs her genitals with a
green cylindrical pillow. She then takes from the night
stand a black vibrator and she sucks the vibrator. She
lubricates the vibrator and rubs it over her breast and
inserts it into her vagina. She appears to reach orgasm.

The next scene shows GEORGE seated at a breakfast
table being served by DONALD. VALERIE enters the scene and
sits at the table across from GEORGE. Some non-sexually
related dialogue transpires and GEORGE leaves for work.

Interviewed on __10/31/75__ at __Memphis, Tennessee__ File # __Memphis 145-233__

by   SA ▮▮▮▮▮▮▮▮ and ▮▮▮▮▮▮▮▮▮▮ b7c   Date dictated __11/3/75__

4

This document contains neither recommendations nor conclusions of the FBI. It is the property of the FBI and is loaned to your agency;
it and its contents are not to be distributed outside your agency.

DONALD approaches VALERIE and verbally indicates
he would like to have sexual contact with her. She
declines and DONALD becomes angry.

The next scene shows VALERIE behind the bar. The
doorbell rings and a young white blonde female enters
the room.

The guest asks VALERIE to come out from behind the
bar in order that the guest can massage VALERIE's neck.
The guest begins the massage and asks VALERIE if VALERIE
has had an affair with another woman. The guest says she
is curious about a relationship between two women and tells
VALERIE that she often wonders what it would be like to
touch VALERIE.

VALERIE pulls up her blouse and the guest rubs
VALERIE's breast with her hand. VALERIE takes off the
guest's white sweater and bra and rubs the guest's breast.
The two embrace and kiss each other. VALERIE then takes off
the guest's slacks and rubs the guest's vagina through her
undergarment, and asks, "Do you like this?" The reply from
the guest is, "It feels wonderful." VALERIE takes off the
guest's undergarments. The guest removes VALERIE's undergarments. At this point the guest performs simulated
cunnilingus on VALERIE. The guest depicts orgasm brought
about by this cunnilingus. A change of camera angle shows
the exposed genitals of the guest and shows actual
cunnilingus of VALERIE on the guest.

After completion of the actual cunnilingus the
guest tells VALERIE that she knows some "real freaky
people who live in a commune." She suggests to VALERIE
that she would invite these people to a party at VALERIE's
house. The guest tells VALERIE "go clean up and I will
call them."

The next scene shows VALERIE nude in the bathroom
of her residence. The guest enters, also nude and asked
what VALERIE is doing. VALERIE shows the guest a white
dildo and inserts it into what appears to be VALERIE's anal
opening. She does this in rhythmic motion. VALERIE and
the guest then rub soap over each others breasts and genitals
and depict an orgasm.

5

x x x x x x x x x x x x x x x x x x x x x x x x x x x x x x x
                                                            x
                                                            x
                                                            x
                                                            x
                                                            x
                                                            x

ME 145-233
3

The next scene depicts an evening in VALERIE's
house. Approximately five couples are in attendance at
what seems to be a party. These individuals were
engaged in various simulated acts of fellatio, cunnilingus
and coitus. Also, a white female nude was shown rubbing
her genitals with a stuffed animal snake. Several of the
men advise her how to rub her genitals and what poses to
strike. Several females were being body painted in the
nude. Several people were seated around a Ouija board,
and one white female becomes "possessed" and she leans
backwards and rubs her genitals. A second white female
begins to kiss and fondle her breast. These females then
remove their clothing and simulate cunnilingus. A white
male who is clothed climbs on top of a white female and
simulates anal intercourse. The camera angle then changes
and shows a closeup of the female genitals. A white female
is then shown performing simulated cunnilingus with a white
female while she herself is receiving simulated cunnilingus
from a white male. On a nearby couch a white couple
is shown with the male performing simulated cunnilingus on
his partner, while she in turn is performing simulated fellatio
on him. Another couple is shown engaged in simulated coitus
with the female on top of the male partner.

At this point the camera angle changes and the
flaccid penis of one of the male guests is shown.

The guests leave VALERIE's home and she remains
there alone. She then experiences a series of "flashbacks,"
showing various sexual activities of the day. She then
states "no, no, I am not a whore, I am not filth."

At this point GEORGE returns home. VALERIE
advises GEORGE that she has not been faithful. They engage
in a conversation indicating all is forgiven and the couple
will spend more time together.

The film then ended at approximately 5:05 p.m.

The next film began at approximately 5:06 p.m.
The film began without any title or credits.

The first scene depicts an airline pilot and
co-pilot in the cockpit of an airplane, which was white in
color, with red trim, preparing for takeoff from the Burbank
Airport.

6

ME 145-233
4

The pilot's name was DICK O'TOOLE, a white male,
approximately 30 years old, brown medium length hair,
wearing a white shirt and black tie. The co-pilot was
identified only as RILEY, white male, approximately 40
years old, brown graying hair with long sideburns,
wearing a black jacket with a white shirt, black tie and
glasses. The two went through a preflight check list
and identify themselves as flight number 117 flying from
Burbank to Georgia.

The scene then changes to the coach section of
the aircraft where a stewardess identified as CHRISTINE,
a white female, brown hair, approximately 30 years of age,
wearing a red blouse, red shorts and gray cap, is instructing
the passengers on flight procedures. Also shown is a white
female stewardess, approximately 28-30 years of age, brown
hair, purple blouse and purple shorts, name unknown.

Over the intercom system the pilot is heard to
state "The stewardesses are here for your gradification and
enjoyment, do with them what you will."

The scene then changes showing the two passengers
on the flight, one passenger is a white female, identified
as HOLLY WOOD, approximately 28-30 years of age, blonde hair,
wearing a gray slip-over blouse with gray hotpants. Also
shown is a white male passenger, identified as JUSTICE
PEACE, approximately 20-22 years of age, black hair, long
sideburns, gray sweater and a black leather coat. HOLLY WOOD
asks JUSTICE PEACE to sit next to her and they engage in
conversation. She states she "owns a string of whorehouses,"
and is going to Georgia to recruit "sweet country girls to
work for her." JUSTICE advises HOLLY he owned massage parlors.

They begin to kiss and fondle HOLLY pulls up
her blouse and he rubs and sucks her breast. He then inserts
his hand inside her clothing and rubs the vagina area. He
then removes her clothing and her genitals are clearly
exposed. He then removes his clothing. His flaccid penis
is shown. He then mounts HOLLY and they engage in simulated
coitus.

7

Creations Employee Handbook

X. FANTASY CALL LIMITS

All calls must adhere to FCC guidelines and our own company policy on content.

1. Under no circumstances, are any of the following subjects to be discussed during your fantasy calls.

   a. No violence or weapons.
   b. No rape fantasy.
   c. No sex with animals.
   d. No incest.
   e. No children.
   f. No drugs.
   g. No brown or red showers.
   h. No amputation or mutilations.

XI. EXCLUSIVE EMPLOYMENT

1. Employees of Creations are not permitted to work for any other company engaged in a similar business without written permission from this company.

AS THE WORM TURNS

16. Suddenly and without warning or provocation, RODMAN abruptly grabbed Plaintiff's bare breast by jamming a $100 bill and his hand down the front of Plaintiff's blouse and holding on to her breast with his cupped hand.

17. Plaintiff backed up quickly while covering her breasts with her hands crossed over her chest, cowering as RODMAN continued to lunge at Plaintiff.

Patterson v. Rodman, Los Angeles Superior Court, 1998

NARRATIVE

ON 8-30-99 I RECEIVED THIS CASE TO FOLLOW UP ON REFERENCE A SEXUAL ABUSE. I REVIEWED THE REPORTS AND NOTICED THAT THE VICTIM WAS LISTED AS OFFICER ███. ███. ACCORDING TO HIS REPORT HE HAD RECEIVED INFORMATION THAT THERE WAS GOING TO BE A GRAND OPENING AT THE "IMAGE" ADULT VIDEO STORE LOCATED AT ҄20 E. RT. 66. SCHMIDT STATED THAT HE HAD INFORMATION THERE WERE GOING TO BE TWO FEMALE PORN STARS PRESENT AT THE GRAND OPENING ON 8-28-99. OFFICER ███████ RETURNED TO THE STORE, IN PLAIN CLOTHES, TO CONDUCT AN UNDERCOVER INVESTIGATION AND DURING THE INVESTIGATION HE NOTICED SEVERAL THINGS OCCUR. OFFICER ███████ WROTE IN HIS REPORT THAT THE TWO WOMEN, IDENTIFIED AS KATYA PONOMAREVA AND MILA SHEGOI, WERE OFFERING TO HAVE PHOTOS TAKEN WITH PATRONS OF THE BUSINESS FOR THE COST OF $5.00. OFFICER ███████ PAID FOR A PHOTO WITH EACH OF THE WOMEN AND DURING THE PHOTO WITH KATYA PONOMAREVA SHE PLACED HER HAND ON THE GROIN OF OFFICER ███████ WITHOUT HIS PERMISSION, SEE THE ATTACHED COPY OF THAT PHOTO.

OFFICER ███████ ALSO INDICATED IN HIS REPORT THAT THE SUBJECT IDENTIFIED AS MILA SHEGOI WAS ON A PLATFORM INSIDE THE BUSINESS. HE DESCRIBED HER AS WEARING A WHITE BRA WITH WHITE PANTIES. HE SAID THAT THERE WERE APPROXIMATELY 20 PATRONS INSIDE THE STORE AT THE TIME AND THAT ONE OF THE PATRONS REQUESTED TO SEE HER "ASSHOLE". OFFICER ███████ OBSERVED MILA PULL HER THONG ASIDE, EXPOSING HER ANUS TO THE CROWD.

ALSO ON 8-28-99 THERE WAS A LIVE REMOTE BEING BROADCAST FROM THE PARKING LOT OF "IMAGE". DURING THE REMOTE ROWDY WALKER AND SAGE WALKER WERE PRESENT. ACCORDING TO THE REPORTS RECEIVED THEY ALLOWED MILA TO SPEAK ON THE RADIO AND DURING THIS TIME MILA MADE SEVERAL OBSCENE AND LEWD COMMENTS. MILA WAS SOLICITING CUSTOMERS TO COME TO "IMAGE" FOR FREE ORAL SEX AND OPPORTUNITIES TO HAVE SEXUAL ENCOUNTERS WITH HER.

DET. PAUL LANGSTON # 5364   **SUPERVISOR: SGT. VESELY # 7031**

I HAD ALSO RECEIVED INFORMATION THAT A CONCERNED CITIZEN, IDENTIFIED AS ███████, HAD CONTACTED THE POLICE DEPARTMENT REFERENCE THE RADIO BROADCAST ON 8-28-99. I RECEIVED A TELEPHONE NUMBER FOR HER AND I CALLED TO SPEAK WITH HER.

I ADVISED ███████ OF WHO I WAS AND THE CASE I WAS CALLING HER ABOUT. ███████ ADVISED SHE HEARD THE KZGL BROADCAST ON 8-28-99 INVOLVING MILA SHEGOI. ███████ ADVISED THE REMOTE WAS "REALLY BAD, "TERRIBLE" AND "OBSCENE". ███████ HAD A DIFFICULT TIME SPEAKING WITH ME ABOUT THE CONTENT OF WHAT WAS SAID OVER THE RADIO AND SAID THAT SHE DIDN'T SAY WORDS LIKE WHAT SHE HEARD. I ADVISED ███████ THIS WAS IMPORTANT AND THAT I NEEDED HER TO TELL ME WHAT SHE HEARD. ███████ WAS EMBARRASSED AND AGREED TO GIVE A WRITTEN STATEMENT OF WHAT SHE HEARD, SEE THE ATTACHED COPY. I CONTINUED TO SPEAK WITH ███████ ABOUT THE CONTENT OF WHAT MILA HAD SAID. ███████ SAID THAT MILA, AT FIRST, WOULD SPELL THE WORDS OUT BUT LATER SHE FORGOT TO SPELL THEM AND SAID THEM IN THEIR ENTIRETY. ███████ SAID MILA SPELLED SUCH WORDS AS C.O.C.K. AND A.S.S. ███████ SAID THAT MILA WOULD ALSO SLIP AND SAY THE WORDS OVER THE AIR AND THAT SHE TALKED ABOUT SWALLOWING SPERM. ███████ ADVISED SHE HAS NEVER SEEN A MOVIE WITH THE TYPE OF LANGUAGE SHE HEARD ON THE RADIO AND SHE WAS CONCERNED ABOUT IT SINCE THE STATION REACHES YOUNGER CHILDREN. ███████ RECALLED THAT MILA TALKED ABOUT SPERM, EJACULATES, AND THAT SHE LOVES THE TASTE OF IT. ███████ ADVISED SHE WAS OFFENDED BY WHAT WAS SAID AND THAT IT WAS VERY EXPLICIT AND GRAPHIC. ███████ SAID THAT SHE RECALLED MILA ASKING PEOPLE TO COME DOWN TO THE BUSINESS FOR ORAL SEX.

███████ SAID SHE WOULD WRITE OUT A STATEMENT AND HAVE IT AVAILABLE FOR ME AT A LATER DATE.

This Arizona police report proves there is actually something more exciting than Casey Kasem's Top 40 countdown on the FM dial.

```
1
2
3
4
5   On 11-03-98 I received this case for investigation.  It was reported that 30-50 high school age
6   girls attended a party.  A male stripper performed at the party and there were reports of
7   possible oral copulation between one of the girls and the stripper, and possible sexual battery
8   between several of the girls and the stripper.  It was reported that the mother of the hostess
9   was present at the time although her knowledge of the performance was unknown.
10
11  A summary of the investigation conducted by Sergeant SOBERANES, Detectives TAMM,
12  BASBAS, and I is as follows:
13
14  Ms. Carye McGRATH is the mother of the hostess, Jane Doe 4 .  ; Jane Doe 3
15  was also found to be a second hostess of the party.  With the permission of her mother,
16  Jane Doe 4 . and Jane Due 3 · planned an all girls sleep over at Doe A .'S house.  The
17  invitation was for all girls attending Amador High School and flyers were made.  The girls
18  had talked about obtaining the services of a male stripper for the party and Doe 4
19  asked her mother.  Her mother denied the request.  Poe 4 . said she felt pressure from
20  the other girls to hire a stripper so she hired one anyway using her mother's credit card to
21  secure his services.
22
23  Doe 4, .. said she told several of the girls that a stripper was going to be at the party
24  and they should inform their parents so that if anyone was uncomfortable with the idea they
25  could leave prior to his arrival.  Some of the girls have confirmed this and some of the girls
26  said they told their parents ahead of time, prior to the party.
27
28  During the night of the party several of the girls report that Ms. McGRATH told them that
29  they were not to lick, touch, or crowd the stripper.  She also told them he was just going to
30  dance around the room.  The girls said this was done about 15 minutes prior to the strippers
31  arrival.  Some of the girls said Ms. McGRATH met with the stripper before the show.  Ms.
32  McGRATH said she had no knowledge that the stripper was there until she heard loud
33  giggling and laughter and went out and saw the stripper already performing in the living
34  room.  She said that she allowed the performance to continue after she saw him dancing in the
35  living room.
36
37  During the show some of the girls said they saw Ms. McGRATH watching the show and
38  some said she was not in the room during the show.  Ms. McGRATH said she was not in the
39  living room during the show.  She said she occasionally walked between the back rooms and
40  the kitchen though.
41
42  Several of the girls report that the stripper touched the genitalia of some of the other girls.
```

Leong   #39   095   11-10-98

1   Three of these girls admitted that the stripper touched their bare breasts. One of the girls said
2   she willingly took her top and bra off and the stripper rubbed her breasts. Two of the other
3   girls said he put his hands down their tops and under their bra to touch and rub their breasts.
4   One of these girls also said he put his hand down her pants, into her underwear and touched
5   the top of her vagina.
6
7   It was reported that one of the girls orally copulated the stripper. Several of the girls said they
8   witnessed this although their stories vary. Some of the girls said the girl just licked the
9   stripper's penis and some said she put his penis into her mouth. Upon questioning of the girl,
10 she denies that either of these occurred. She insists that the stripper's penis was not near her
11 mouth.
12
13 We had also heard reports of drugs and alcohol being served. All of the girls that we spoke to
14 said drugs and alcohol were not served and many of them said they did not know of anyone
15 bringing any in. Some said 4-5 girls brought and consumed their own alcohol. The names of
16 the girls who did this stayed consistent by the witness's accounts.
17
18 In regards to the identification of Steve MITCHELL, Sergeant SOBERANES obtained a
19 business card with his picture and pager number on it from one of the girls she interviewed.
20 The pager number on the card matched the pager number listed in the original report ((925)
21 472-   ). I paged the number on the first night of the investigation and MITCHELL
22 returned my page and he eventually gave me his cell phone number ((510) 701-   ). I have
23 since called MITCHELL back on his cell phone on three occasions and spoken to him .
24
25 MITCHELL said he was hired by Strip O Gram for this party. He said as far as he knew all of
26 the girls at the party were 18-19 years old. He said he was at school so I suggested that we
27 meet the following day to discuss this case. MITCHELL said he would call back with a time
28 and place to meet. MITCHELL had given me a middle name of Michael and a DOB of
29 04-13-69. A DMV check on the name and birthday given by MITCHELL proved negative.
30
31 After failing twice to give me a time and place to meet, we obtained a subpoena on 11-05-98
32 directed at Cellular One requesting the disclosure of the name and account information related
33 to the cell phone number given to me by MITCHELL. The information provided by Cellular
34 One showed that John V. GIORVAS (address of   Ct. Alamo CA 94507) is
35 associated with the cell phone number (510) 701-   A DMV check showed GIORVAS
36 has a CDL number of C0376576 (address of   Ct San Ramon CA 94583).
37
38 Detective TRYPHONAS called DMV and ordered a color photo of GIORVAS and also a
39 faxed copy of the photo. On 11-05-98 we obtained a fax from DMV of GIORVAS' photo.
40 The fax photo of GIORVAS and the photograph of MITCHELL on his business card were of
41 the same person with the exception of his hair length. During our interviews with the girls,
42 Detective TAMM and I showed several of the girls the business card of Steve MITCHELL

Leong   #39   095   11-10-98

DRUNKEN SANTA'S COMING TO TOWN

Who do you know with a liver that's huge,
A big red nose and guzzles down booze?
Drunken Santa's coming to town.

He's ringing a bell and holding a cup.
Playing Santa Claus beats sobering up.
Drunken Santa's coming to town.

He gets himself kicked out of bars
For passing deadly gas.
He came with two boots leaves with three,
One wedged up his ass.

Dogs lift their legs to the jolly drunk elf
But he doesn't care, he pees on himself.
Drunken Santa's coming to town.

Mommy, Mommy, can I sit on Santa's lap, please.
Sure honey, go ahead.
Oh, Mommy, Santa smells. Ewwww.
What do you want for Christmas?
I want to go home.
But I'm Santa Claus. (Burp)

He likes to drink a six pack
And hang out at the malls.
He'll give your kid a candy cane
That he used to scratch his balls. (Burp)

He wears a red hat, black belt and a scarf.
His beard should be white but its covered with barf.
Santa's gonna show up,
Stagger 'round and throw up.
Drunken Santa's coming to town.

After several companies that publish classic Christmas songs learned that a lewd holiday parody album was being distributed, they successfully filed a copyright infringement lawsuit complete with exhibits containing the offending lyrics. While defaming the likes of poor Santa and Rudolph, the parodist somehow chose not to lampoon "Come All Ye Faithful."

SEXUAL BATTERY.
Ritchie aka Vicious

DON JOHNSON

Scott Weiland (M 30)

8 NICHOLSON,
Mr. Robin Leach   WOULD YOU LIKE TO SUCK MY COCK?

Mr. Leach   shoot him or kill him.

CELEBRITIES

12 NICHOLSON

revealing their bare breasts and buttocks to Mr. Leach
14   Mr. Leach   NICHOLSON

exposed themselves
Mr. Leach.   Criminal Trespass

BEHAVING

He thought he had "pee'd" himself.
Mark Wahlberg

17 NICHOLSON   Mr. Leach.

18   Wahlberg   performance of sexual acts   NICHOLSON.

19 NICHOLSON
Wahlberg

BADLY

hit him over the head with the stick.
playing bongo drums.

22   NICHOLSON.   BOUGHT DRUGS

23   McConaughey, Matthew W/M (11-4-69)   NICHOLSON
Mr. Leach. she hit him and he hit her.

Mr. Leach exposed themselves to restaurant staff   Mr. Leach
Mr. Leach

26 NICHOLSON

Mr. Leach

28   NICHOLSON

very intoxicated

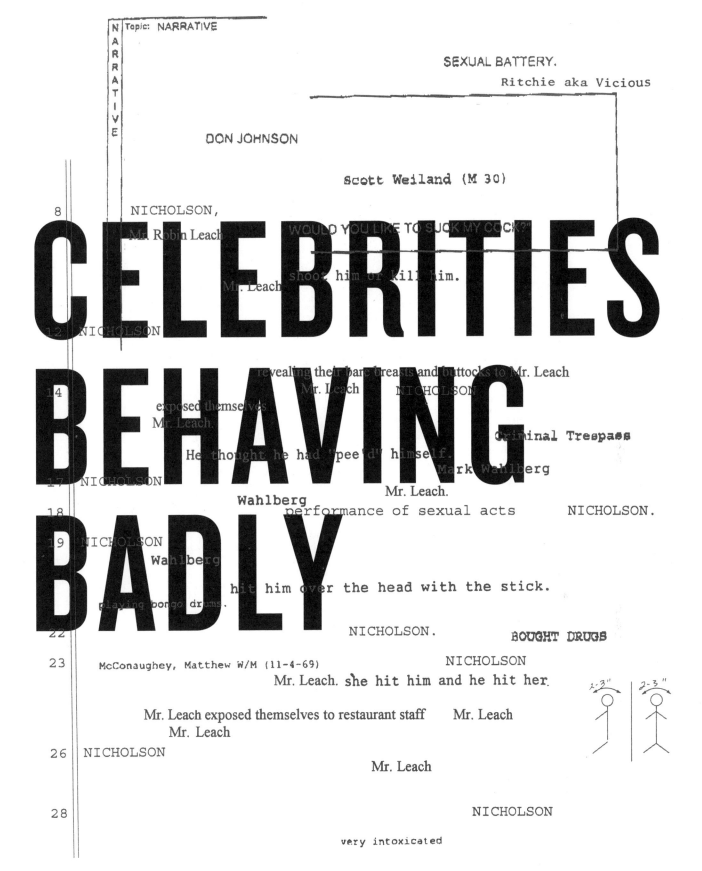

Here's some advice for detectives trying to break a tough
case: Watch a few episodes of *Entertainment Tonight*.
If you go more than a week without eyeballing the suspect,
you're probably not really paying attention.

Cause Number: 356822

THE STATE OF TEXAS   ) (IN THE MUNICIPAL COURT
) (CITY OF AUSTIN
COUNTY OF TRAVIS   ) (IN TRAVIS COUNTY, TEXAS

AFFIDAVIT FOR WARRANT OF ARREST AND DETENTION

Undersigned Affiant, Who After Being Duly Sworn By Me, On Oath, Makes The
Following Statement:

I have good reason to believe and do believe that McConaughey, Matthew W/M (11-04-69)

On or About The 25th Day of October 1999, In the incorporated limits of the
city of Austin, County of Travis and the State of Texas, did then and there
commit the offense of:

Resisting Transportation - Class A

My belief of the foregoing statement is based upon personal knowledge.
On 10-25-99 at about 2:37am I was dispatched to a DOC - Noise call at 2002
Meadowbrook Dr (final location was actually 2004 Meadowbrook Dr.) I had officer
G. Stephenson #4071 riding with me. We were both wearing standard issue APD
uniform with our badges prominently displayed.

On arrival to the location I could easily hear very loud music coming from 2004
Meadowbrook Dr. There was no apparent front door to the residence, but there
was a path leading to a wrought iron gate on the south side of the residence.
As we got closer to the house I could hear music along with what sounded like
bongo drums and someone clapping with the music. We went throught the unlocked
wrought iron gate looking for a door. After this gate there was a small set of
steps that led to a door that was dark (no porch light and no light coming from
inside.) There was also a half-wall on the left side of the area and a wooden
gate on the right side. I looked over the half-wall and could see a room on the
other side. Through the window and the door was open(there was a screen door
that was closed over the doorway) I could see a nude, white male dancing and
playing bongo drums. I decided to try to make contact with the subject to get
him to turn down the radio and stop playing the drums. I went through the
second gate (which was unlocked also) and approached the door. As I approached
I could see that there was another white male in the room. He was dancing and
clapping his hands to the music. The music was so loud that I knew they would
not hear me if I knocked or hollered at them. I flashed my flashlight back and
forth across the room about 8 to 10 times to try to get their attention. They
did not notice the flashing light. From the door I could see what I recognized
to be a marijuana bong sitting on the coffee table. It was filled with water
and had black residue in the bowl. I then decided to make entry to the
residence to get the music turned off and to identify the residents. I checked
the screen door to see if it was unlocked. It was. I opened the screen door
and started to enter the house. I could immediately smell a faint odor of
marijuana. I stepped into the room. The naked subject saw me after I was
already inside and he turned off the radio. He began yelling at us. He said,
"You can't be in here! Get the Fuck out of the house! Why are you here?" The
other subject was also yelling similar phrases. I told them that we had a
complaint about the loud music.

I could tell that both subjects were very intoxicated. They both had very
slurred speach. They swayed while standing still. There was a strong odor of
alcoholic beverage coming from both of them. While onscene I observed that they
both had glassy and very bloodshot eyes.

You can bet that the next time actor Matthew McConaughey gets naked, breaks out the marijuana, and starts pounding on his bongos, he'll lock the front door. He was fined $50 for the nocturnal revelry.

At this point I was acting as if I had not seen the paraphernalia in order to
try to gain their cooperation with the DOC-Noise complaint. I asked who lives
at the house and was met with more profanity. I asked for the subjects'
identification. The nude subject yelled, "You're violating our rights! You
can't come in my house like this!" I said, "I just need to see some ID from
ya'll." Both subjects continued yelling phrases similar to those above. The
subject nearest to me was moving around alot. He was stepping back and forth
and looking around. Due to the low light conditions (low lights and candles) I
could not see very well around the entire room. There were shelves, tables,
couches, a bed, and the drums that could all easily conceal any possible
weapons. I decided that due to the subjects' lack of cooperation I would put
them both in handcuffs for our safety while I further investigated and tried to
get them identified. I placed Hauser in handcuffs and quickly frisked him for
weapons. I then asked him to sit down on the floor. He cooperated physically,
but continued yelling that we were not supposed to be in the house and that we
were violating his rights. I told Stephenson to stay near Hauser and keep an
eye on him. I then stepped across the room towards the nude subject.

While I was going across the room I glanced at the coffee table and observed a
shallow bowl that had what I recognized to be marijuana stems and seeds in it.
I also saw a "one-hitter", which is an item of paraphernalia that is commonly
used to store marijuana. One side of it typically contains the marijuana and
the other side contains a metal cigarette-like device that is used to smoke one
"hit" of marijuana at a time.
I asked the nude male several times to put some pants on (there was a pair of
pants next to him on the floor.) He responded by saying, "Fuck you." I told
him that he needed to put on a pair of pants or I would have to put him in
handcuffs with nothing on. He then reached out with his left hand as if to push
me while saying, "Fuck You!" I deflected his hand by grabbing it and twisting
it around behind his back. I then handcuffed him. I told him to sit on the
ground (so he could not move around much while I tried to continue to
investigate and identify the subjects.) He would not sit down, so I pushed him
down to a sitting position by pushing on a pressure point above his collar bone.
He got almost to a sitting position and then suddenly shot back up to a standing
position. I again ordered him loudly to sit down. I pushed him down again and
this time he got to a sitting position. I asked where his ID was and he said,
"Take the cuffs off and I'll go get it." I told him it was too late for that
and that I needed to get his ID for him. I looked closer at the coffee table
and observed a moneyclip. Some cash was wrapped around a TX Driver's License.
I retrieved the DL and was able to then identify the subject as:

McConaughey, Matthew W/M (11-4-69).

He asked why he was under arrest. I told him that he was under arrest for
Possession of Drug Paraphernalia. After another officer arrived on the scene I
was able to wrap a long sleeve shirt around his waist to cover him. I decided
to go ahead and take him out to the patrol unit. As I walked him along the
walkway towards the front of the house he dragged his feet and tried to push
backwards against me constantly. He kept yelling, "This is bullshit!" When we
got to the wrought iron gate he put his left foot up against the door jamb and
shoved backwards very hard. This caused his back to slam into my chest, causing
me to nearly fall over backwards. I had to step back several steps and the
other officer had to grab McConaughey's right arm in order to catch us both from
falling. We then walked him to the patrol unit. I opened the back right door
and asked him to sit in the car. He refused. He just stood there facing us. I
then ordered him to get into the unit. He said, "Fuck You!" and jerked his body
towards us. I had to take him by the hair and try to bend him down into the
backseat. He put his foot on the bottom of the door jamb and pushed very hard
against it. This caused his body to forcefully push into mine. His right
shoulder struck my chest, causing me to be pushed backwards about a step. I had

to use my knee to push him in the hip area to bend his body backwards into the
seat. We were then able to push him into the unit.

McConaughey was booked into jail for Resisting Transportation. He intentionally
obstructed a person he knew to be a peace officer from transporting him by using
force against the peace officer.

and conditions of employment which included expected employee conduct and behavior. Among other issues discussed were employee/customer and employee/employee relations, and alcohol awareness training.

Although each employee had a somewhat different perspective of and exposure to the events in question, the consensus of opinion among the sixteen (16) who were at Delmonico Steakhouse on the evening of May 31 as to the details and sequence of events is as follows.

> Mr. Robin Leach arrived at Delmonico Steakhouse for dinner at approximately 8:30 p.m. on May 31, 1999, and was seated in the KT. Five (5) female companions arrived to join him at various times within the next 15-30 minutes. Mr. Leach had made reservations several days earlier.
>
> The meal consisted of several courses commencing at approximately 9 p.m. Starting at approximately 9:30 p.m. and continuing on an intermittent basis for approximately one (1) hour, several management and front line employees witnessed the females revealing their bare breasts and buttocks to Mr. Leach and the kitchen staff. At times Mr. Leach would photograph the females while they exposed themselves and the women also took photographs of each other and Mr. Leach. Some of the females physically touched each others breasts. While this activity was ongoing several employees, including restaurant management staff, applauded and vocally encouraged continuation of the activity. One of the females departed the restaurant during this period of time leaving a total of four (4) female guests and Mr. Leach.

Photographs taken on July 1, 1999 of the KT from the KT entrance door and the kitchen area, and photographs of the kitchen and back service bar areas taken from inside the KT appear as **Exhibits 4 and 5**, respectively.

The employees interviewed continued by stating:

> At approximately 10:30 p.m. the dessert course was served to the KT by several employees. The dessert consisted of a variety of food items, some specifically requested by Mr. Leach. For a period of time, estimated to have been approximately 15-20 minutes in duration, all of the female companions of Mr. Leach exposed themselves to restaurant staff and Mr. Leach in a lewd way. Mr. Leach and the females engaged in applying these dessert food substances to certain body parts of the females and were observed by staff to then orally consume the food substance. Mr. Leach was observed to fondle

7

Here's hoping that peach flambé wasn't one of the desserts Robin Leach slathered on his harem.

! ! ! ! ! ! !

BLOOMFIELD TWP. POLICE DEPT.
200 Telegraph Rd., P.O. Box 489, Bloomfield Hills, MI 48303-0489
Phone: 810-433-7755   ORI # MI6326200

INCIDENT / PROSECUTION REPORT

PO # _____

☐ PRIMARY ☐ SUPP   PAGE 1 OF _

01	DATE. 05 24 97	DAY SAT	SHIFT 03	PLAT 03	BADGE 1 136	BADGE 2	UCR CLR CLR97	ADMIN	YEAR	INCIDENT # 10354

02	RECEIVED 2120	DISPATCHED 2120	ARRIVED 2120	COMPLETED 2345	DATE(S) OCCURRED 052497		TIME(S) OCCURRED 2120	HOUR 21	DAY SAT

( )

08 test, Mr Dick was asked to take the following
09 sobriety tests:
10   Alphabet: Mr Dick was asked to recite the
11 alphabet. Mr Dick attempted the alphabet, but
12 when he reached the letter "O" he then stated
13 "Q,R,Z." Mr Dick stated to Writer ████████████
14 ████████████████████████████████
15   Count Backwards: Mr Dick was asked to count
16 backwards from 87 to 74. Mr Dick attempted this,
17 but stated, "79, 78, 70, 69." Mr Dick once again
18 advised Writer ████████████████████.
19 ████████
20   Stand on one leg: Writer asked Mr Dick to
21 stand on one leg & count to 15. Mr Dick
22 attempted this, but was unable to keep his
23 balance.
24   Heel to toe: Mr Dick was asked to walk
25 heel to toe. Mr Dick attempted this, but could
26 not place his heel to his toe & keep his
27 balance.
28

E ven at his most inspired, *Home Improvement* star Tim Allen (real name: Timothy Alan Dick) has never been quite as entertaining as he was during this 1997 sobriety test.

AIKEN COUNTY SHERIFF'S OFFICE
INCIDENT REPORT

AGENCY I.D.
SCO 0020000

CASE NUMBER 0.0.0.0.9.0.7.1.9.

NCIC 24

INQ. / **ENTD.** S

INCIDENT TYPE	COMPLETED	FORCED ENTRY	PREMISE TYPE	UNITS ENTERED	TYPE VICTIM
1. KIDNAPPING	☑YES ☐NO	☐YES ☑NO	Hom	O	☑Individual ☐Business ☐Financial Inst.
2. ASSAULT WITH INTENT TO KILL	☐YES ☑NO	☐YES ☑NO	Hom	O	☐Government ☐Relig. Orgn. ☐Soc./Public
3.	☐YES ☐NO	☐YES ☐NO			☐Other ☐Unknown ☐Police Off.

INCIDENT LOCATION (SUBDIVISION, APARTMENT AND NUMBER, STREET NAME AND NUMBER)
430 DOUGLAS ROAD BEECH ISLAND, SC

ZIP CODE 29841 **WEAPON TYPE** KNIFE

INCIDENT DATE	24 HR. CLOCK	TO	DATE	24 HR. CLOCK	DISP. DATE	DISPATCH DATE/TIME 24 HR. CLOCK DISP. TIME	TIME ARRIVED	DEPART. TIME	LOCATION NO.
07/03/00	0900				7/13/00	0850	0850	1000	14U13

COMPLAINANT'S NAME (LAST, FIRST, MIDDLE) SAME AS VICTIM

RELATIONSHIP TO SUBJECT #1 #2 #3

RESIDENT ·J S O U

RACE SEX AGE / **ETH.**

DAYTIME PHONE / **EVENING PHONE**

NARRATIVE

MR. BROWN WAS CARRYING A SUIT ON A HANGER. MR. BROWN ASKED MR. EUBANKS IF HE SAW THE SUIT AND MR. EUBANKS REPLIED "YES SIR". MR. BROWN STATED "THAT MEANS I'M A GOVERNMENT AGENT, AND I CAN LOCK YOU UP YOU SON-OF-A-BITCH WHITE TRASH FOR TRESPASSING AND SNEAKING AROUND ON MY PROPERTY".

MR. EUBANKS ATTEMPTED TO EXPLAIN TO MR. BROWN ABOUT THE COMPLAINT OF HAVING NO LIGHTS, AT WHICH TIME MR BROWN STATED " I TOLD YOU THAT I COULD LOCK YOU UP, YOU DAMN WHITE TRASH". MR. BROWN HUNG THE SUIT OF CLOTHES ON THE PORCH RAILING THEN CAME TOWARDS MR. EUBANKS SWINGING A KNIFE IN HIS LEFT HAND. MR. EUBANKS STATED THAT THE KNIFE APPEARED TO BE A STEAK KNIFE WITH A BROWN HANDLE, APPROXIMATE 2" OR 3" OF THE BLADE WAS VISABLE FROM MR. BROWNS HAND. MR. BROWN TOLD MR. EUBANKS THAT THIS WOULD BE HIS LAST DAY AT THE POWER COMPANY THAT HE WAS GOING TO BE FIRED. MR. BROWN TOLD MR EUBANKS TO CONTACT HIS SUPERVISOR AND THAT HE COULDN'T LEAVE. MR. EUBANKS WALKED TO HIS TRUCK AND CONTACTED HIS SUPERVISOR MR. CLAYTON QUATTLEBAUM (642·6252) BY RADIO. MR. QUATTLEBAUM ADVISED MR EUBANKS THAT IF HE COULD LEAVE TO DO SO AND THAT MR. ALTEES HICKS (642·6253) SCE+G SECURITY WAS BEING NOTIFIED.

AT THIS TIME A WORKER FOR MR. BROWN WALKED UP TO MR. EUBANKS TRUCK AND ASKED IF THERE WAS A PROBLEM WITH THE ELECTRICITY. MR EUBANKS ADVISED THE WORKER - (B/M 27·30 YEARS OF AGE 6' 140 LBS) THAT HE HAD A NO LIGHT COMPLAINT AND THAT MR. BROWN HAD PULLED A KNIFE ON HIM. THE WORKER STATED THAT MR. BROWN HADN'T BEEN ACTING RIGHT LATELY AND FOR MR. EUBANKS TO LEAVE. MR. EUBANKS LEFT ABOUT 0940 HRS.

ADMINISTRATIVE

SUBJECT IDENTIFIED	SUBJECT LOCATED			
☑YES ☐NO	☑YES ☐NO	☐ACTIVE ☐ADM. CLOSED ☐UNFOUNDED	☐ARRESTED UNDER 18 ☐ARRESTED 18 AND OVER	☐EX-CLEAR UNDER 18 ☐EX-CLEAR 18 AND OVER

REASON FOR EXCEPTIONAL CLEARANCE: 1. ☐ OFFENDER DEATH. 2. ☐ NO PROSECUTION. 3. ☐ EXTRADITION DENIED. 4. ☑ VICTIM DECLINES COOPERATION. 5. ☐ JUVENILE - NO CUSTODY

REPORTING OFFICER(S)	DATE	UNIT NUMBER	APPROVING OFFICER	DATE	UNIT NUMBER
EASTLAKE- G M	7/13/00	434	Billy F. Lucy	07/13/00	2709

FOLLOW-UP INVESTIGATION ☑YES ☐NO **OFFICER** EASTLAKE

While remaining the hardest working man in show business, James Brown can still find time to threaten some "damn white trash" with a steak knife. No charges were filed against JB.

CRIMINAL COURT OF THE CITY OF NEW YORK
COUNTY OF NEW YORK

THE PEOPLE OF THE STATE OF NEW YORK

-against-

1. Scott Weiland (M 30)

Defendant.

MISDEMEANOR

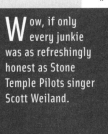

Wow, if only every junkie was as refreshingly honest as Stone Temple Pilots singer Scott Weiland.

STATE OF NEW YORK)
) ss.:
COUNTY OF NEW YORK)

Page 1 of 2

Police Officer Robert Clark, shield #2381 of the PSA4, being duly sworn, deposes and says as follows:

On June 1, 1998, at about 1455 hours at 20 AVENUE D in the County and State of New York, the defendant committed the offenses of:

1. PL 220.03   Criminal Possession Controlled Substance 7th
2. PL 140.15   Criminal Trespass 2nd Degree

in that the defendant knowingly and unlawfully possessed a controlled substance; and the defendant knowingly entered and remained unlawfully in a dwelling.

The offenses were committed under the following circumstances:

Deponent states that he observed the defendant inside of the lobby at the above location, a public housing development, an apartment building where people reside and that said location is posted with signs saying, "No Trespassing" and "Tenants and their Guests Only." Deponent states that he is further informed by the defendant himself who states in substance, NO I DON'T LIVE IN THE BUILDING; NO I'M NOT VISITING ANYONE; I JUST BOUGHT DRUGS.

Deponent further states that he is a custodian of such property and that defendant did not have permission to enter or remain on the property.

Deponent states that he recovered 10 glassines of heroin from defendant's waistband liner.

(a) Count I:

At approximately 9:00 p.m. on April 8, 1988 Thanh Lam, a Vietnamese adult male who resides in Dorchester, traveled by car to 998 Dorchester Avenue, Dorchester, Massachusetts. At 998 Dorchester Avenue, Thanh Lam left his car carrying two cases of beer. As he crossed the sidewalk, Mark Wahlberg attacked Thanh Lam. Wahlberg was carrying a large wooden stick, approximately five feet long and two to three inches in diameter. Wahlberg approached Thanh Lam calling him a "Vietnam fucking shit", then hit him over the head with the stick. Thanh Lam was knocked to the ground unconscious. Th stick broke in two and was later recovered from the scene. Thanh Lam was treated overnight at Boston City Hospital.

11. After he was placed under arrest and informed of his rights, the Defendant Wahlberg referred to one of the victims as a "slant-eyed gook mother-fucker". He also stated that he "hit the gook in the head with a stick".

VOLUNTARY DISCLOSURE SHEET SUPPLEMENT

Defendant made various statements to police officers and detectives at the Hotel Chelsea.

To the first police officers he said in substance that:

> He didn't know what happened - he wasn't there.
> He discovered the body about 10:30 AM.
> He wished they would shoot him or kill him.
> He also identified himself and the deceased.

To the detectives he said in substance that:

> He and the deceased had taken tuinal that night and he went to sleep about 1 AM. Nancy was in the bed with him when he went to sleep. Nancy was sitting on the edge of the bed flicking a knife. They had had an argument.

> He claimed when he woke up in the morning the bed was wet with blood. He thought he had "pee'd" himself. He found the deceased in the bathroom sitting on the floor (same position as found by police). She was breathing. She had a stab wound in her stomach.

> He left her. He went out to get her methadone - at Lafayette Street. When he returned she was full of blood. He washed off the knife and he attempted to wash her off. When he could not wash the blood off her he called for help. He did not know what happened to her. He had slept the entire night through. At various times he said "my baby is dead" or words to that effect. He denied stabbing her (various times).

> The defendant also said that he did not remember what their argument was about and that she hit him and he hit her on top of the head and knocked her onto the bed - but he did not knock her unconcious. He said "I stabbed her but I didn't mean to kill her. I loved her, but she treated me like shit."

> At other times the defendant said the deceased must have fallen on the knife and that she must have dragged herself into the bathroom.

> When asked why he left the deceased in the bathroom, wounded, and went out to get his methadone he said "Oh! I am a dog" or similar words.

7 friend when she came to the RESIDENCE. During this telephone

8 call, NICHOLSON, having told plaintiff that she could bring along

9 her friend, informed plaintiff that he wanted them to wear little

10 black dresses and no stockings. Having donned the requested black

11 dresses, plaintiff and her friend drove to the RESIDENCE, calling

12 NICHOLSON from the vehicle to inform him that they were on their

13 way. When they arrived at the RESIDENCE, plaintiff and her

14 friend were greeted at the door by NICHOLSON who, after offering

15 them a drink, invited plaintiff and her friend upstairs to the

16 bedroom. At or about this time, plaintiff confirmed with

17 NICHOLSON that both she and her friend would receive the sum of

18 $1,000.00 each for the performance of sexual acts with NICHOLSON.

19 NICHOLSON reaffirmed this agreement to pay each of the women the

20 said sum, and indicated that he would "take care of it later."

21   5.   At the said RESIDENCE, plaintiff and plaintiff's friend

22 did perform sexual acts with NICHOLSON. At some point in time,

23 during the course of sexual acts between NICHOLSON and plaintiff,

24 plaintiff's friend left the bedroom.

25   6.   At or about 7:00 a.m., plaintiff, observing that

26 NICHOLSON was fatigued, asked him to "take care" of her and her

27 friend as promised and give them the agreed to amount of $1,000.00

28 each. In response to plaintiff's request, NICHOLSON became loud

# # # #

# # # # # #

# # # # # # # #

1 and abusive, demanding to know what plaintiff was talking about,

2 stating that he had never paid anyone for sex as he could get

3 anyone he wanted as a sexual partner.   Plaintiff informed

4 NICHOLSON that she knew he had paid others to perform sexual acts

5 with him and attempted to use the telephone to request help from

6 a friend who was acquainted with NICHOLSON.   At this point,

---

6 Plaintiff, terrified for her physical safety, and unable to leave

7 as the friend remained in a state of undress, reached for a

8 telephone to call for help.   When plaintiff attempted to use the

9 telephone to call the police, NICHOLSON threatened plaintiff with

10 a raised arm and clenched fist.   He was enraged and yelled that he

11 would give plaintiff a reason to call the police.   NICHOLSON

12 further threatened to throw plaintiff's person over Mulholland

13 Drive and then told plaintiff that he would call the police

14 himself.   These threats terrified plaintiff who feared even more

15 physical violence upon her person by NICHOLSON.   Plaintiff,

16 frightened and in physical pain, pleaded with NICHOLSON to let her

17 leave.   In answer to her plea, NICHOLSON physically took hold of

18 plaintiff and violently threw her out of the RESIDENCE.

15   24.   JOHNSON continued to touch NAPOLI, touching her face,

16 attempting to kiss her, and then, against NAPOLI's will, forcibly

17 pushed his hand down inside her pants.   JOHNSON forcefully

18 penetrated NAPOLI's vagina with his finger, pulled it out, licked

19 his finger, and told NAPOLI that she tasted good and that she was

20 "well trimmed."   JOHNSON continued to try to kiss NAPOLI, and

21 NAPOLI continued to resist the physical advances and sexual

22 assault of JOHNSON.

When two former assistants sued Don Johnson for sexual harassment, they offered a peek at the actor's suave pickup lines and chick-magnet maneuvers. Johnson settled the cases out of court.

11   30.   Upon arriving at the front of JOHNSON's residence, the

12 security guard for the residence came outside to escort JOHNSON

13 into the house.   JOHNSON did not get out of the car and told the

14 security guard to go back inside.   JOHNSON told MURRAY that he

15 wanted to make love to MURRAY.   JOHNSON again grabbed at MURRAY's

16 skirt against MURRAY's wishes, forcibly pushed the skirt above her

17 waist, forcibly grabbed her tights, pulled them away from her

18 waist, and looked at her pubic area.   JOHNSON said, "That's much

19 too long," and "I'm going to have to trim that for you."   MURRAY

20 grabbed JOHNSON's wrist and pushed his hand away from her and

21 prevented him from fondling her pubic area.   JOHNSON refused to

22 exit the Town Car, and continued his attempts to kiss her and

23 touch her despite her protests and physical resistance.

San Francisco Police Department
INCIDENT REPORT

010112504

| N | Topic: NARRATIVE |

ON SATURDAY, 01/27/01, AT APPROXIMATELY 1853 HRS., (V) ▊▊▊▊▊▊▊▊▊▊▊▊ WALKED INTO NORTHERN STATION TO REPORT A SEXUAL BATTERY.

(V) TOLD ME THAT SHE HAD JUST FINISHED HAVING DINNER AT MAS SAKE, LOCATED AT 2030 LOMBARD STREET. (V) LEFT HER TABLE IN ORDER TO GO TO THE RESTROOM PRIOR TO LEAVING THE RESTAURANT. AT THE TIME, THE RESTAURANT WAS FULL OF PEOPLE. (S) DON JOHNSON WAS STANDING NEAR THE WOMEN'S RESTROOM. AS (V) APPROACHED THE WOMEN'S RESTROOM, (S) JOHNSON REACHED OUT AND GRABBED (V) RIGHT ARM AND SAID, "DO YOU KNOW WHO I AM." (V) REPLIED, "YES, I DO." (S) ADDED, "YOU HAVE REALLY NICE TITS. THEIR REAL AREN'T THEY? YOU KNOW, IT'S ALL IN HOW THEY FEEL." (V) PULLED AWAY FROM (S), BACKED UP AND SAID, "YOU'RE A DISGUSTING PIG." (S) GRABBED (V) LEFT ARM, PULLED HER CLOSE TO HIM, PUT HIS MOUTH ON (V) LEFT EAR AND SAID, HOW WOULD YOU LIKE TO SUCK MY COCK?" (V) SMELLED A STRONG ALCOHOLIC BEVERAGE ON (S) BREATH. (V) REPLIED, "WHAT, ARE YOU ASKING EVERY WOMAN IN THIS PLACE?" (S) SAID, "NO, MOST OF THE WOMEN IN THIS PLACE ARE WHORES. YOU (IN GENERAL) WOULDN'T TAKE THEM HOME. YOU, I'D TAKE HOME." (V) PULLED AWAY FROM (S) AND SAID, "YOU'RE GOING DOWN." (V) THEN TURNED AND WALKED AS FAST AS SHE COULD TOWARDS THE FRONT OF THE RESTAURANT. IN THE PROCESS, (V) SLIPPED AND FELL, BRUSING/SCRATCHING HER LEFT KNEE AND LEFT ELBOW. (V) SAID THAT THE BRUSES/SCRATCHES TO HER LEFT KNEE AND LEFT ELBOW AS WELL AS THE DISCOLORATION ON HER LEFT BICEP WERE NOT THERE PRIOR TO HER ENCOUNTER WITH (S).

(V) STATED THAT AFTER SHE RETURNED TO THE MEMBERS OF HER PARTY, SHE PROCEDED TO TELL THEM ABOUT THE ABOVEMENTIONED INCIDENT. THE MEN IN THE PARTY MADE THEIR WAY TO THE REAR OF THE RESTAURANT IN ORDER TO FIND (S) WHO (V) SAID THEY SAW FLED THROUGH THE KITCHEN AND OUT OF THE BACK DOOR. AFTER THE MEN RETURNED TO (V) LOCATION, THEY WENT TO THE OWNER OF THE RESTAURANT AND TOLD HIM WHAT HAD OCCURRED.

(W1) ▊▊▊▊▊▊▊▊▊▊ TOLD ME THAT SHE WAS STANDING IN LINE TO USE THE LADIES ROOM. SHE NOTICED THAT (S) JOHNSON WAS STANDING NEARBY TALKING WITH (V). (W1) TURNED AROUND TO FACE THE LADIES ROOM DOOR. SECONDS LATER, (W1) TURNED BACK AROUND AND BOTH (V) AND (S) WERE STILL ENGAGED IN CONVERSATION. (W1) THEN WENT INSIDE OF THE LADIES ROOM. WHEN (W1) RETURNED, BOTH (V) AND (S) WERE GONE. (W1) RETURNED TO THE OTHER MEMBERS OF HER PARTY.

(W2) ▊▊▊▊▊▊▊▊ SAID THAT HE NEVER SAW (S). HOWEVER, (W2) SAW THAT (V) ELBOW WAS BLEEDING AND THAT SHE WAS UPSET. (W2) ADDED THAT (V) TOLD HIM (S) JOHNSON HAD PROPOSITIONED HER. AFTER (V) EXPLAINED THE DETAILS OF THE PROPOSITION, (W2) SAID THAT HE AND (W3) ▊▊▊▊▊▊▊ WENT TO FIND (S) AND TELL HIM THAT WHAT HE DID WAS INAPPROPRIATE. THEY NEVER FOUND (S).

(W3) ADVISED ME THAT HE DIDN'T SEE WHAT OCCURRED BETWEEN (V) AND (S). (W3) REPORTED THAT (V), "WAS EMOTIONAL, IN TEARS, AND A STATE OF SHOCK." (W3) SAID THAT HE FOLLOWED (W2) IN ORDER TO LOCATE (S). THEY NEVER FOUND (S) INSIDE OF THE RESTAURANT. AFTER RETURNING TO THE MEMBERS OF HIS PARTY, (W3) SPOKE TO THE OWNER (ROBERT JONES) REGARDING THE INCIDENT.

cident # 010112504

H ere's one woman's account of an alleged brush with a boozy Don Johnson in a San Francisco sushi bar. The actor denied the hallway solicitation and prosecutors declined to press charges.

Before embarking on a strenuous cocaine and booze rampage, which young celebrity made sure to carbo-load beforehand, fueling up with a traditional Sunday afternoon spaghetti meal?

DRUG INFLUENCE EVALUATION

EVALUATOR: R.D. HAMILTON OBS

BOOKING NO. 5345382

DR. 97-08 18449

Page 6 of 8

ARRESTEE'S NAME (LAST, FIRST, MI)

AGE	SEX	RACE
27	M	CAUC

ARRESTING OFFICER (NAME, SERIAL #, DIV.) WLA 8A35
BEHNKE, A. #27916 FLORES, J #33231

E EXAMINED/TIME/LOCATION
8-11-97 1200 Hrs SANTA MONICA UCLA MED CENTER

BREATH RESULTS: ☐ Refused
Results .24% d .25% Instrument # 4948
UCLA STA

CHEMICAL TEST ☐ Both Tests ☐ Refused
☒ Urine ☐ Blood

MIRANDA WARNING GIVEN: ☐ Yes ☒ No
Given by: DET PHILLIPS

What have you eaten today? SPAGHETTI
When? 5PM SUN

What have you been drinking? How much? LOTS I DON'T REMEMBER.
Time of last drink? 4AM 8/1/97

Time now? UNK
When did you last sleep? 9-10AM SAT
How long? 2 HRS.

Are you sick or injured? ☐ Yes ☒ No

Are you diabetic or epileptic? ☐ Yes ☒ No

Do you take insulin? ☒ No

Do you have any physicial defects? ☐ Yes ☒ No

Are you under the care of a doctor/dentist? ☐ Yes ☒ No

Are you taking any medication or drugs? ☐ Yes ☒ No

ATTITUDE COOPERATIVE

COORDINATION POOR

SPEECH Slow/Slurred

BREATH STRONG Alcoholic

FACE FLUSH/MOIST

CORRECTIVE LENS: ☒ None ☐ Glasses ☐ Contacts, if so ☐ Hard ☐ Soft

Eyes: ☐ Normal ☒ Bloodshot ☒ Watery

Blindness: ☒ None ☐ L. Eye ☐ R. Eye

Tracking: ☒ Equal ☐ Unequal

PUPIL SIZE: ☒ Equal 4-5 ☐ Unequal (explain)

HGN Present: ☒ Yes ☐ No

Able to follow stimulus: ☒ Yes ☐ No

Eyelids: ☒ Normal ☐ Droopy

PULSE & TIME	HGN	Left Eye	Right Eye
1. 1204 , 96	Lack of Smooth Pursuit	✓	✓
2. 1215 , 99	Max. Deviation		
3. 1330 , 93	Angle of Onset	30%	30%

Vertical Nystagmus? ☐ Yes ☐ No

Convergence Right Eye Left Eye

ONE LEG STAND NOT OBS

BALANCE EYES CLOSED 2-3" 2-3"

WALK AND TURN TEST NOT OBS

Cannot keep balance
Starts too soon

	1st Nine	2nd Nine
Stops Walking		
Misses Heal-Toe		
Steps off Line		
Raises Arms		
Actual Steps Taken		

L R
☐ ☐ Sways while balancing.
☐ ☐ Uses arms to balance.
☐ ☐ Hopping.
☐ ☐ Puts foot down.

INTERNAL CLOCK: ☒ Estimated as 30 sec.

Describe Turn NOT OBS

Cannot do Test (explain)

Type of Footwear BARE FEET

○ Right △ Left
Draw lines to spots touched
NOT OBS

PUPIL SIZE	Room Light	Darkness	Indirect	Direct
Left Eye	6	7.5	7	3.5
Right Eye	6	7.5	7	3.5

NASAL AREA SLIGHT REDNESS

ORAL CAVITY

HIPPUS ☐ Yes ☒ No

REBOUND DILATION ☐ Yes ☒ No

Reaction to Light NEAR NORMAL

RIGHT ARM

LEFT ARM

CLEAR

BLOOD PRESSURE: 164 , 69
TEMP 98.2°

ATTACH PHOTOS OF FRESH PUNCTURE MARKS

MUSCLE TONE: ☒ Near Normal ☐ Flaccid ☐ Rigid

Comments:

at medicine or drug have you been using? COCAINE
How much? 2 LINES
Time of use? 5:00 AM
Where were the drugs used? (Location) #1405 10445 WILSHIRE BL, LA

DATE/TIME OF ARREST 8-11-97 0745

TIME DRE NOTIFIED 0945

EVAL START TIME 1200 Hrs

TIME COMPLETED 1900 Hrs

CONTROL #

EXAMINING OFFICER SGT R. D. HAMILTON

SERIAL NO. 20690

DIVISION WILS

UNAVAILABLE DATES PAST.

REVIEWED BY Sgt Guy 27046

LAPD 08.40.2 (9/89)

duct tape

pubic hairs

cockroach

surgical towel

circumcision

HOT GREASE

THAT'S NOT RIGHT

rodent.

Beanie Baby

foreign object

What happened to service with a smile?
Some days it seems like there's a conspiracy
against the poor consumer, with burger
flippers and doctors alike part of the jihad.
Mom was right, you can't trust anybody.

DEPT 163

DATE	SHIFT	DAY OF WEEK	BADGE	DATE OCCURRED	PLAT	TWP	CLASS	COMPLAINT NUMBER
010300	02	MONDAY	219	123099	19	08	2310	99-132275

SUPPLEMENT INVESTIGATION: On date 01/03/00, I spoke with Rhonda Newberry of the, Oakland County Mental Health Department, phone 745-4900. Ms.Newberry stated that she is the case manager of Robert Nitz. Ms. Newberry stated that Robert Nitz has attempted self-inflicted wounds before to get out of arrest. She stated that he cut himself on DUI traffic stops by Centerline and by White Lake Police Departments. She stated that instruments used in those incidents were a plastic spoon and a comb. Ms. Newberry is concerned that this incident would get him out of any criminal charges. She stated that he is not mentally ill but he is manipulative. I informed Ms. Newberry that Robert Nitz was arrested on a misdemeanor warrant for Centerline Police. She was informed that after Nitz injuried himself he was transported to Pontiac Osteopathic Hospital and he was released pending issuance of a warrant. She was advised to contact the Oakland County Prosecutors Office and talk with them about his case.

On date 01/04/00, I spoke with Deputy Cejmer by phone. Deputy Cejmer informed me that he arrested Mr. Nitz on the misdemeanor warrant from Centerline Police. He stated that while enroute to the Oakland County Jail, Mr. Nitz begun to bang his head against the shield window. Deputy Cejmer also stated that Mr. Nitz layed on the back seat and begun to kick the rear passenger door window. Deputy Cejmer stated that the window was knocked off track. Deputy Cejmer stated that Mr. Nitz then broke Deputy Cejmer's chain handcuff. Deputy Cejmer stated that Mr. Nitz then used the broken handcuff as a knife and Mr. Nitz begun to cut a big hole into his stomach. Deputy Cejmer stated that Mr.Nitz then placed his hand into the big stomach hole and Nitz started to pull out his stomach and intestines. Deputy Cejmer stated that blood was spraying out of his stomach and Mr.Nitz was attempting to throw blood and stomach material at the responding Firemen and Deputies. Deputy Cejmer stated that Mr. Nitz also broke out of his restraints in the AMR ambulance and again placed his hand into his stomach.

On date 01/04/99, Detective Wilson was notified by Pontiac Osteopathic Hospital that Mr.Nitz is currently in a patient and he is in stable condition in section 7west.

On date 01/04/99, Sergeant Norman advised me that he had dispatch place a premis alert on Mr. Nitz address in Highland for future police response.

STATUS: OPEN____ CLOSED ⨉ WARRANT OBTAINED_____

SIGNED,_____

OAKLAND COUNTY SHERIFF DEPARTMENT

Hey, it takes some nerve to throw your intestines at a group of firemen and cops. According to this Michigan police report, Robert Nitz actually had guts to spare.

101 CLOSES

ASSUME THE SALE, THE ONLY REASON THAT YOUR CUSTOMER CAME IN THE STORE IS BECAUSE THEY NEED A MATTRESS.

PEACH CLOSE; THE MANUFACTURE MADE A MISTAKE AND SENT SOME OF THESE MODELS TO THE WAREHOUSE, BUT IN A PEACH COVER! I CHECKED EARLIER THIS MORNING AND THEY STILL HAD A COUPLE LEFT AT A DISCOUNTED PRICE. YOU'LL NEVER SEE THE FABRIC UNDER THE MATTRESS PAD AND SHEETS! MIGHT AS WELL SAVE A LITTLE BIT OF MONEY? RIGHT? LET ME CALL THE WAREHOUSE AND HAVE IT RESERVED FOR YOU NOW!

HOTEL CLOSE: WE HAD AN ORDER FROM THE RITZ-CARLTON HOTEL PUT ON HOLD FOR 150 OF THIS PARTICULAR MATTRESS. WE WERE BLOWING THEM OUT AT THE HOTEL DISCOUNT PRICE. I JUST MIGHT BE ABLE TO GET YOU THAT SAME DEAL IF WE'RE LUCKY. HOWEVER I MIGHT NEED YOU TO TAKE DELIVERY ON IT AS SOON AS POSSIBLE BECAUSE WE NEED THAT VALUABLE SPACE INOUR WAREHOUSE.

FINANCE CLOSE; WE ARE CURRENTLY OFFERING 90 DAYS SAME AS CASH FINANCING. I WISH YOU HAD BEEN HERE LAST WEEK WHEN WE WERE OFFERING 6 MONTHS NO DOWN NO INTEREST. I'D REALLY LIKE YOU TAKE ADVANTAGE OF THAT PROMOTION. PERHAPS, I COULD GIVE MY DISTRICT MANAGER A CALL. IF HE GIVES ME THE O.K., WOULD YOU LIKE TO TAKE IT TODAY?

OUT OF STOCK CLOSE: I BETTER CALL THE WAREHOUSE TO SEE IF THEY HAVE ANY LEFT IN STOCK! LIKE I MENTIONED EARLIER, THIS IS ONE OF OUR BEST SELLING MODELS. THE PROBLEM IS THAT WE HAVE 30 OTHERS STORES SELLING THAT SAME MODEL. (PRETENDING THAT YOU'RE ON THE PHONE WITH THE WAREHOUSE)YOU'RE IN LUCK TODAY!! WE HAVE ONLY 3 LEFT! AND THEY CAN ALSO DELIVER WITHIN THE WEEK!

PRESUMPTIVE CLOSE; (GRAB AN INVOICE AND A CLIPBOARD AND START WRITING) WHAT IS YOU LAST NAME? AND WHERE WOULD YOU LIKE THIS TO BE DELIVERED? HOW DOES WEDNESDAY SOUND? PERFECT! ($$$)

COUPON CLOSE: I NORMALLY WOULDN'T DO THIS BUT YOU FOLKS ARE SUCH NICE PEOPLE. I WANT TO MAKE SURE YOU GET A COMFORTABLE MATTRESS. I'M ALMOST SURE THAT I STILL HAVE A COUPON LEFT IN MY DESK. I KNOW YOU REALLY LIKE THIS MATTRESS. LET ME GIVE YOU THE COUPON.

PREVIOUS SALE CLOSE: I'D REALLY HATE TO SEE YOU LEAVE WITHOUT BUYING A MATTRESS FROM THE GALLERY. I'LL TELL YOU WHAT I'M GOING TO DO FOR YOU. GIVE ME JUST ONE MOMENT. LET ME LOOK THROUGH ALL THE OLD ADVERTISEMENTS AND SEE IF I COULD SAVE YOU SOME MONEY. I JUST MIGHT BE ABLE TO GET MY DISTRICT MANAGER TO HONOR THE HUGE SALE WE HAD LAST HOLIDAY. IF I CAN DO THAT, WOULD YOU TAKE IT TODAY?

January 23, 1975

SECRET

No. 204 By ⟨signature⟩

Mr. C. A. Tucker:

Our attached recommendation to expand nationally the successfully tested "Meet the Turk" ad campaign and new Marlboro-type blend is another step to meet our marketing objective: To increase our young adult franchise. To ensure increased and longer-term growth for CAMEL FILTER, the brand must increase its share penetration among the 14-24 age group which have a new set of more liberal values and which represent tomorrow's cigarette business.

Presently, almost two-thirds of the CAMEL FILTER business is among smokers over 35 years of age, more than twice that for Marlboro. While "Meet the Turk" is designed to shift the brand's age profile to the younger age group, this won't come over night. Patience, persistence, and consistency will be needed. There may even be temporarily a softness in CAMEL FILTER's growth rate as some of the older, more conservative CAMEL FILTER smokers are turned off by the campaign and younger, more liberal smokers begin to come into the brand's franchise. Test market results suggest, though, that this risk is small.

The current media spending level will be maintained since test market shipments indicate no significant short-term volume gains from increased spending. Other competitive brands such as VANTAGE, Newport, and Virginia Slims with sharply directed advertising have demonstrated significant growth rates attainable with CAMEL FILTER's media spending level. We would prefer, as we did for VANTAGE, to demonstrate an increased growth rate with this campaign/blend and then give consideration to asking for extra monies.

J. F. Hind

JFH:jh

Attachment

SCS77 5557

- Do not wear your uniform when deadheading. Avoid identifying yourself as an AA employee, especially in First Class. Due to the large fares paid by first class passengers, be sensitive to the fact that some of these people resent sharing these accomodations with employees.

- Finally, some generalizations about your Latin passengers. Expect a maximum of 20 to 30% North Americans on any load. The large majority will be Latin Americans. Just like the domestic passenger, they want to know what's going on - where they are, why the delay, etc. They distrust baggage handlers and will try to bring everything into the cabin with them. Large shopping bags are common for carrying items on board. They expect not to depart on time. In fact, it's rumored that they will call in a false bomb threat to delay a departure if they think they'll be late. Due to the involved security problems at most airports and a possible long walk from the terminal (no jetways), they like a drink in the plane prior to takeoff. Unruly and/or intoxicated passengers are not infrequent. Your flight attendants, especially the old pros, know your passengers better than you do. If they ask for back-up to resolve a situation, believe that they know what they're talking about, and provide prompt assistance. Latin passengers like to see the Captain both in flight and on the ground. Take every opportunity to interact with your passengers as long as it doesn't distract from your flight responsibilities. Finally, remember that all other things being comparable, the Latin passenger has chosen to fly AA because they trust you more than Latin pilots.

Note to American Airlines: In the future, you may want to avoid committing racist, xenophobic slurs to paper. Not surprisingly, this training manual was recalled.

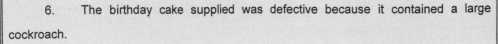

20   5.   On or about June 30, 1998, Defendant Francisco Lopez d/b/a Baskin Robbins

21   supplied a birthday cake, which had been manufactured on its premises, and/or under the

22   direction and control of Defendant Baskin Robbins USA, to Andrea Read of Santa Fe, New

23   Mexico.

24   6.   The birthday cake supplied was defective because it contained a large

25   cockroach.

*

Smith stated on 09/10/00 he had shaved part of his groin as well as the back of his neck and saved the hairs in a cake box. Smith stated he put down a layer of cake batter in a pan, and placed his pubic hairs and head hairs in a corner of the cake so he would know where they were. Smith stated he then placed the rest of the cake batter in and baked the cake. Smith stated he only intended for hairs to be in two pieces of the cake, but they must have gotten through the rest of the cake when he went to put the cake in the oven and the batter sloshed around in the pan. I asked Smith what his intentions were with these two pieces of cake, and he stated that he wished for Boos and Normand to eat them, so he could have the personal satisfaction of knowing they ate his pubic hairs. Smith stated he then baked the cake, frosted it and placed sprinkles and other various decorations on the cake. Smith stated on 09/11/00 he took the cake to his class and began to cut it up. Smith stated that

*

18.   After receiving the serving of nacho chips from an employee other than Jones who was attending the drive-thru window, Plaintiff consumed several of the nacho chips, and then noticed a clear, slimy substance on the nacho chips, that appeared to him to be human saliva.

*

dogs from the grill in the Clubhouse. When Mr. Lee unwrapped a portion of the foil, he saw that the "hot-dog" was covered with mustard, and he then proceeded to take a bite. When he bit down he discovered, to his horror, that the bun did not contain a "hot-dog" at all, rather it contained a dead mouse, inside a hot-dog roll, covered with mustard.

T hink that those stories of people finding disgusting items in their food are just urban myths? Take a look at these revolting allegations from court and police files. Then pass the Pepto-Bismol.

*
*
*
*
*
* * * * *   * * * * *

* *
                                                                                  *
                                                                                  *
                                                                                  *

---

3.   On or about January 6, 1996, the Plaintiff, Jane Doe purchased a box of Cheese

Nips from a Stop & Shop Supermarket located in Westport, Connecticut.

4.   A few days after purchasing said box of Cheese Nips, the Plaintiff began eating

the crackers by reaching her hand into the box and then placing the crackers into her mouth.

While in the process of eating the crackers, the Plaintiff unknowingly placed a bloody first aid

bandage in her mouth which was mixed in with the crackers located in the box. The Plaintiff

then began to chew on the crackers and bloody first aid bandage for a period of time until she

realized it was not a cracker. The Plaintiff, upon feeling this foreign object, removed it from her

---

                                        *

According to Sgt. Bahr, he immediately felt swelling and a burning sensation in
his mouth so he unwrapped one of Chalupas and observed a white powdery or
granular substance mixed in with the other Chalupas ingredients. Said powdery
substance was also found in the other Chalupa. Bahr reports that said white
powdery substance smelled like bleach, chlorine or some type of chemical. At
that point, Sgt. Bahr states that his mouth was very sore, his tongue and mouth
felt very dry and burning.

---

                                        *

---

8.   The plaintiff purchased the nacho meal for the ordinary purpose of consumption.

9.   Plaintiff began to consume the nacho meal while inside Defendant's restaurant.

While consuming the meal, Plaintiff bit into a tough object, which she believed to be gristle from

the meat. Plaintiff chewed on the tough object for 15 to 30 seconds. Plaintiff felt the tough

object scrape the inside of her mouth. Plaintiff removed the tough object from her mouth and

recognized the object as the severed foot of a small rodent.

---

                                        *

---

* * * * * * * * * * *   he received personal injuries when he was caused to eat a "Big Mac"

purchased from McDonald's Restaurant, located at 1547 Montgomery

Highway, Hoover, Alabama, that contained a condom.

After reading this, you may want to think twice about asking for, say, extra pickles on your Hardee's Monster Burger. So much for service with a smile.

Qty. **4.**

Drug Unit Type:

Weight: **0.00**   Unit of Measure:

Description:

BROOMS

Value Stolen or Damaged: **$0.00 Unknown**   Value Recovered: **$0.00 Unknown**

Disposition of Evidence / Property: **Property Room**   Full-Automatic Firearm: Victim / Complaint Signed Signature Card: **NA**

Property Received From: **HARDEE'S**

ADDITIONAL INFORMATION

OFFICERS WERE DISPATCHED TO A REPORT OF A BATTERY AT LIL CHAMP, 907 LANE AVE. S.
UPON ARRIVAL I MET PARAMEDICS OF RESCUE 31 WHO WERE TREATING THE VICTIM FOR BURNS. AFTER
TREATMENT, THE VICTIM WAS ABLE TO GIVE AN ACCOUNT OF THE INCIDENT. THE VICTIM, MS. HOUSTON,
SAID SHE WAS IN THE DRIVE-THROUGH WITH HER FRIEND ORDERING FOOD.   MS. HOUSTON SAID A
DISAGREEMENT AROSE WITH THE EMPLOYEE AND MS. HOUSTON SAID SHE WENT INSIDE TO SEE THE
MANAGER ABOUT THE CONDUCT OF THE EMPLOYEE. MS. HOUSTON SAID THAT AS SHE STOOD AT THE
COUNTER DEMANDING TO SEE THE MANAGER, THE EMPLOYEE (SUSPECT) THREW HOT GREASE IN HER
FACE. MS. HOUSTON SAID SHE WAS BLINDED BY THE GREASE AND TRIED TO GET TO A SINK TO PUT
WATER ON HER FACE. MS. HOUSTON SAID THAT THE SUSPECT THEN ATTACKED HER WITH A BROOM AND
STARTED BEATING HER IN THE HEAD WITH IT. MS. HOUSTON SAID SHE WAS ABLE TO GET FREE AND RAN
ACROSS THE STREET TO THE LIL CHAMP TO CALL FOR HELP.
WITNESS #1 WAS WITH THE VICTIM AND SAID SHE SAW THE SUSPECT HITTING THE VICTIM WITH THE
BROOM INSIDE THE RESTAURANT.
WITNESS #2 SAID HE WAS IN THE BACK OF THE STORE AND HEARD A COMMOTION AND CAME FORWARD
TO SEE THE SUSPECT BEATING THE VICTIM WITH THE BROOM.
WITNESS #3 SAID HE WAS IN THE MANAGER'S OFFICE AND HEARD A COMMOTION AND CAME OUT TO
INVESTIGATE AND SAW THE VICTIM AND SUSPECT STRUGGLING NEAR THE FRONT COUNTER. HE SAID THE

4.   On February 17, 2000, at approximately 8:10 a.m., the plaintiff, Eric N. Meek, M.D., pursuant to instructions given to him by the anesthesiologist in charge, namely, Robert A. Stein, Jr., M.D., proceeded to surgical room No. 6 at Mercy Hospital Medical Center to assume anesthesiology care in connection with an orthopedic surgical case that was in progress.

5.   Surgical suite No. 6 was being utilized at the time by the defendant, Scott Neff, M.D. On the before-mentioned date and time, the defendant, Scott Neff, M.D., was performing orthopedic surgery on a patient. Upon entering surgical suite No. 6, the defendant, Scott Neff, M.D., pointed a blood laden Pulsevac hose at the plaintiff, Eric N. Meek, M.D., and squirted blood laden liquid from the Pulsevac machine on the face, eye and neck of the plaintiff, Eric N. Meek. Upon feeling this liquid on his face, eye and neck, Eric N. Meek ducked and knelt on the floor. While on the floor, the defendant, Scott Neff, M.D., continued to squirt the plaintiff, Eric N. Meek, with the blood laden liquid.

6.   The liquid solution which was being poured on the plaintiff, Eric N. Meek, M.D., by the defendant, Scott Neff, M.D., was coming from the hip of the patient upon which Scott Neff was performing the operation.

Wasn't this a scene from *The Three Stooges Go to Medical School?* Or perhaps it was Rip Taylor's guest appearance on *ER.* Dr. Neff denied the Pulsevac prank.

2

this community. On February 18, Plaintiff kept a dental appointment with Defendant who, without informing plaintiff of her intentions and without sufficient inquiry into the general health of plaintiff as related to the capacity to withstand such treatment, proceeded to pull sixteen (16) teeth in the one sitting on that date, stopping only when plaintiff could stand no more and refused to allow further extractions. Plaintiff lost consciousness as she left the office and had to be transported to the St. Francis Hospital. Plaintiff was subsequently informed that the defendant had intended to pull all of her teeth on February 18, 1994.

)
)
)
)
)

6.   That on or about May 6, 1997, the Plaintiff, Margo West, was admitted

to St. Vincent Infirmary Medical Center for the purpose of undergoing a

hysterectomy. The surgery was performed by Sharon Keith, M.D., Defendant, and

others, on that same date and Plaintiff remained in the hospital until on or about

May 13, 1997, for the purpose of recuperation. Unbeknownst to Plaintiff, a surgical

towel was left in her abdomen when the incision was closed.

)
)
)
)
)

Suffolk, ss.

**Board of Registration
in Medicine**

**Adjudicatory Case
No. 98-32-DALA**

_____

In the Matter of	)
	)
Tod F. Forman, M.D.	)
_____	)

FIRST AMENDED STATEMENT OF ALLEGATIONS

(

Patient D

14. On January 19, 1998, Patient D presented to Dr. Forman with symptoms of an upper respiratory infection. She was then age 19, overweight and suffering from bipolar disorder (a.k.a. manic-depressive illness).

15. After observing that Patient D had gained two pounds, Dr. Forman told her that she was becoming "bigger than a whale" and that she would become unattractive to boys if she gained any more weight. Then Dr. Forman refused to examine her because she owed him ten dollars from previous visits.

(

> The doctors described here should heed the advice, "Physician, heal thyself." Because they might not be seeing too many other patients.

30. Dr. Forman informed Patient J that the student was going to perform the vaginal examination while he supervised her. Upon noticing during the examination that Patient J was wearing blue toenail polish on her feet, which were then in the stirrups, Dr. Forman told Patient J that the effect was too young for her. When she defended her taste, he remarked "you'd better not tell me you have a belly ring" to which Patient J replied that in fact she did have a navel ring and began defending this choice also. Dr. Forman then said "let me see" as he pulled her robe wide open, exposing her fully, head to toe, and looked at her navel and remarked "very sexy." Then, noticing her genital area, he remarked "and, she's shaved too. God, I love that."

31. After the student obtained the PAP smear and completed the vaginal examination, Dr. Forman examined Patient J's breasts. While he did so, he declared to the student that Patient J was "pear-shaped" and very healthy and that "she's going to bury at least three husbands." When the student asked, "how do you know?", Dr. Forman replied, "Oh, I can tell. I can read breasts."

While the investigation into these five complaints was open and ongoing, on 09/22/98, at approximately 1145 hours, your affiant met with the sixth and newest victim in this case, ████████████████████████ advised this detective that she also had recently seen an infertility doctor and once again had her prescription needs filled at the Eckerds at 7030 Jog Road. All the victims in this case stated that they would receive a phone call from a person who sounded like a young W/F. In these phone calls, the suspect would say things to the victims, referring to their infertility problem. These statements included, but were not limited to "infertile bitch", "why don't you go lay an egg", and "I heard the stork passed you over."

As this investigation continued, it became obvious that the suspect(s) had selected the victims due to their infertility treatments and that the number of people that had access to this information would be limited as all victims stated that the infertility treatments were a personal issue, which only they and their respective husbands had knowledge of.

Based on this information, on 09/29/98, at approximately 1100 hours, this detective accompanied by Det. Griffin met with the suspect in this case, Veronica Smith, at her place of employment. Veronica Smith, after being confronted with the information we had, subsequently agreed to voluntarily accompany myself and Det. Griffin back to the Palm Beach County Sheriff's Office Detective Bureau.

Upon our arrival at the Detective Bureau, the suspect, Veronica Smith, was mirandized, during which time she provided myself and Det. Griffin with a taped confession. In her taped confession, suspect Smith admitted to obtaining the victim's information ████████ pharmacy computer at the Eckerd's Pharmacy. She further stated that she selected these victims based on their infertility problems and the medications that they were consuming for their infertility treatments. The suspect further stated that she would write down the victim's home phone numbers and then take them home and sometimes call the victims from her residence and sometimes from the pay phones outside of the Eckerd's Pharmacy ████████ spect stated that she was jealous of the victims and specifically targeted them due to the treatments. The victim further confessed that she obtained a calling card in hopes of disguising the place from which the harassing phone calls originated. The suspect also states that besides the six reports on file at the Sheriff's Office relating to the harassing phone call complaints, there may be as many as 20 victims in total which she selected from the computer at Eckerds because of their infertility or prenatal treatments.

It's frightening to think what Smith would have done to some flaccid guy carrying a Viagra prescription.

2.

Mr. Banks was admitted to Earl K. Long Medical Center on August 14, 1995, for an aortic femoral by-pass operation scheduled to take place on August 15, 1995.

3.

When Mr. Banks awoke from surgery on August 15, 1995, he discovered that he had been circumcised and the aortic femoral by-pass operation he was scheduled to undergo had not been performed.

4.

At no time prior to surgery did Mr. Banks consent to a circumcision nor was he informed of any possibility that a circumcision would be performed.

Talk about not knowing someone's ass from his elbow. The defendants claimed the clip job was a surgical necessity.

AS THE WORM TURNS

3. On April 19, 1998, inside of the Las Vegas Hilton Hotel and Casino, Defendant, without cause, consent, or provocation; sexually assaulted Plaintiff by physically grabbing her left breast and shaking it.

4. At the same time as sexually assaulting Plaintiff, Defendant made the following lewd comments in the presence of numerous spectators:

a. "Damn woman, you got some big titties";

b. "Gee woman, you must be pregnant"; and

c. "Most women with titties that big are pregnant."

Defendant Name: Smith, Michelle
Docket Number:

POLICE

CRIMINAL COMPLAINT

AFFIDAVIT of PROBABLE CAUSE

Ed Bloskey witnessed Michelle Smith mentally abuse John Murphy by telling him there was gas in his room, use the birdcage to detect gas. Threaten him with the unions being after him. The molly McGuires were coming after him and using a alarm clock to torment him. The alarm clock would be placed in his room and the timer set. Michelle Smith would find it and tell him it was a bomb. He witnessed Smith telling Gilda Costanzo that her car was being towed away to deliberately upset her. He witnessed Smith give vodka to resident Julia Hutchey. Hutchey had previous problems with alcohol and most all of the residents on the third floor (alzheimers) they were on medications. He saw Michelle place salt on the food of resident Wally Strempek, knowing that he was not allowed salt in his diet. He witnessed Michelle Smith tell resident Mary Zahornacky that her sister was found dead, dismembered and that she would have to identify the body. Ed Bloskey stated that the acts of abuse he related were a normal course of conduct for Michelle Smith & Linda Brown. The acts of abuse took place most every night that they worked. He stated that when first approched by staff members for a statement, he lied. He did so at the request of Michelle Smith after receiving threats of violence directed at himself and his wife. He was followed and called repeatedly by Michelle Smith at home and work. She went as far as to threaten to blow his head off with a gun if he said anything about her. When driving home from work with his wife and child
Michelle Smith pursued them in her personal vehicle. On Davis Street in the City of Scranton, his wife at the wheel, Smith attempted to force their car off the road, they stopped and called police. This incident took place on the 25th of January 1998. On the previous day Smith called Mrs. Bloskey at her place of employment and stated that Ed was harassing her and she would have him arrested.

Susan Pierson stated that she witnessed Michelle Smith abuse Wally Strempek by deliberately messing up his food trays. She would pour the beverage over the food, making it unfit for consumption. She witnessed Michelle tell Gilda Costanzo that her prized possession, a vehicle was being towed away for parking violations or that it had been stolen. Smith would trash the room of Elenor Dougherty and blame it on Gilda Costanzo, in an effort to make them argue. She witnessed Smith tell John Murphy that Jimmy Hoffa, Molly McGuires wer after him. He didn't pay his rent and they were throwing him out on the street. The alarm clock being placed in his room and telling him she found a bomb. Pierson stated that Michelle Smith was especially cruel in her abusive actions. Linda Brown was involved in the incidents although Michelle Smith seem to be the leader. Susan Pierson stated that she initally told her supervisors at the facility that she knew nothing about abuse of residents. She did so at the request of Michelle Smith. Smith called her and threatened to make a false accusation to the Bureau of Children & Youth. She feared that Smith would have Children & Youth take her child away from her. After learning that the District Attorneys Office was investigating, she decided to tell the truth.

Holly Dyshuk stated that most of what she knew regarding resident abuse was indirect, she recalled seeing Michelle Smith coming out of Mary Zahornacky's room laughing. Dyshuk stated that as Smith came out she heard Mary crying and saying "Mother of God, our Helen is dead".

Based upon the facts set forth in this affidavit I ask that warrants be issed for the arrest of Michelle SMITH & Linda BROWN.

AFFIDAVIT of PROBABLE CAUSE

On 8 DEC 1998 between 1130-1230hrs, Michele KISER discovered that an "Angel Halo" *Beanie Baby* doll was missing from her ill daughter's hospital room located in the Pediatric Rehab Floor of the Hershey Medical Center., KISER immediately reported the missing property to on-duty registered nurse Nancy WAGNER due to the fact that the doll was the property of her ill daughter, and that it had sentimental value to her. WAGNER, who had suspicions that a floor licensed practical nurse (PINKNEY) may have taken the doll, searched through PINKNEY's black lunch bag which was located in the staff lunch room. WAGNER's search subsequently revealed that the doll was located within the bag wrapped in a white paper towel. WAGNER later observed PINKNEY relocate the lunch bag from the lunch room to PINKNEY's vehicle which was parked on the hospital's third floor parking garage.

Having witnessed this act, WAGNER notified Hershey Medical Center Security Chief Peter RIDGE. RIDGE then contacted Derry Township Police to request investigation and intervention in this matter. At 1500hrs, RIDGE and myself met with PINKNEY in the hospital and advised her of the allegations made against her. I informed PINKNEY that I would be obtaining a search warrant for her vehicle in order to locate the stolen property. I also advised PINKNEY of her right to provide police with a voluntary consent to search her vehicle in lieu of the search warrant. PINKNEY replied that she did not have the doll in her vehicle and that she would take RIDGE and myself to her car to prove it. Once at her vehicle (1987 Cadillac PA reg: BAM8672), I inquired with PINKNEY as to whether she would provide consensual search. PINKNEY then began to shout at RIDGE, Derry Twp. Police Officer GASPICH, and myself proclaiming that our interaction with her is unjustified. PINKNEY then proceeded to her car, unlock the door and attempt to enter the driver's seat of the vehicle at which time she was stopped by GASPICH and myself and advised that she would be detained at the scene until a search warrant was obtained. PINKNEY continued to shout at us using profanity. She made several attempts to re-enter her car, and she physically pushed GASPICH and myself on two occasions to get into her vehicle. PINKNEY was then escorted away from her vehicle as she continued to try and push past the officers and flail her arms in attempts to bypass us. PINKNEY was then advised that she would be placed under arrest if she continues to act disorderly. PINKNEY then stated, "ok, I admit it........I made a big mistake" at which time she voluntarily unlocked her trunk and opened it allowing me to search. My search revealed a black lunch bag which when unzipped, contained an "*Angel Halo*" Beanie Baby doll wrapped in a white paper towel.

At approximately 1515hrs, PINKNEY was advised that she was being placed under arrest for theft at which time she began shouting at officers using profanity. PINKNEY was ordered to stop acting in a disorderly manner, but she continued to shout and attempt to leave the scene. Both GASPICH and myself attempted to secure PINKNEY's hands in order to handcuff her; however, she broke free from our grasp and flailed her arms about striking GASPICH and myself. PINKNEY was eventually handcuffed and transported to DTPD for prisoner processing.

I verify that the facts set forth in this affidavit are true and correct to the best of my knowledge or information and belief. This verification is made subject to the penalties of Section 4904 of the Crimes Code (18 PA. C.S. 4904) relating to unsworn falsification to authorities.

5/11/99
(Date)

_____ (Roche)
(Signature of Affiant)

SWORN AND SUBSCRIBED BEFORE ME ON THIS ___12th___ DAY OF ___May___ 1999.

12-3-04
(Magisterial District)

_____ (SEAL)
(Issuing Authority)

1. <u>An 8 month old infant was duct taped to a wall to see if the infant would "stick."</u>

On March 2, 2000, the OCCS investigator interviewed Diane, the Center's Director. Suzanne, the Center's owner, was present during the interview. Diane claimed that JW's father mentioned to her one morning about two months ago that duct tape works on everything. Diane also claimed that they joked about whether a child would "stick" to a wall with duct tape. Diane reported that, during the afternoon, she was joking with Natercia and Francesca about the duct tape. Diane further informed the OCCS investigator that she said, "I wonder if it works." Diane admitted that she put the duct tape on JW's arms while Francesca held JW's arms. Diane stated that the duct tape became loose very quickly. Diane stated that she had only duct taped the arms to the wall and placed the tape on JW's shirt. Diane stated that she did mention it to JW's father at the end of the day and "he laughed at me."

JW's father stated to the OCCS investigator that, when he dropped JW off at the Center on the day JW was duct taped, the infants were noisy. Diane indicated to JW's father that she wished she could tape them to the wall. JW's father jokingly responded "well, duct tape works on everything." JW's father stated that this is a phrase that he is accustomed to using. JW's father reported that, when he arrived to pick up JW, Diane told him that JW had a miserable day and that she had duct taped JW to the wall. JW's father explained that he thought that Diane was joking and, therefore, did not believe her. JW's father reported that he later found out from Natercia that this had indeed occurred.

Francesca reported that during one morning at the Center, she observed Diane and a parent talking about duct tape working on everything. In the afternoon, Francesca heard Diane say, "I wonder if duct tape would work". Francesca saw Diane go into her Office and come back with duct tape. Diane then duct taped JW's arms and waist to the wall. When JW got one of her arms free, she was taken out of the tape. JW was not crying when this occurred. Diane thought it was funny. Diane did tell JW's father that she had duct taped JW to the wall but he thought that it was a joke. Francesca stated that she did not inform Suzanne, the owner about the duct tape incident.

Joleen volunteered information to the OCCS investigator regarding the duct taping of JW without being directly asked about the incident by the OCCS investigator. Joleen reported that, about a month ago, she went into the infant room between 1:30 p.m. and 2:00 p.m. because she was on break. Joleen stated that she "saw a baby taped to the wall." Joleen remembers saying "how mean." Diane told Joleen that "I did not do this to be mean." Joleen recalls the infant's arms being taped but could not remember if the waist or any other part of the body was taped. Joleen stated that she immediately went to her room (toddler room) after she observed this and she mentioned it to DC (former toddler teacher). Joleen explained that she did not bring this to Suzanne's attention because Suzanne is friendly with Diane.

Kerry stated that she had heard rumors about the duct taping but did not feel comfortable discussing this with the OCCS or DSS investigators.

Natercia reported that, during the end of January 2000 or beginning of February 2000, she was sitting on a mat in the infant room with JW. JW kept on climbing and bouncing on the mat that

Next time, the Massachusetts day care workers mentioned in this state investigative report might try a staple gun—it doesn't leave sticky stuff on the wall.

was against the wall while JW held onto Natercia's hand. Diane was in the room and she stated "I wonder if she (referring to JW) would stick to the wall. I bet she would because she is tiny and petite." Diane laughed. Diane walked out of the room and came back with duct tape. Diane pulled out a long piece of duct tape, ripped it with her teeth and placed the first piece on either JW's waist or legs, she could not recall which. Diane placed three long pieces of duct tape across JW's waist, legs and arms. After Diane taped JW to the wall Natercia stated that Diane was "laughing hysterically." Natercia reported that one piece of the tape started to come apart and then Natercia took the duct tape off JW. JW was holding on to Natercia's right hand throughout the incident. Natercia denied that she or Francesca held JW while Diane taped JW." Natercia stated that the other witnesses to this incident were Francesca, who was in the room when this occurred, and Joleen, who came into the room while the child was taped but did not witness the entire event.

Natercia reported that when JW's father came in to the Center to pick up JW, Diane told JW's father, in a joking manner, that she had duct taped JW to the wall. It appeared that JW's father did not take Diane's comments seriously, and allegedly responded in a joking manner, "well sometimes I would like to stick her to the wall."

Five of the six staff interviewed by the OCCS investigator confirmed that an infant was duct taped to a wall while in the Licensee's care. The sixth staff member refused to comment on the incident. Additionally, the infant's father confirmed that Diane admitted to him that she had duct taped his child to the wall.

}
}
}
}
}
}
}
}
}
}
}
}
}
}
}
}
}
}
}
}

The former minister of a large Atlanta church was embalmed and buried by SCI through its Spring Hill location. It was a high profile funeral which included news media. Mr. Barnes walked up to the reposing room to pay his respects to the decedent before the crowd got there. Mr. Barnes walked into the back of the reposing room, and found Bill Oakley, the Assistant Manager, and another funeral director placing the casket in the reposing room. As Mr. Barnes stood there, Oakley began rubbing the decedent's crotch saying, "I bet you've never been rubbed like this by a queen before." Mr. Barnes was repulsed and disgusted by this sexually perverted behavior.

Thankfully, dead men tell no tales. Otherwise, this poor preacher might certainly have something to testify about. Oakley denied the post-mortem grope.

AS THE WORM TURNS

4. On April 19, 1998, inside of the Las Vegas Hilton Hotel and Casino, Defendant, without cause, consent, or provocation, sexually assaulted Plaintiff by physically grabbing her by either side of the breasts and lifting her off the ground.

5. That when Defendant lifted Plaintiff by the breasts, it caused the underwire of Plaintiff's bra to be pushed into Plaintiff's right breast causing pain, discomfort, and bruising.

Wilcox v. Rodman, U.S. District Court, District of Nevada, 1998

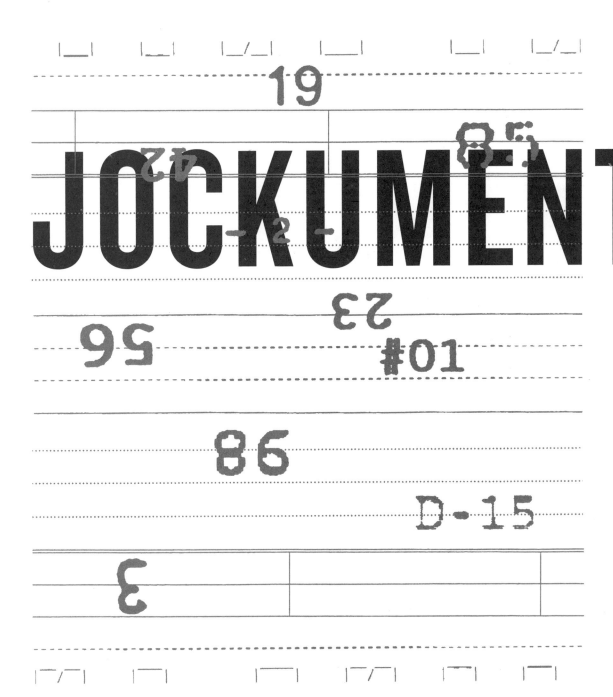

JOCKUMENTS

A graceful double play. A thrilling touchdown pass. A gravity-defying dunk. Well, ESPN can have that crap. Because the star athlete's post-game activities are far more entertaining.

ORLANDO POLICE DEPARTMENT   Date Created: 10/26/97
                                                  Page: 1

Aggravated Battery   Case No: 97-391218

Primary Victim: LUGO,JORGE,,

Date/Time Reported: 10/26/97 1:19 Hrs.   Dispatch Incident Type:
Date/Time Occurred: 10/26/97 1:19 Hrs.   BATTERY
Date/Time Between : 10/26/97 2:00 Hrs.   Unit No: 579
Location Occurred : 129 W CHURCH ST
Cross Street . . :
Grid: GRID#-1346   Sub-Grid: GRID 1346C   District: D-15

Reporting Officer : 5274 WILLIAMS,JEFFERY,A,
Primary Unit Assigned to Investigate: Homicide   Approving Ofcr:
Scene Processed by: 2978 MCGUIRE,SUZANNE,C,   Event Log NO
Assigned Investigators: Special Circumstance:

Stat|___| Disp|__| Date|_/_| Invt|____| Asmt Type|__| Date|_/_|
Case Status: CHRG AFFDT Disposition: ARREST   Disp. Date: 10/26/97

                              COPY
Distribution
NONE

Case Narrative
On 10/26/97, this officer was working off duty at 129 West Church
Street (Church Street Station). Between 2300 and 2330 the arrestee
entered Phineas Phoggs, a dance club, at Church Street Station. Up
until approximately 0150 hours, there had been no problems at the
club. The arrestee even came out and signed several autographs for
fans.

At approximately 0145 hours, the club began to empty out. A steady
stream of people were coming out. At approximately 0200 hours,
while standing at the front door of the club, I observed a Hispanic
male running towards the door with a black male chasing him. I
grabbed the Hispanic male and had him under control and bent over.
The next thing I knew, the arrestee, who was chasing him, was next
to me on my left and grabbed the victim by the left arm. I then
said, "Charles, I will handle this, let go. Charles, let me take
care of this." Charles then said to me, "I will not hurt him, I
just want to talk to him."

As I stood up, I held onto the victim with my right hand. I looked
over my shoulder at the crowd, which was closing in on us. I
reached with my left hand up to my Church Street radio to call
Officer Sharpe, at which time I felt the victim being pulled from
my grasp. I looked up and saw the arrestee holding the victim up
in the air by his arms, at which time the arrestee threw the victim
into a plate glass window. All of this occurred within a matter of
seconds.

After the arrestee threw the victim through the glass, I grabbed
the arrestee and pulled him away from the victim who had slumped to
the ground and was bleeding from a laceration on his upper right

Charles Barkley's
career statistics:
23,757 points.
12,546 rebounds.
4,215 assists.
One man thrown
through a plate glass
window.

Aggravated Battery   Case No: 97-391218

arm. Unknown people began trying to help the victim as I attempted
to keep the arrestee away. Two times the arrestee came back over
to the victim. On the first occasion the arrestee bent down and
stated, "You got what you deserve. You don't respect me. I hope
you're hurt." I got the arrestee away. He then stepped back to
the victim and stated, "For all I care, you can lay there and
die."

After this, unknown persons got the arrestee and tried to get him
to leave the area. He got approximately a half a block away before
Officer Sharpe and several other officers were able to stop him.
While Officer Sharpe was getting control of the arrestee, several
people approached the victim and were saying, "You deserve what
happened and you should be dead." I repeatedly had to get between
bystanders and the victim. An unknown Church Street employee got a
towel and provided it to two unknown people, possibly friends of
the victim, who were rendering first aid to the victim.

OFD Engine #101 and Rescue #1 responded and rendered first aid.
Rural Metro #126 responded and transported the victim to ORMC.
This officer was advised by Sergeant Beavers that the victim would
most likely be released.

Post Miranda, I interviewed the arrestee. The arrestee, in the
presence of Officer Cooney, was read his Miranda Warnings, waived
those rights, and stated he would talk to me and write a
statement.

Post Miranda, the arrestee wrote a statement which read that he was
sitting at a table with three women when the victim allegedly threw
ice at the arrestee and the three witnesses. The arrestee then
chased the victim out of the front door where he grabbed him and
threw him into a window.

Witnesses Felicano, Telfer, Leiba, Carrington, and Ashley all
stated that the victim had thrown ice and a glass at the arrestee
and three of the witnesses which resulted in one of the witnesses
being struck in the face with the glass.

Also, witness Rodriguez stated that prior to the arrestee going
after the victim, that they had argued and the arrestee pushed her
twice, one of which resulted in her cutting her leg. She further
stated he had no authority to touch her.

Officer Sharpe charged the arrestee with Resisting Without
Violence, OPD case #97-3   78. Damage to the window was
approximately $2,000. CST McGuire responded and took photos of the
scene, the victim, witness Rodriguez, and the arrestee.

kh/2968/102697/0547 hours/n

COPY

INDIANA YOUTH CENTER
Commissary Order Ticket

DOC No — 922335   Name — TYSON MICHAEL   Dorm — O

Order No — 231898   Date — 11/28/94   I.T.F. Amount $3,238.60

Qty. Ordered	Item Description	Item Number	Unit Cost	Extended Cost
1. 2	Coffee 3oz	1160	1.75	3.50
2. 36	Diet Cola (Singles) *36	1270	.20	7.20
3. 2	Tea Bags Keefe, 48 ct.	1140	1.05	2.10
4. 2	Cheese 8oz Tub Jalapeno	2070	1.45	2.90
5. 2	Chips Nacho Tortilla * 3	2140	1.15	2.30
6. 4	Chips Potato * bags *	2190	.90	3.60
7. 8	Honey Bears	2130	1.10	8.80
8. 1	Picante Sauce (Hot)	2250	1.25	1.25
9. 2	Generic Ritz Crackers	2220	1.50	3.00
10. 24	Soup, Shrimp — Dry	2650	.45	10.80
11. 15	Tuna Fish	2360	.75	11.25
12. 2	Bread Wheat * Limit of *	4090	1.05	2.10
13. 1	Chap Stick	5070	.75	.75
14. 2	Deodorant Roll-On	5290	1.00	2.00
15. 1	Q-Tips	5300	.85	.85
16. 1	Shower Shoes Xlrg *Lim 2	5360	.70	.70
17. 2	Soap Irish Spring	5180	.55	1.10
18. 2	Toothbrush	5440	.35	.70
19. 2	Toothpaste Close Up	5680	1.10	2.20
20. 10	Schick Disp. Razor Lim 10	5910	.20	2.00
21. 6	Battery Radio AAA *6	6270	.45	2.70
22. 2	Handkerchiefs White	6060	.45	.90
23. 1	Loose Leaf Paper *200*	6160	.90	.90
24. 1	Plastic Thermo-Mug 22oz	6290	1.10	1.10

Total Purchases $74.70

Balance $3,163.90

To survive in jail, you've got to act tough (or have an endless supply of loose cigarettes). Unless, of course, you're Mike Tyson. Then you can order Honey Bears and Irish Spring soap from the prison commissary without fear of becoming somebody's bitch.

Signature _____

DISTRICT COURT OF MARYLAND FOR .... (City/County)

LOCATED AT (COURT ADDRESS)

RELATED CASES: ....

DISTRICT COURT
CASE NUMBER
0D00054096

COMPLAINANT/APPLICANT

Name (Print): Richard Dale Hardick

Address (Number and Street): 8117 Will-Mil Ter

City, State, and Zip Code: Monrovia MD 21770   Telephone: 301-865-XXXX

Agency, Sub-Agency, and I.D. #   (Officer Only)

DEFENDANT

Name (Print): Michael Gerard Tyson

Address (Number and Street): 8313 Persimmon Tree Rd

City, State and Zip Code: Bethesda, MD 20817   Telephone: 301-365-6673

CC#: G98208583

DEFENDANT'S DESCRIPTION: Driver's License # Unknown .... Sex M Race B Ht 5 Wt 11

Hair Black Eyes Brown Complexion .... Other .... D.O.B 6/30/66 .... ID

APPLICATION FOR STATEMENT OF CHARGES   Page 1 of 3

I, the undersigned, apply for a statement of charges and a summons or warrant which may lead to the arrest of the above named Defendant because on or about August 31, 1998

Date

at Shady Grove Road near Muncaster Mill Rd, Gaithersburg, MD, the above named Defendant

Place

Assaulted me by Kicking me in the groin. This occurred while I was

(Concise statement of facts showing that there is probable cause to believe that a crime has been committed and that the Defendant has committed it):

driving home from work using Shady Grove Road. As I was approaching Muncaster, I was in the left hand lane. Traffic was very heavy — creeping with many stops. A green late model convertible was in front of me. During one of the occasions the traffic was stopped, a car behind me hit my car in the rear. My car was forced into the car in front of me.

(Continued on attached .... pages) (DC/CR 1A)

I solemnly affirm under the penalties of perjury that the contents of this Application are true to the best of my knowledge, information and belief.

....
Date   Officer's Signature

I have read or had to me and I understand the Notice on the back of this form.

X) September 2, 1998   X) Richard Dale Hardick
Date   Applicant's Signature

Subscribed and sworn to before me this 2 day of September 19 98

Time: 9:23 A. M.   Judge/Commissioner Michael D. Johnson   I.D. 1527

I understand that a charging document has been issued and that I must appear for trial ☐ on ....

Date

at ...., ☐ when notified by the Clerk, at the Court location shown at the top of this form.

Time

....
Applicant's Signature

☐ I declined to issue a charging document because of lack of probable cause.

....
Date   Commissioner   I.D.

Witnesses' Names and Addresses:

Name | Number and Street/Agency/Sub-agency/I.D. | City, State, Zip

Name | Number and Street/Agency/Sub-agency/I.D. | City, State, Zip

Name | Number and Street/Agency/Sub-agency/I.D. | City, State, Zip

DC/CR 1 (Rev. 8/94)

TRACKING NUMBER

COURT COPY

Traffic may have been creeping along on Shady Grove Road, but when motorist Richard Hardick got into a fender bender, he discovered that Mike Tyson was unsafe at any speed.

DISTRICT COURT OF MARYLAND FOR _____ (City/County)

LOCATED AT (COURT ADDRESS)

DISTRICT COURT
CASE NUMBER
0D0005*40*96

DEFENDANT'S NAME (LAST, FIRST, M.I.)

Tyson, Michael Gerald

That car was driven by a black Female And Mr. Tyson was the passenger. I immediately got out of my car And asked the driver behind why he hit me. I do not recall if he answered me. I then went to the front of my car to assess if there was Any damage. I could not see Any but I was not able to get close. Mr. Tyson, I believe, asked me why I hit his car. I said something to the effect that the man behind me pushed me into his car. Mr. Tyson began to approach the driver behind me who at that time was outside his car on the drivers side. Mr. Tyson then was being restrained by a man who I did not know And the woman driver of the Tyson car. Despite being restrained, Mr. Tyson hit the man in the face. I do not recall if the man fell to the ground. Immediately I got back into my car because I feared what Mr. Tyson would do next. I put the key into the ignition to get power to my window, I locked the door And closed the windows. Briefly thereafter the man who tried to restrain Mr. Tyson Approached my driver side window. He Acted like he wanted to talk to me so I lowered my window. He reached in immediately and took my keys out of the ignition. He said that I was not going Anywhere. I said something to the effect that I did not intend to leave. He then asked for my driver's

September 2, 1998
Date

Richard Dale Hardick
Applicant's Signature

TRACKING NUMBER

DC/CR 1A (Rev. 8/94)

COURT COPY

DISTRICT COURT OF MARYLAND FOR .... (City/County)

LOCATED AT (COURT ADDRESS)

DISTRICT COURT CASE NUMBER
0D000540096

DEFENDANT'S NAME (LAST, FIRST, M.I.)

Tyson, Michael Gerael

APPLICATION FOR STATEMENT OF CHARGES (CONTINUED) Page 3 of 3

license. I gave it to him. I then thought that Mr. Tyson had calmed down and we could proceed with the exchange of information (insurance, driver's license, etc). I got out of my car (I can unlock the door without the key) and stood near the passenger door. Mr Tyson then started toward me — he was in the medial strip. The woman driver and the same man who restrained Mr Tyson previously did so again. Mr. Tyson was able to continue to approach me despite the restraint. When he got close, his arms, I believe, were being restrained and he kicked me in the groin. I immediately double over in pain and fell to the ground. I stayed there until the police came. While I was on the ground in the medial strip, Mr. Tyson and the woman driver left the scene. After talking to the police I drove myself to Montgomery General Hospital in Olney. I was treated and released.

September 2, 1998
_____
Date

Richard Dale Hardick
_____
Applicant's Signature

TRACKING NUMBER

DC/CR 1A (Rev. 8/94)

COURT COPY

front of the house. As I contacted Silver I immediately saw he had blood dripping from the area of his nose over his lip. He also had a swollen area on his left cheeck.

Silver was very excited and told me that Tonya Harding had just punched him in the face and she was out of control inside the house. He also said she threw a metal object at his face, which caused the swelling. Silver advised she was throwing stuff and he could not calm her down. Silver said he did not want anyone arrested and he would leave if we wanted him to. He then said that he had two witnesses in the barn that saw the whole incident.

At this point Harding came out of the residence and she was also excited and was speaking loudly. Harding told me that Silver held her down on the ground and she punched him in the face to get him off of her. She said that she punched him to defend herself. I asked her about hitting him with a metal object and she replied that she did throw a round thing toward his motorcycle. Harding said the object just happened to hit Silver instead of the motorcycle. Harding told me she had just returned from playing video poker in Oregon with Silver before the incident occurred.

Officer Justis and Sergeant Lackey arrived and Officer Justis continued talking with Silver while Sergeant Lackey talked with Harding. I then went and talked with the two witnesses in the barn, Deven Schroeder and Perry Demarco. Schroeder said that he and Demarco where by the barn when Harding and Silver pulled up in their vehicle and parked inside. Schroeder said they got out of the car and Harding started hitting Silver. Schroeder stated, " She started beating the shit out of him...he wouldn't hit her. He held her arms." Demarco told me Harding picked up a wheel cover and threw it at Silver and it hit him in the face. He pointed out the wheel cover which has a dent in the side. Demarco said the dent was caused from hitting Silver's face. The wheel cover was seized as evidence. See attached property report.

I asked Schroeder how many times Harding hit Silver and he said she repeatedly hit him all over. Demarco said he guessed she punched him ten times. Schroeder said Silver knew not to hit Harding and he said Silver was yelling at her, " Go ahead and hit me bitch. I got witnesses right here." I asked what broke the fight up and they told me Harding ran off toward the house.

After listening to Harding's, Silver's and the witness' statements, I found there were some inconsistencies. The witnesses said the assault started immediately after Harding and Silver got home and out of their vehicle. Harding also said they had just gotten back from being out. However, according to the witnesses, Harding was never on the ground being held down by Silver. They said Silver was holding Harding's arms to keep her from hitting him. According to the witnesses, Harding initiated the incident, while Harding says she was defending herself from Silver holding her.

Next, I went back to Sergeant Lackey's location and told Harding about the strict domestic violence laws in Washington. Harding told me she did not want Silver to be arrested. I told Harding she was the one under arrest for assaulting Silver and she started crying and told me she punched him because he held her down. At approximately 2014 hours I read Harding her Constitutional Rights from my pocket Miranda card. Harding said

Officer: S Keathery   Incident Report   Case# 00-0036
Page 2

she understood her rights and I told her she only had to talk to us if she wanted to. Harding was crying and shook her head yes.

While talking with both Harding and Silver it was obvious they were both intoxicated. I could smell a strong odor of intoxicants on Silver's breath and Harding's eyes were red and watery, her speech was slurred, she was talking loudly, and she stumbled while she walked. Sergeant Lackey could smell a very strong odor of intoxicants on Harding's breath.

Harding was taken into custody and was immediately transported to the Camas Police Department. While in the booking room Harding again repeated, " What was I suppose to do? He pushed me to the ground and I punched him in the face." Harding was cited for Assault IV-DV and issued a No Contact Order. Harding was released to her godparents, Greg and Linda Lewis. While we were discussing the incident with Greg and Linda Lewis, Linda asked Harding if her hand hurt because it looked bruised. Harding said that it hurt from punching Silver in the face. Harding also commented about how she also broke a nail from hitting him. I looked at Harding's right hand and it was red and there was a small scratch on her middle knuckle.

While I was transporting Harding, Officer Justis stayed at the incident location and took photographs of Silver's injuries. The photographs were taken as evidence, see attached property report. In addition, See Officer Justis' supplemental report concerning statements made by Silver.

At approximately 2200 hours I called the dispatcher at CRCA and inquired about the 911 call. I talked with Holly Starr. Starr told me that she answered the phone on the back line, which she said was 696-4461. Starr said a male caller initially told her that he needed the police out here and asked her about the laws for domestic violence. She said he hung the phone up and she heard a noise like a fax machine. Starr said she stayed on the line in case the phone was picked back up. She said it was picked up and a female who identified herself as Tonya Harding told her she needed the police because " he forced me to defend myself." Starr then told me she heard the male yelling in the background saying she punched him in the face. Starr said Harding was concerned about the media finding out and requesting that we keep the call quiet.

While assisting Harding right after she was released with a civil standby, Officer Justis gave Silver a copy of the domestic violence victim's handout form and a copy of the No Contact Order.

< < < < < < <

> >

Which was Tonya Harding's more impressive feat: nailing a triple salchow or breaking only one nail during this 2000 beating of her boyfriend?

Officer: S. Keatley   Incident Report   Case# 00-0636

IN THE COUNTY COURT,
IN AND FOR DADE COUNTY, FLORIDA

THE STATE OF FLORIDA,   )   CASE NO.: M99-6410
          Plaintiff,   )   JUDGE: THOMAS
)
vs.   )   DISCOVERY UNDER FLORIDA
)   CRIMINAL PROCEDURE RULE 3.220
ROBINSON, EUGENE   )
          Defendant(s).   )   DEMAND FOR NOTICE OF ALIBI UNDER
_____/   FLORIDA CRIMINAL PROCEDURE RULE 3.200

FILED

MAR 0 2 1999

CLERK

COMES NOW KATHERINE FERNANDEZ RUNDLE, State Attorney of the Eleventh Judicial Circuit of Florida, by and through the undersigned Assistant State Attorney, and files this Discovery, Statements of Particulars and Demand for Notice of Alibi under Florida Criminal Procedure Rules 3.220 and 3.140(n) as follows:

1.   The persons, known to the State at this time, that have information which may be relevant to the offense charged, and to any defense with respect thereto, are as follows:

1. OFF. WANDER #01-7348 MIAMI P.D.	2. OFF. CASIANO #01-909 MIAMI P.D.
3. OFF. DINTER #01-1474 MIAMI P.D.	4. OFF. GOMEZ #01-2369 MIAMI P.D.
5. OFF. PICHEL #01-5642 MIAMI P.D.	6. LT. M. GARCIA #01-2167 MIAMI P.D.

[ ] Evidence which may be introduced at trial

[X] A copy of the Defendant's prior criminal history in Miami Dade County.

[X] A copy of the Arrest Form (if any) is attached.

[ ] A copy of the Information (if any) is attached.

[ ] A copy of the Police Report (if any) is attached.(See Exhibit A attached). Paragraphs designated by an asterisk (*) apply to the reciprocal provisions pursuant to rule 3.220 of the Florida Rules of Criminal Procedure only.

[X] Statements of the Defendant.
MR. ROBINSON WAS READ HIS RIGHTS BY LT. MARIO GARCIA AT THE CENTRAL DISTRICT. MR ROBINSON ACKNOWLEDGED THAT HE UNDERSTOOD HIS RIGHTS. AFTERWARDS HE MADE THE FOLLOWING STATEMENTS, "LORD JESUS, WHAT DO I TELL MY WIFE AND KIDS. I AM A BORN AGAIN CHRISTIAN. I HAVE ACCEPTED THE LORD AS MY SAVIOR. I DIDN'T MEAN TO DO IT. I HAVE DISAPPOINTED MY TEAM, MY COACH AND MY GOD. I WAS GIVEN THE BART STARR MAN OF THE YEAR AWARD".
Police case Number: 0301913-Y

2.   Pursuant to Rule 3.220 (a) (1) of the Florida Rules of Criminal Procedure, the State will disclose to the defense counsel and permit him to inspect, copy, test, and photgraph the material and information, if any, provided for in paragraph (ii) through (xi), upon request, within five (5) days of receipt of this Discovery at a mutually convenient place.

One day before Super Bowl XXXIII, police charged Atlanta Falcon Eugene Robinson with soliciting a prostitute. As to his question about what he'd tell his wife, "Honey, we're not going to Disney World" might have been appropriate.

( )
( )
( ) ( ) ( ) ( ) ( ) ( ) ( ) ( )

ARREST WARRANT APPLICATION
JD-CR-64   Rev 10-93
R BK. 593, 593A, 594
GEN STAT 54-2a

STATE OF CONNECTICUT
SUPERIOR COURT

Supporting Affida___
☐ YES

NAME AND RESIDENCE (Town and Residence)

Wesley Spears   76 Brightwood Lane   West Hartford, Ct.

COURT TO BE HELD AT ___
West Hartford

APPLICATION FOR ARREST WARRANT

TO: A Judge of the Superior Court

The undersigned hereby applies for a warrant for the arrest of the above-named accused on the basis of the facts set forth in the

☒ affidavit below   ☐ affidavit(s) attached

DATE & SIGNATURE	DATE 12/18/96	SIGNED (Prosecutorial Official)

AFFIDAVIT   (Page #13)

The undersigned, being duly sworn, deposes and says:

21. cont... for one Mr. Shelman Spears, 70 Elizabeth Avenue, Bloomfield, Ct. Shalija stated she avoided further contact from Spears and shortly after received an eviction notice from him. She felt the notice was an attempt by Spears to scare her because it was not properly served. She later received a second notice which was in proper form and then formal eviction proceedings began.

22. That on June 24, 1996 the Affiants met with Camby and his Attorney/Agent, Bryant for the purpose of taking a written statement from Camby. Prior to taking the statement Camby was advised that new information had been obtained that conflicted with his earlier accounts in reference to his relationship with Spears. Camby admitted that he left certain details out of his complaint because he was concerned with protecting UMASS from possible NCAA violations. He indicated that his contact with Spears prior to becoming a free agent could result in serious sanctions against the school's basketball program. Camby agreed and his attorney encouraged him to be completely accurate in his written statement. He indicated that the first time he had met Spears was in December when Tamia Murray brought him to his dorm at UMASS. Camby stated that Spears and Murray arrived with a woman whom he had never met before and has since forgotten her name. Camby stated that after they brought the woman to him at the dorm, both Spears and Murray left him alone with her. While they waited outside in the hallway, Camby stated he had intercourse with the woman. Later that same night, Spears again left the room and Camby, Murray and another UMASS basketball player, Charlton Clark, had group sex with the girl. The affiants showed Camby Spears' business card which had been turned over by Shalijia Castaneda. Camby examined the card and stated that the number on the reverse side of it was his beeper number which he had put on the card and given to the woman Spears brought to his dorm.

DATE & SIGNATURE	DATE 11/26/96	SIGNED (Affiant)
JURAT	SUBSCRIBED AND SWORN TO BEFORE ME ON (Date) 11/26/96	SIGNED (Judge, Clerk, Comm. Sup. Ct., Notary Pub.) G. Brigandi

G. BRIGANDI
NOTARY PUBLIC
MY COMMISSION EXPIRES NOV. 30, 1999

FINDING

The foregoing Application for an arrest warrant, and affidavit(s) attached to said Application, having been submitted to and considered by the undersigned, the undersigned finds from said affidavit(s) that there is probable cause to believe that an offense has been committed and that the accused committed it and, therefore, that probable cause exists for the issuance of a warrant for the arrest of the above-named accused.

DATE & SIGNATURE	DATE 12-18-96	SIGNED (A Judge of the Superior Court)

New York Knicks star Marcus Camby has many fine basketball skills. But back in his days at the University of Massachusetts—when he was being improperly courted by a prospective agent—he was particularly adept at the triple team.

John G. Koeltl
Attorney

<u>Steinbrenner offer of proof</u>

On October 9, 1973, Edward Bennett Williams, Vincent Fuller, and Jack Vardaman came to the office to talk with McBride and Koeltl. Williams explained the substance of the testimony which Steinbrenner could provide us if we were willing to allow Steinbrenner to plead guilty to a one count felony violation of 18 U.S.C. Section 610.

Williams indicated that Steinbrenner would testify to his conversations with Kalmbach and Tom Evans in relationship to the solicitation of Steinbrenner. Williams stated that Steinbrenner could provide us with the name of a corporation which had provided services to CREP and which had then billed other corporations for alleged services rendered. In other words, Steinbrenner could provide us with more than a dozen companies which had been involved in 610 violations.

Williams indicated that Steinbrenner had heard that the Teamsters had given more than a million dollars, that the million dollars had then been kept at the Hotel Pierre, and that someone from the Teamsters had then stolen it back again.

Steinbrenner could also provide us with reliable hearsay on a number of companies which appeared to have been involved in 610 violations. (Williams indicated that Merrill Lynch had substantial difficulties in the campaign finance area.)

Files
Chron
Circ.
Koeltl

Steinbrenner could also provide us with information as to the sale of a couple of ambassadorships. Specifically, Williams discussed a March 6 stag dinner at the White House where several prominent people were simply kept off the guest list deliberately.

With respect to Melcher, Williams does not know what Steinbrenner's testimony would be.

Facing the possibility of jail time for his illegal contributions to Richard Nixon's reelection campaign, New York Yankees owner George Steinbrenner offered to turn snitch. This internal memo was prepared by Watergate prosecutors, who rejected Steinbrenner's overtures.

- 2 -

Williams indicated that Steinbrenner received nothing for his contribution. Originally, Steinbrenner had intended to obtain an ambassadorship for someone else (probably ███████████).

With respect to Tom Evans, Williams indicated that the only information was that Evans had told Steinbrenner not to come in. There were extensive conversations between Evans and someone at American Shipbuilding at this time; Williams believes the conversations were between Melcher and Evans. Vardaman indicated that Melcher's secretary had stated that Melcher had a great many conversations with Evans at this time.

Wheels and Tires
Custom built BRABUS 3 pc. 3 point stars 18". Custom wheels built using two sets to make one . Chromed finish. PERELLI 335 P - Zeros in front(18"x 13"), (18"x 10) in front.

$13,200

Brake System
Custom 14" Front brake system for increased stopping power, by ALCON stainless steel brake lines. Works with existing ABS.

$5500

Gauge faces
Custom Colored burgundy gauge faces with parchment lettering on all dash dials.

$600

Carbon Fiber
Carbon fiber finish all stock interior wood: 2 Door Rails, 2 Door Handles, 2 Door Inserts, 2 Seat switch back plates, 4 dash rails, 2 piece Center Console, 2 rear Quarter Door Rails, Steering Wheel, Shift Knob, 3 piece rear seat Console, Rear seat Tambour Door, Rear Ash tray cover.
Carbon Fiber finish custom Pieces: 2 Seat backs, Lumbar control area, 2 Video Bezels for rear video, Front navigator, and video bezels/ enclosure, 4 Door Pocket Covers, 4 Grips, 2 Remote mirror corners, 4 headrest mounts, Center Armrest and Latches, Gauge bezel, Rear light bezels, Cellular Phone Handset. Rear air Vents.

$13,700

Computer Chip Upgrade
Upgrade engine management system, will run on 92+ Octane only, adds 40 horsepower. due out 1/97.

$695

Secret compartment
Located in area specified by customer, opened electronically via hidden switch, location revealed on delivery.

$750

> **T**his invoice details the customization of a tricked-out Mercedes-Benz ordered by Los Angeles Laker Shaquille O'Neal. As for that secret compartment, Shaq was probably planning to store his Oscar for *Kazaam* in there.

ARREST WARRANT APPLICATION
JD-CR-64   Rev. 10-93
PR. BK. 593, 593A, 594
GEN. STAT. 54-2a

STATE OF CONNECTICUT
SUPERIOR COURT

FOR COURT USE ONLY
Supporting Affidavits Sealed
☐ YES   ☐ NO

DOB: 11-16-77   BPD# 97-00706

NAME AND RESIDENCE *(Town)* OF ACCUSED	COURT TO BE HELD AT *(Town)*	G.A. NO.
BAIUL, OKSANA, 14 RIVERWALK DR., SIMSBURY	WEST HARTFORD	16

APPLICATION FOR ARREST WARRANT

page 1 of 3

TO: A Judge of the Superior Court

The undersigned hereby applies for a warrant for the arrest of the above-named accused on the basis of the facts set forth in the . . .

☐ affidavit below . . .   ☐ affidavit(s) attached.

DATE & SIGNATURE	DATE 1/14/97	SIGNED *(Prosecutorial Official)*

AFFIDAVIT

The undersigned, being duly sworn, deposes and says:

1. That I, Officer Eric M. Kovanda, am a regular member of the Bloomfield Police Department and have been a member of said department since August 17, 1995. That this Affiant is currently assigned to the Patrol Division.

2. On 01-12-97 at about 02:25, this Affiant was dispatched to investigate a report from a concerned citizen of what she believed sounded like a car that was out of control, followed by what sounded like a crash in the area of 5 Burr Road.

3. I located a vehicle off the roadway and in the woods off the right, eastern shoulder of Simsbury Road, approximately 314 feet north of Burr Road. I observed a man and woman at the edge of the roadway and went to check them for injuries.

4. I observed that the woman had suffered a laceration to the back of her head and began to apply a dressing to her wound. During this encounter with the woman I smelled a very strong odor of alcoholic beverage about her breath.

5. I asked the man if anyone else was in the vehicle. He stated that there was not. I asked him if he was hurt and he replied that he was not. I asked him what happened and he stated that she had lost control of the vehicle. I asked him what her name was. He stated that her name was Oksana Baiul.

6. A van pulled up to the scene of the accident. A party later identified as Dana Johnston exited the van and ran up to Baiul. I had an opportunity to interview her briefly. Johnston told me that Baiul had

---

10. That calculations performed on the measurement of yaw marks left by the vehicle on Simsbury Road between Mountain Road and Burr Road, indicated a speed of 97.11 mph. That calculations performed on the measurement of yaw marks left by the vehicle on Simsbury Road north of Burr Road indicated a speed of 85.46 mph.

DATE & SIGNATURE	DATE 1-14-97	SIGNED *(Affiant)* Ofc. E Kovanda #107
JURAT	SUBSCRIBED AND SWORN TO BEFORE ME ON *(Date)* January 14, 1997	SIGNED *(Judge, Clerk, Comm. Sup. Ct., Notary Pub.)* Sgt. R. Schmidt #98

FINDING

The foregoing Application for an arrest warrant, and affidavit(s) attached to said Application, having been submitted to and considered by the undersigned, the undersigned finds from said affidavit(s) that there is probable cause to believe that an offense has been committed and that the accused committed it and, therefore, that probable cause exists for the issuance of a warrant for the arrest of the above-named accused.

DATE & SIGNATURE	DATE 1/14/97	SIGNED *(A Judge of the Superior Court)*

(OVER)

---

11. That I interviewed Ms. Baiul at St. Francis Hospital on 01-12-97 at about 09:00, at which time I still detected an odor of alcoholic beverage about her breath. Ms. Baiul told me that she remembered losing control of the vehicle, but that she did not remember much else about the accident. When I asked her if she remembered where she went after leaving the Hartford Civic Center, she said she was going home. I asked her the name of the bar that she and her friends had stopped at before heading home, and she told me that I would have to talk to her Manager. I did not interview Ms. Baiul any further.

Olympic skating champion Oksana Baiul gets high marks for the degree of difficulty in driving 97 mph drunk, but low scores for her sloppy execution.

Urinating in Public
Nature of Occurrence

2-13-99
Date of this Supplement

99-03629
D.R. Number

On <u>02-13-99</u> at approximately <u>1:10</u> ^{A/m} hours I was on routine bicycle patrol in the area of <u>7300 E STETSON</u> in full uniform on my Police mountain bike. From approximately <u>5 (flyds)</u> away, I observed the suspect, later identified as <u>KERRY L.</u> <u>WOOD</u> (DOB <u>061677</u>), URINATING ON THE WALL OF THE BUSINESS THAT IS ON THE WEST END OF THE CITY LOT. AS I PULLED UP HE CONTINUED TO URINATE FOR APPROXIMATELY 30 MORE SECONDS. I COULD SEE THE URINE AS IT SPLATTERED ON THE WALL AND RAN DOWN ONTO THE GROUND.

The suspect stated " I CANT STOP NOW, I HAVE TO FINISH." HE ALSO ASKED WHAT THE FINE WAS.

The suspect's demeanor was COOPERATIVE.

The suspect identified him/herself with TX DRIVERS LICENSE w/PHOTO.
The suspect was cited on citation # 1411725 for violation of Scottsdale City Code 19-19, (Urinating in Public) and released at the scene with a signed promise to appear in Scottsdale City Court.

_____489_____
Reviewing Supervisor

BROWN 511
Reporting Officer

```
REPORT ID# : 246326.A118
      DR# : 10077
     DATE : 01-18-01
     TIME : 2045
```

On 01-18-01/1744 hours, PVPD dispatch reports a domestic violence case in progress at ███ E. Joshua Tree Ln, Town of Paradise Valley, Az., 85253, the Kidd residence. Myself along with officer's M. Kulak, F. Hoekstra and lead officer M. Woytonik responded. PVPD dispatch has Mrs. Kidd on the phone waiting our arrival.

Upon my arrival, officer Kulak is standing at the front door with Mrs. Kidd. Kulak told me that Officer Hoekstra is in the kitchen with Mr. Kidd. I stopped and talked with Mrs. Kidd who appeared visibly upset and crying. She told me that she and her husband Jason Kidd, had been arguing since returning home.

At approximately 17:00 PM. Mrs. Kidd decides to go to the gym to workout and asked Jason if he would watch and feed their son TJ. Mrs. Kidd makes a plate for TJ and sits him in the high-chair in the kitchen. Jason then takes a french fry from the plate of TJ, Mrs. Kidd tells Jason not to eat any of TJ's food because there wasn't very much. Jason then turns towards Mrs. Kidd and spits the french fry at Mrs. Kidd striking her in the face. Mrs. Kidd turns away from Jason, Jason then strikes Mrs. Kidd in the face while holding a container of yogurt in his hand.

Mrs. Kidd then ran for her bedroom and locked the door. Jason then kicked the door open to gain entry. Mrs. Kidd then retreated to the bathroom and again locks the door. Jason just stood there and called her names. Mrs. Kidd then called the police, however she hangs up prior to dispatch answering the phone. PVPD dispatch then calls back the number and talks with Jason. Mrs. Kidd also gets on the phone line and states that she called for police assistance. PVPD police were then dispatched to the Kidd residence.

I looked for injuries on Mrs. Kidds face, I could see a small scratch under her nose on the right side of her lip. She then showed me a small scratch located on the bottom of her lip inside of her mouth. I asked Mrs. Kidd if she wanted any medical attention? She declined my offer. Officer Woytonik was then called to bring a polaroid to take pictures of her injuries.

I then went into the kitchen and found Jason sitting at the kitchen table. He appeared calm and quiet. Based on Mrs. Kidds statement and the injuries consistent to her statement I informed Jason Kidd that he was under arrest for domestic violence, for assaulting his wife. Jason was cooperative and didn't resist. He had no visible signs of injuries nor did he complain of any. Refer to officer Kulaks report for further details of his involvement in this case.

NBA All-Star Jason Kidd is not much of a rebounder, but don't get in his way if there's a scramble for a loose french fry. Armed with a yogurt container, the point guard's a terror.

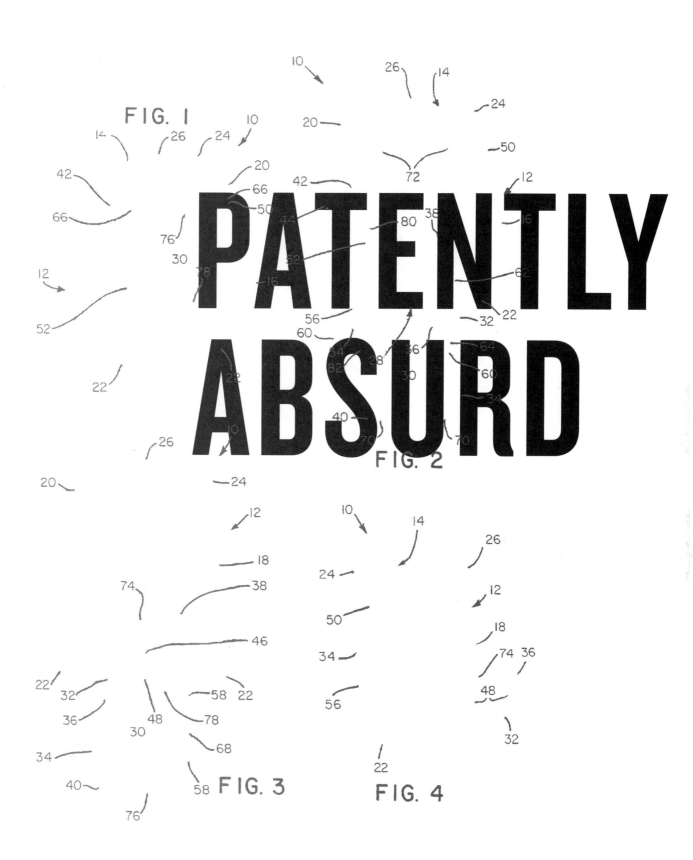

Want to be an inventor?
Just come up with a gizmo that is insane, offensive, or incomprehensible and that patent number is probably yours. Better yet, if the item somehow involves male genitalia, you're virtually guaranteed the coveted digits.

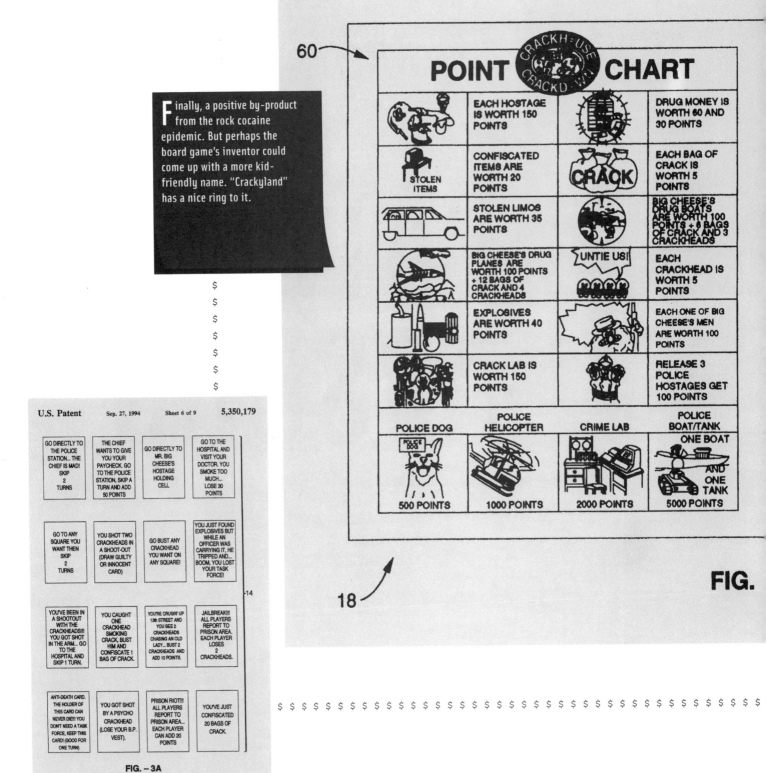

Finally, a positive by-product from the rock cocaine epidemic. But perhaps the board game's inventor could come up with a more kid-friendly name. "Crackyland" has a nice ring to it.

60

POINT CHART

CRACKHOUSE
CRACKDOWN

	EACH HOSTAGE IS WORTH 150 POINTS		DRUG MONEY IS WORTH 60 AND 30 POINTS
STOLEN ITEMS	CONFISCATED ITEMS ARE WORTH 20 POINTS	CRACK	EACH BAG OF CRACK IS WORTH 5 POINTS
	STOLEN LIMOS ARE WORTH 35 POINTS		BIG CHEESE'S DRUG BOATS ARE WORTH 100 POINTS + 6 BAGS OF CRACK AND 3 CRACKHEADS
	BIG CHEESE'S DRUG PLANES ARE WORTH 100 POINTS + 12 BAGS OF CRACK AND 4 CRACKHEADS	UNTIE US!	EACH CRACKHEAD IS WORTH 5 POINTS
	EXPLOSIVES ARE WORTH 40 POINTS		EACH ONE OF BIG CHEESE'S MEN ARE WORTH 100 POINTS
	CRACK LAB IS WORTH 150 POINTS		RELEASE 3 POLICE HOSTAGES GET 100 POINTS

POLICE DOG	POLICE HELICOPTER	CRIME LAB	POLICE BOAT/TANK
POLICE DOG			ONE BOAT AND ONE TANK
500 POINTS	1000 POINTS	2000 POINTS	5000 POINTS

18

FIG.

$ $ $ $ $ $ $

U.S. Patent   Sep. 27, 1994   Sheet 6 of 9   5,350,179

GO DIRECTLY TO THE POLICE STATION... THE CHIEF IS MAD! SKIP 2 TURNS	THE CHIEF WANTS TO GIVE YOU YOUR PAYCHECK. GO TO THE POLICE STATION, SKIP A TURN AND ADD 50 POINTS	GO DIRECTLY TO MR. BIG CHEESE'S HOSTAGE HOLDING CELL	GO TO THE HOSPITAL AND VISIT YOUR DOCTOR. YOU SMOKE TOO MUCH... LOSE 30 POINTS
GO TO ANY SQUARE YOU WANT THEN SKIP 2 TURNS	YOU SHOT TWO CRACKHEADS IN A SHOOT-OUT (DRAW GUILTY OR INNOCENT CARD)	GO BUST ANY CRACKHEAD YOU WANT ON ANY SQUARE!	YOU JUST FOUND EXPLOSIVES BUT WHILE AN OFFICER WAS CARRYING IT, HE TRIPPED AND... BOOM, YOU LOST YOUR TASK FORCE!
YOU'VE BEEN IN A SHOOTOUT WITH THE CRACKHEADS!!! YOU GOT SHOT IN THE ARM... GO TO THE HOSPITAL AND SKIP 1 TURN.	YOU CAUGHT ONE CRACKHEAD SMOKING CRACK, BUST HIM AND CONFISCATE 1 BAG OF CRACK.	YOU'RE CRUSIN' UP 13th STREET AND YOU SEE 2 CRACKHEADS CHASING AN OLD LADY... BUST 2 CRACKHEADS AND ADD 10 POINTS.	JAILBREAK!!! ALL PLAYERS REPORT TO PRISON AREA. EACH PLAYER LOSES 2 CRACKHEADS.
ANTI-DEATH CARD. THE HOLDER OF THIS CARD CAN NEVER DIE!!! YOU DON'T NEED A TASK FORCE, KEEP THIS CARD! (GOOD FOR ONE TURN)	YOU GOT SHOT BY A PSYCHO CRACKHEAD (LOSE YOUR B.P. VEST).	PRISON RIOT!!! ALL PLAYERS REPORT TO PRISON AREA... EACH PLAYER CAN ADD 20 POINTS.	YOU'VE JUST CONFISCATED 20 BAGS OF CRACK.

—14

FIG. – 3A

$ $

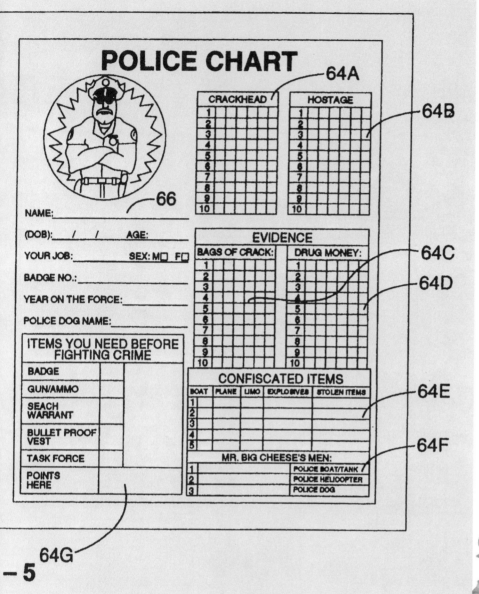

POLICE CHART

NAME: _____ —66

(DOB): __/__/__ AGE: _____

YOUR JOB: _____ SEX: M☐ F☐

BADGE NO.: _____

YEAR ON THE FORCE: _____

POLICE DOG NAME: _____

CRACKHEAD —64A

| 1 |
| 2 |
| 3 |
| 4 |
| 5 |
| 6 |
| 7 |
| 8 |
| 9 |
| 10 |

HOSTAGE —64B

| 1 |
| 2 |
| 3 |
| 4 |
| 5 |
| 6 |
| 7 |
| 8 |
| 9 |
| 10 |

EVIDENCE —64C

BAGS OF CRACK:	DRUG MONEY:	—64D
1	1	
2	2	
3	3	
4	4	
5	5	
6	6	
7	7	
8	8	
9	9	
10	10	

ITEMS YOU NEED BEFORE FIGHTING CRIME

BADGE	
GUN/AMMO	
SEACH WARRANT	
BULLET PROOF VEST	
TASK FORCE	
POINTS HERE	

CONFISCATED ITEMS —64E

	BOAT	PLANE	LIMO	EXPLOSIVES	STOLEN ITEMS
1					
2					
3					
4					
5					

MR. BIG CHEESE'S MEN: —64F

1	POLICE BOAT/TANK
2	POLICE HELICOPTER
3	POLICE DOG

—64G

—5

SUMMARY OF THE INVENTION

The present invention is both a board game apparatus designed for educating its players against the scourge of crack cocaine and its accompanying criminal lifestyle, as well as a method for playing the board game apparatus. Broadly, the board game apparatus, entitled "Crackhouse Crackdown", includes a playing board divided into four main regions having a continuous pathway which meanders through each of the four main regions. A start position and an end position are placed at opposite ends of the pathway, wherein the start position is placed adjacent to the first of the four main regions. In the first main region are a plurality of playing positions indicating "prerequisite items" which a player, assuming the role of a police officer, must obtain first, as prerequisites for gaining entrance into the other three main regions which comprise the playing board. These "prerequisite items" include a bullet proof vest, a police badge, armaments, a task force comprised of a plurality of police officers, and a search warrant.

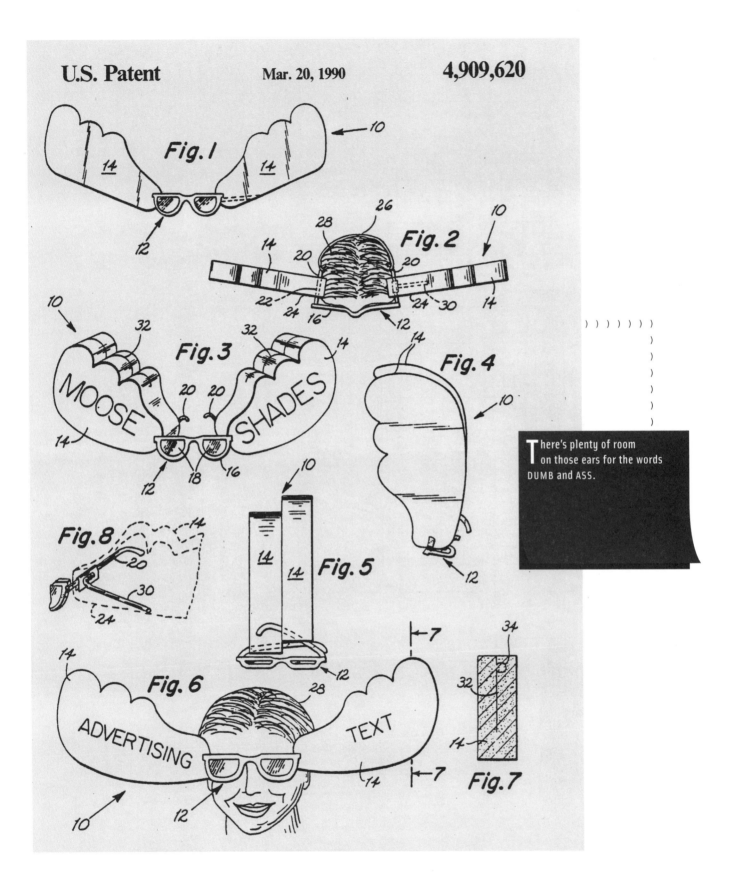

Fig. 1

Fig. 2

Fig. 3

Fig. 4

Fig. 5

Fig. 6

Fig. 7

Fig. 8

MOOSE SHADES

ADVERTISING TEXT

There's plenty of room on those ears for the words DUMB and ASS.

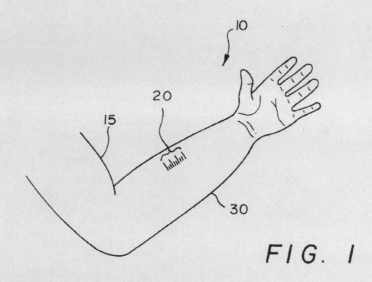

FIG. 1

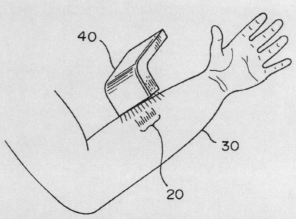

FIG. 2

Invisible or not, tattoos as a form of ID might not go over well with anyone who's ever cracked open a history book.

1

**METHOD FOR VERIFYING HUMAN
IDENTITY DURING ELECTRONIC SALE
TRANSACTIONS**

BACKGROUND OF THE INVENTION

1. Field of the Invention

The present invention relates to the identification of humans. More particularly, the present invention relates to the application of invisible, indelible tattoos on humans for purposes of identification in order to conduct monetary and credit transactions in a secure manner.

United States Patent [19]

Welch

[11] **Patent Number:** **Des. 398,994**

[45] **Date of Patent:** **∗∗Sep. 29, 1998**

[54] **HUMAN GAS FILTER PAD FOR WEARING IN THE UNDERWEAR**

[76] Inventor: **Michael J. Welch**, 42 Cottage St., Wilmington, Mass. 01884

[∗∗] Term: **14 Years**

[21] Appl. No.: **70,095**

[22] Filed: **Apr. 29, 1997**

[51] **LOC (6) Cl.** **24-04**
[52] **U.S. Cl.** **D24/124**
[58] **Field of Search** D24/124, 126, D24/125, 183; 5/636, 638, 641, 652, 652.1, 485; D6/502, 596, 601

[56] **References Cited**

U.S. PATENT DOCUMENTS

D. 309,689   8/1990   Bool D6/601
D. 331,968   12/1992   Bosley D24/126
D. 338,797   8/1993   Huls D6/601
D. 342,181   12/1993   White D6/601
5,706,535   1/1998   Takashima 5/485

Primary Examiner—Stella Reid

[57] **CLAIM**

The ornamental design for a human gas filter pad for wearing in the underwear, as shown.

DESCRIPTION

FIG. **1** is a front elevational view of a human gas filter pad for wearing in the underwear, showing my new design;
FIG. **2** is a back elevational view thereof;
FIG. **3** is a left side elevational view thereof;
FIG. **5** is a top plan view thereof; and,
FIG. **6** is a bottom plan view thereof.

1 Claim, 3 Drawing Sheets

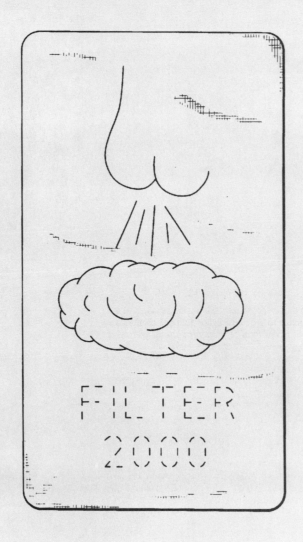

Putting aside for a moment whether Filter 2000 has merit, just how did the inventor convince Jennifer Lopez to pose for the patent drawing?

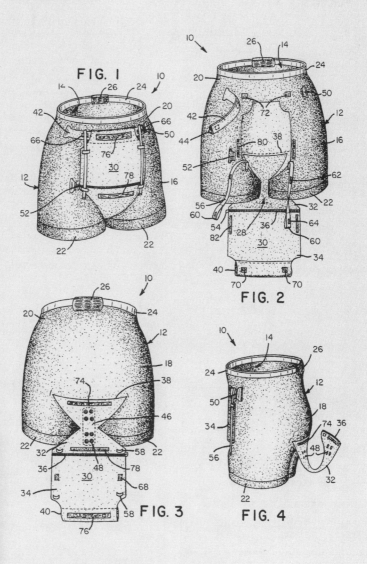

FIG. 1

FIG. 2

FIG. 3

FIG. 4

While this undergarment looks bulky (not to mention impregnable), some Hanes Control Top hosiery might help eliminate unsightly Kevlar panty lines.

SUMMARY OF THE INVENTION

In light of the foregoing need, it is a principal object of the present invention to provide a lightweight and comfortable undergarment in the form of pants for personal protection against sexual assault. When worn under an article or clothing such as trousers or a skirt, the protective undergarment is a hidden deterrent capable of significantly decreasing the likelihood of a successful sexual assault upon a wearer.

It is another object of the invention to provide a protective undergarment of the type described that permits a wearer to urinate or defecate without the garment being fully removed or soiled. To this end, a protective flap for selectively closing an elongated opening in the pants is a feature of the invention. The protective flap has a tubular sleeve at its free end through which a waist belt may be selectively drawn and locked. To attend to bodily functions, the belt need merely be unlocked and withdrawn from the tubular sleeve for the protective flap to be removed from the elongated opening.

United States Patent [19]

Bell

[11] **Patent Number:** 5,531,230

[45] **Date of Patent:** Jul. 2, 1996

[54] **STRAP SECURED CONDOM**

[76] Inventor: **Ray W. Bell**, 4601 W. Bellarose St., Tallahassee, Fla. 32310

[21] Appl. No.: **502,377**

[22] Filed: **Jul. 14, 1995**

[51] Int. Cl.⁶ **A61F 6/02**; A61F 6/04
[52] U.S. Cl. **128/842**; 128/844; 128/918
[58] Field of Search 128/842, 844, 128/918; 604/347–353

[56] **References Cited**

U.S. PATENT DOCUMENTS

5,121,755 6/1992 Hegedusch 128/844

5,158,556	10/1992	Starley	128/842
5,201,327	4/1993	Johnson	128/844
5,327,911	7/1994	Pien	128/844
5,437,286	8/1995	Stratton	128/844

Primary Examiner—Michael A. Brown

[57] **ABSTRACT**

A condom for securely receiving the male sexual organ. The inventive device includes a condom having a cylindrical sheath closed at a distal end and open at a proximal end thereof. Straps extend from the proximal end of the condom and can be positioned about a waist of a male wearer to secure the condom from unintentional removal.

1 Claim, 3 Drawing Sheets

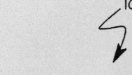

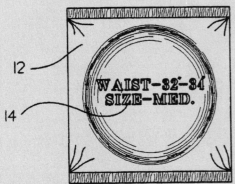
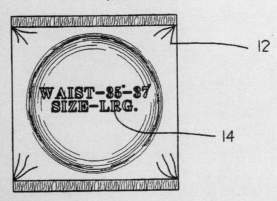
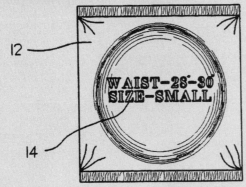
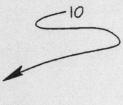

A s Bette Davis once said, "Fasten your seat belts, it's going to be a bumpy night."

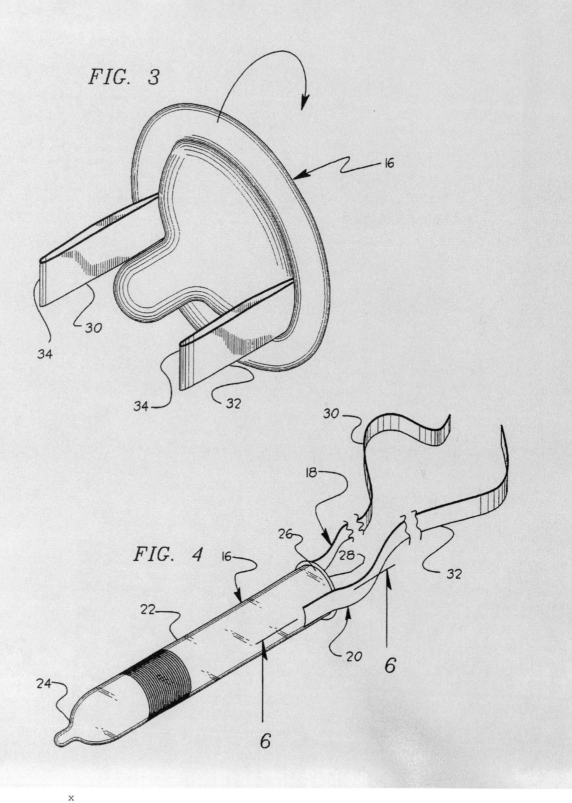

FIG. 3

FIG. 4

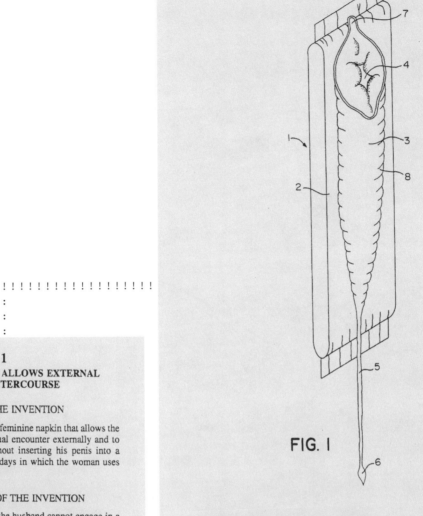

FIG. I

! ! ! ! ! ! ! ! ! ! ! ! ! ! ! ! ! !
:
:
:

1
FEMININE NAPKIN ALLOWS EXTERNAL SEXUAL INTERCOURSE

FIELD OF THE INVENTION

This invention relates to a feminine napkin that allows the husband to engage in a sexual encounter externally and to have sexual enjoyment without inserting his penis into a woman's vagina during the days in which the woman uses feminine napkins.

BACKGROUND OF THE INVENTION

There are times in which the husband cannot engage in a sexual encounter with his wife, for example, when she is in the menses period, having continuous bleeding from her womb, during the period following delivery, when she suffers from vaginitis or a womb ulceration which may become more serious if she engages in a sexual encounter, when there is fear of transfer of infection between the two parties, or in other situations in which a doctor forbids sexual intercourse between the husband and his wife. This also can occur when the woman uses the rhythm method to prevent pregnancy without using contraceptives so that sexual relations are stopped for certain days, or when the woman cannot satisfy the excessive desire of her husband for sex.

As a result, the wife suffers from the feeling of depression since she cannot satisfy her husband's sexual desire, and also results in the husband becoming nervous and frustrated for he cannot satisfy his sexual desire. This causes some husbands to the use isolators and to engage in sexual relations during menses, which may result in infections to the wife. Some husbands may also seek sexual enjoyment from other sources, which affects family relations and raises the possibility of transferring sexual diseases. Many divorce cases and familial disputes occur during the periods when couples are forced to stop love making.

Apparently American inventors are just too busy perfecting the next Pentium chip or building cold fusion devices. Because it fell to a Saudi Arabian to invent this divorce-preventing device.

! ! ! ! ! !   ! ! ! ! ! ! !

:
:
:
:
:

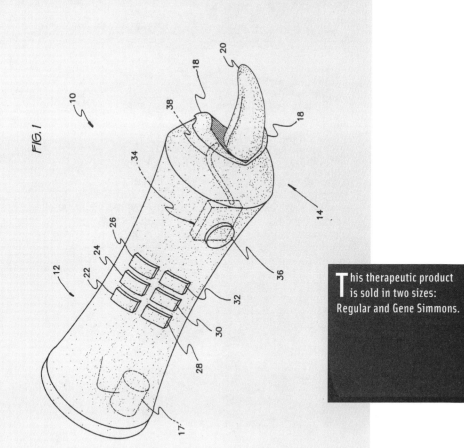

FIG.1

This therapeutic product is sold in two sizes: Regular and Gene Simmons.

BACKGROUND OF THE INVENTION

1. Field of the Invention

The present invention relates to a portable vibratory feminine stimulator for use in marital and sexual therapy.

2. Description of the Prior Art

Within the last several decades, the existence and desirability of the female orgasm has been virtually universally accepted by civilized society. Yet it is equally well established that a large percentage of women do not orgasm regularly during sexual intercourse, the use of ordinary vibrators or the use of self-stimulation. Indeed, a substantial minority of women report that they rarely, if ever, orgasm through the aforementioned three methods and only orgasm through the means of cunnilingus. For a substantial number of married couples, this can lead to tension and frustration which, in turn, leads to marital discord, especially if the husband has a dislike for performing cunnilingus or an inability to perform cunnilingus. Assuming that this is not a result of lack of facility on the part of the husband or intractable trauma based psychological problems on the wife's part, orgasmic therapy with a device which can perform a simulation of cunnilingus can replace or substantially supplement traditional marital therapy for such troubled couples.

United States Patent [19]

Szekely

[11] **Patent Number:** 5,472,399

[45] **Date of Patent:** Dec. 5, 1995

[54] **APPARATUS FOR EXERCISING THE PENIS**

[76] Inventor: **Andre Szekely**, Box 25, Benton Hollow Rd., Woodbourne, N.Y. 12788

[21] Appl. No.: **426,873**

[22] Filed: **Apr. 24, 1995**

[51] Int. Cl.⁶ **A63B 21/00**
[52] U.S. Cl. **482/121**; 482/148; 600/38
[58] Field of Search 482/121, 122, 482/124, 79, 80, 30, 31, 32, 44, 148; 600/38–40

[56] **References Cited**

U.S. PATENT DOCUMENTS

2,830,816	5/1958	Uhl	482/80
3,814,420	6/1974	Encke	482/79
3,937,462	2/1976	Kusmer	482/121
5,069,445	12/1991	Mai	482/30
5,160,303	11/1992	Smith	482/44

Primary Examiner—Stephen R. Crow
Attorney, Agent, or Firm—Levine & Mandelbaum

[57] **ABSTRACT**

Apparatus for exercising the penis has a torsion bar with an anchored end and a free end, and a fulcrum rod movably mounted above the torsion bar for adjusting the downward resistive force of the free end. Padding is provided at the free end against which the penis can be flexed for improving circulation and strengthening the muscles to improve and maintain sexual function.

5 Claims, 1 Drawing Sheet

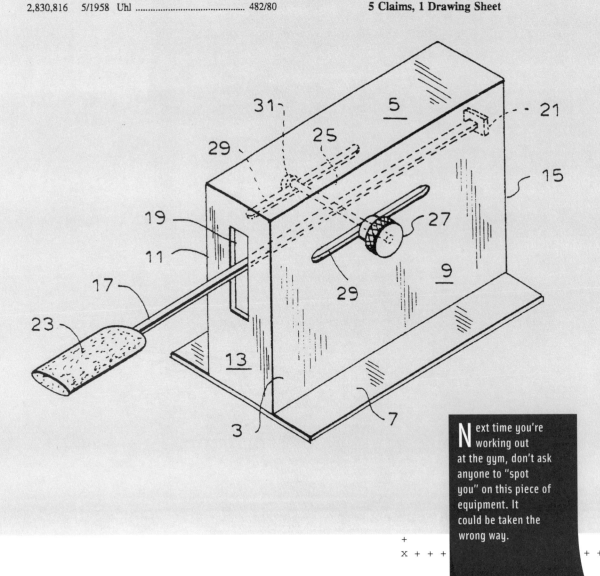

Next time you're working out at the gym, don't ask anyone to "spot you" on this piece of equipment. It could be taken the wrong way.

United States Patent [19]

Monostory

[11] **Patent Number:** **Des. 289,031**

[45] **Date of Patent:** ✶✶ **Mar. 31, 1987**

[54] **JET POWERED SURFBOARD**

[76] Inventor: **Egon Monostory,** 3743 Robertson Blvd., Culver City, Calif. 90230

[**] Term: **14 Years**

[21] Appl. No.: **633,391**

[22] Filed: **Jul. 23, 1984**

[52] **U.S. Cl.** **D12/307;** D21/236

[58] **Field of Search** D21/228, 229, 236, 237; D12/307; 114/270; 441/74, 65

[56] **References Cited**

U.S. PATENT DOCUMENTS

D. 276,994	1/1985	Montgomery et al.	D12/307
4,274,357	6/1981	Dawson	114/270
4,350,113	9/1982	Moreau et al.	114/270

Primary Examiner—James M. Gandy
Assistant Examiner—Kay H. Chin
Attorney, Agent, or Firm—Kelly, Bauersfeld & Lowry

[57] **CLAIM**

The ornamental design for a jet powered surfboard, as shown.

DESCRIPTION

FIG. **1** is a perspective view of a jet powered surfboard showing my new design;

FIG. **2** is a left side elevational view thereof;

FIG. **3** is a right side elevational view thereof;

FIG. **4** is a top plan view thereof;

FIG. **5** is a bottom plan view thereof;

FIG. **6** is a front end elevational view thereof; and

FIG. **7** is a rear end elevational view thereof.

From the people who brought you the rocket-powered kite.

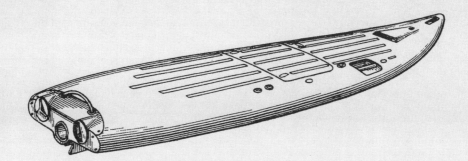

United States Patent [19]

Chatman

[11] **Patent Number:** **5,161,288**

[45] **Date of Patent:** **Nov. 10, 1992**

[54] **MULTI-OCCUPANCY CASKET**

[76] Inventor: **Charles Chatman**, 1566 Dianne Cir. East, Memphis, Tenn. 38114

[21] Appl. No.: **714,559**

[22] Filed: **Jun. 13, 1991**

[51] Int. Cl.⁵ A61G 17/00
[52] U.S. Cl. 27/2
[58] Field of Search 27/1–8, 27/18, 19, 35

[56] **References Cited**

U.S. PATENT DOCUMENTS

3,997,949	12/1976	Waltz	....	27/2
4,962,574	10/1990	Estes	....	27/2

Primary Examiner—Richard E. Chilcot, Jr.
Attorney, Agent, or Firm—Leon Gilden

[57] **ABSTRACT**

A casket construction includes a central container cavity, including at least one support member directed medially of the container cavity, wherein the support member includes a respective first and second coplanar support, with a medially directed coplanar connecting rib accommodating support of a plurality of individuals upon the respective first and second support plates permitting positioning of the leg portions of the individuals below the support member within the container cavity. A plurality of lids are provided to provide selective access to each individual upon each respective support plate. The invention further includes a cover housing, wherein the cover housing is mounted upon a medial ledge positioned below an upper top surface of the side walls, wherein the housing includes furled cover webs extendable from within the housing to selectively cover discrete portions of individuals mounted upon the support member. The invention further includes a partition wall directed orthogonally between opposed end walls and medially between the side walls to permit positioning of a further support member in coplanar relationship relative to the support member to accommodate a further plurality of individuals thereon within a single casket construction.

6 Claims, 4 Drawing Sheets

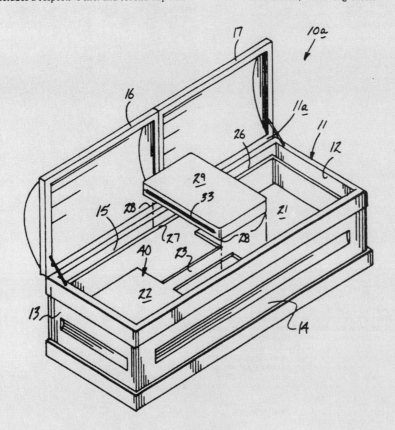

Christ, most people can't stand the idea of carpooling, so who'd want to double up while taking a dirt nap? And as for that drip pan idea, bravo. Nobody wants to visit the family crypt and step in a puddle of Grandma.

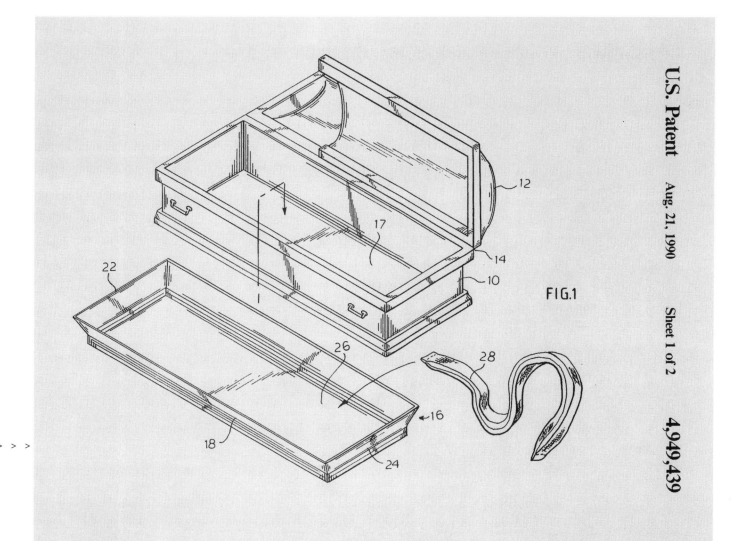

FIG.1

1

DRIP PAN FOR CASKETS

This is a continuation of co-pending application Ser. No. 914,241 filed on Oct 2, 1986 now abandoned.

BACKGROUND OF THE INVENTION

Above-ground burials in mausoleums have become very popular. It is well known to those skilled in the art that there are several causes of the decomposition of bodies placed in mausoleums. Some of these are related to the embalming and others to atmospheric conditions. It is not uncommon for the liquid products within the casket incident to decomposition to eventually penetrate through caskets containing the deceased and drip onto the floor causing severe consternation to the family, relatives and friends that may from time to time visit the mausoleum of the deceased.

OBJECTS AND SUMMARY OF THE INVENTION

It is an object of the present invention to provide a reliable and efficient sealing drip pan for a casket to trap and collect body liquids of decomposition and prevent their penetration and dripping from the casket.

An additional object of the present invention is to provide a drip pan that will make a proper seal between the casket side and end walls.

An additional objection of the present invention is to provide an absorbent pad for the pan to absorb liquid and which may also have a deodorant material to mask the odors of decomposition should they manage to escape from the casket.

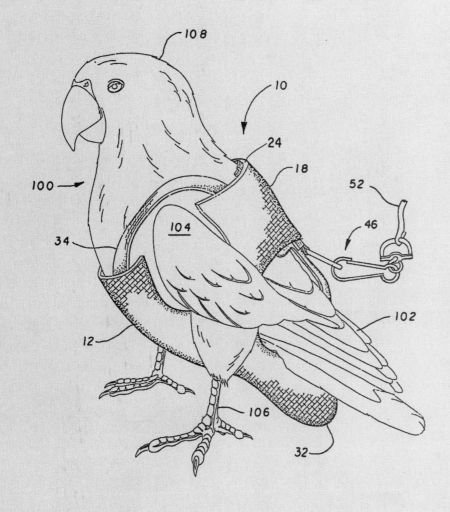

FIG. 1

Want to know why the uncaged bird sings? Because she is wearing a stylish Lycra crap sack that reins in "falling excrement." Yes, Polly wanna Pamper.

SUMMARY OF THE INVENTION

10   The present invention is a sanitary apparatus configured for a pet bird to wear. The sanitary apparatus, otherwise referred to as a bird diaper, is formed from a stretchable and absorbent material. The bird diaper covers a bird's chest, back, urogenital area and anus. The bird diaper also a pair of

15   openings for the bird's wings and legs and an aperture for the bird's tailfeathers. The bird diaper is thus configured to allow the pet bird to freely fly around the owner's house while protecting the bird owner's property from falling excrement.